Social Dramas

Also by New Academia Publishing

SOCIAL PROPRIETIES: Social Relations in Early-Modern England (1500-1680), by David A. Postles

SOCIAL GEOGRAPHIES IN ENGLAND 1200-1640, by David A. Postles

MISSED OPPORTUNITIES? Religious Houses and the Laity in the English High Middle Ages, by David A. Postles

SHAKESPEARE'S THEATER OF LIKENESS, by R. Allen Shoaf

NATIONALISM, HISTORIOGRAPHY, AND THE (RE)CONSTRUCTION OF THE PAST, Claire Norton, ed.

www.newacademia.com

Social Dramas

Literature and Language in Early-Modern England

by David A. Postles

New Academia Publishing
Washington, DC

Copyright © 2010 by David A. Postles

New Academia Publishing, 2010

All rights reserved. No part of this book may be reproduced or transmitted in any form or by any means, electronic or mechanical, including photocopying, recording, or by any information storage and retrieval system.

Printed in the United States of America

Library of Congress Control Number: 2010937254
ISBN 978-0-9828061-5-9 paperback (alk. paper)

New Academia Publishing, LLC
P.O. Box 27420
Washington, DC 20038-7420
www.newacademia.com - info@newacademia.com

Contents

Abbreviations vii
List of Tables and Figures xv
Acknowledgments xvii

Introduction 1

1. Language, Literature and Life 9
2. Flatcaps, Fashioning and Civility 43
3. Conjugal Relations 61
4. Money Matters 79
5. *Eastward Ho*. Credit in Virginia 99
6. Northern Speech 123
7. The Drama of the Cockfight 141

Conclusion 153
Works cited 156
Index 171

Abbreviations

1 Plays

[Date] indicates the approximate date of first performance or printing.

Middleton's plays are collected together in *Thomas Middleton: The Collected Works*, edited by G. Taylor and L. Lavagnino (Oxford: Oxford University Press, 2007).

Alchemist	Ben Jonson, *The Alchemist*. In *Ben Jonson Five Plays*, edited by G. A. Gilkes. Oxford: Oxford World's Classics, 1981 [1610].
Bartholomew Fair	Ben Jonson, *Bartholomew Fair*. In *Ben Jonson Five Plays*, edited by G. A. Gilkes. Oxford: Oxford World's Classics, 1981 [1614].
Changeling	Thomas Middleton and William Rowley, *The Changeling*. In *Five Jacobean Tragedies Middleton/Webster*, edited by Andrew Hadfield. Ware: Wordsworth Classics, 2001 [1622].
Chaste Maid...	Thomas Middleton, *A Chaste Maid in Cheapside*, edited by Alan Brissenden. London: A. & C. Black, 2002 [1613].
Cynthia's Revels	Ben Jonson, *Cynthia's Revels* <www.gutenberg.org/etext/3771>[1601].
Devil is an Ass	Ben Jonson, *The Devil is an Ass*, edited by Margaret J. Kidnie. Oxford: Oxford World's Classics, 2000 [1616].

Duchess of Malfi	John Webster, *The Duchess of Malfi*, edited by Brian Gibbons. London: A. & C. Black, 2001 [1614].
Eastward Ho	George Chapman, Ben Jonson, and John Marston, *Eastward Ho*. In *The Roaring Girl and Other City Comedies*, edited by James Knowles. Oxford: Oxford World's Classics, 2001 [1605].
Englishman for My Money	Anonymous, *An Englishman for My Money; or, A pleasant Comedy called A Woman will have her Will*, edited by W. W. Greg. Oxford: Malone Society Reprints, 1912 [1616].
Epicoene	Ben Jonson, *Epicoene, or, The Silent Woman*. In *Ben Jonson The Alchemist and Other Plays*, edited by Gordon Campbell. Oxford: Oxford World's Classics, 1995 [1609].
Every Man in His Humour	Ben Jonson, *Every Man in His Humour*. In *Ben Jonson Five Plays*, edited by G. A. Gilkes. Oxford: Oxford World's Classics, 1981 [1598].
Every Man Out of His Humour	Ben Jonson, *Everyman Out of His Humour* <www.gutenberg.org/etext/3695> [1599]
Faire Quarrell	Thomas Middleton and Thomas Rowley, *A Faire Quarrell*.Bodleian Library, Oxford: Bookstack Mal. 233 [1617].
Game at Chess	Thomas Middleton, *A Game at Chess*, edited by T. H. Howard-Hill. Manchester: Manchester University Press, The Revels Plays, 1993 [1624].
Gammer Gurton's Nedle	William Stevenson, *Gammer Gurton's Nedle*. In *Four Tudor Comedies*, edited by William Tydeman. London: Penguin, 1984 [1575].
Honest Whore I	Thomas Dekker (with Thomas Middleton), *The First Part of the Honest Whore*. In *Thomas Dekker The Honest Whore Parts One and Two*, edited by Nick de Somogyi. London, Nick Hern Books, 1998 [1604].

Honest Whore II   Thomas Dekker, *The Second Part of the Honest Whore*. In *Thomas Dekker The Honest Whore Parts One and Two*, edited by Nick de Somogyi. London, Nick Hern Books, 1998 [1605].

Jovial Crew   Richard Brome, *A Jovial Crew*, edited by Ann Haaker. London: Edward Arnold, 1968 [1641].

Knight of the Burning Pestle   Francis Beaumont, *The Knight of the Burning Pestle*. In *Renaissance Drama: An Anthology of Plays and Entertainments*, edited by Arthur F. Kinney. Oxford: Blackwell, 1999 [1606].

Like Will to Like   Ulpian Fulwell, *Like Will to Like*. In *Two Moral Interludes,* edited by P. Happé, H. R. Woodhuyse and J. Pitcher. Oxford: Malone Society Reprints, 1991 [1568].

Mad World...   Thomas Middleton, *A Mad World, My Masters*. In *Thomas Middleton A Mad World, My Masters and Other Plays*, edited by Michael Taylor. Oxford: Oxford University Press, 1995 [1606].

Malcontent   John Marston, *The Malcontent*, edited by Bernard Harris. London: A. & C. Black, repr. 1987 [1603].

Michaelmas Term   Thomas Middleton, *Michaelmas Term*. In *Thomas Middleton A Mad World, My Masters and Other Plays*, edited by Michael Taylor. Oxford: Oxford University Press, 1995 [1605].

New Inn   Ben Jonson, *The New Inn, or, The Light Heart*, edited by Margaret J. Kidnie. Oxford: Oxford World's Classics, 2000 [1629].

No Wit...   Thomas Middleton, *No Wit, No Help Like a Woman's*. In *Thomas Middleton A Mad World, My Masters and Other Plays*, edited by Michael Taylor. Oxford: Oxford University Press, 1995 [1613].

Pedlar's Prophecy	Thomas Creede, *The Pedlar's Prophecy*, edited by W. W. Greg. Oxford: Malone Society Reprints, 1914 [1595].
Poetaster	*Poetaster, Or, The Arraignment*, edited by Margaret J. Kidnie. Oxford: Oxford World's Classics, 2000 [1601].
Revenger's Tragedy	Thomas Middleton, *The Revenger's Tragedy*. In *Five Jacobean Tragedies Middleton/ Webster*, edited by Andrew Hadfield. Ware: Wordsworth Classics, 2001 [1606].
Roaring Girl	Thomas Dekker and Thomas Middleton, *The Roaring Girl, or, Moll Cutpurse*. In *The Roaring Girl and Other City Comedies*, edited by James Knowles. Oxford: Oxford World's Classics, 2001 [1611].
Sejanus	Ben Jonson, *Sejanus his Fall*, edited by Margaret J. Kidnie. Oxford: Oxford World's Classics, 2000 [1603].
Shoemaker's Holiday	Thomas Dekker, *The Shoemaker's Holiday, or, The Gentle Craft* In *The Roaring Girl and Other City Comedies*, edited by James Knowles. Oxford: Oxford World's Classics, 2001 [1599].
Staple of News	Ben Jonson, *The Staple of News*, edited by Anthony Parr. Manchester: Manchester University Press, The Revels Plays, repr. 1999 [1626].
Trick...Old One	Thomas Middleton, *A Trick to Catch the Old One*. In *Thomas Middleton A Mad World, My Masters and Other Plays*, edited by Michael Taylor. Oxford: Oxford University Press, 1995 [1605].
Volpone	Ben Jonson, *Volpone, or, The Fox*. In *Ben Jonson Five Plays*, edited by G. A. Gilkes. Oxford: Oxford World's Classics, 1981 [1606].
Weakest Goeth to the Wall	Anonymous, *The Weakest Goeth to the Wall*, edited by Jill L. Levenson. New York and London: Garland Publishing Inc., 1980.

Westward Hoe	Thomas Dekker and John Webster, *Westward Hoe*. In *The Dramatic Works of Thomas Dekker*, edited by F. Bowers. Cambridge: Cambridge University Press, 1955 [1604]
White Devil	John Webster, *The White Devil*, edited by Christina Luckyj. London: A. & C. Black, 1996 [1612].
Wily Beguilde	Anonymous, *Wily Beguilde*, edited by W. W. Greg. Oxford: Malone Society Reprints, 1913 [1602]
Witch of Edmonton	William Rowley, Thomas Dekker, and John Ford, *The Witch of Edmonton*, edited by Peter Corbin and Douglas Sedge. Manchester: Manchester University Press, 1999 [1621].
Woman Killed with Kindness	Thomas Heywood, *A Woman Killed With Kindness*, edited by Brian Scobie. London: A. & C. Black, 1985 [1603].
Women Beware Women	Thomas Middleton, *Women Beware Women*, edited by J. R. Mulryne. Manchester: Manchester University Press, The Revels Plays, 1975 [1621].

2 General

Bruster, *Shakespeare and the Question of Culture*	Douglas Bruster, *Shakespeare and the Question of Culture: Early Modern Literature and the Cultural Turn*. Basingstoke: Palgrave Macmillan, 2003.
Chakravorty, *Society and Politics*	Swapan Chakravorty, *Society and Politics in the Plays of Thomas Middleton*. Oxford: Oxford University Press, 1996.
Clarke, *Renaissance Drama*	Sandra Clarke, *Renaissance Drama*. Cambridge: Polity Press, 2007.
Crystal, *"Think on My Words"*	David Crystal, *"Think on My Words": Exploring Shakespeare's Language*. Cambridge: Cambridge University Press, 2008.

Dillon, *Cambridge Introduction*	Janette Dillon, *The Cambridge Introduction to Early Modern Theatre*. Cambridge, Cambridge University Press, 2006.
Goodman, *British Drama Before 1660*	Jennifer R. Goodman, *British Drama Before 1660*. Boston, MA: Twaine Publishers, 1990.
Greenblatt, *Renaissance Self-fashioning*	Stephen Greenblatt, *Renaissance Self-fashioning: From More to Shakespeare*. Chicago: University of Chicago Press, 1980.
Gurr, *Shakespearean Stage*	Andrew Gurr, *The Shakespearean Stage, 1574-1642*. Cambridge: Cambridge University Press, 1982.
Hattaway, *Introduction to Early Modern English Literature*	Michael Hattaway, *An Introduction to Early Modern English Literature*. Oxford: Blackwell Publishing, 2005.
Kinney, *Renaissance Drama*	Arthur F. Kinney, ed., *Renaissance Drama: An Anthology of Plays and Entertainments*. Oxford: Blackwell Publishing, 1999.
Lakoff and Johnson, *Metaphors*	George Lakoff and Mark Johnson, *Metaphors We Live By*. Chicago: University of Chicago Press, 1980.
McLuskie, *Dekker & Heywood*	Kathleen McLuskie, *Dekker & Heywood*. Basingstoke: Macmillan Press Ltd., 1994.
Manley, *Literature and Culture*	Laurence Manley, *Literature and Culture in Early Modern London*. Cambridge: Cambridge University Press, 1994.
Muldrew, *Economy of Obligation*	Craig Muldrew, *The Economy of Obligation: The Culture of Credit and Social Relations in Early Modern England*. Basingstoke: Palgrave, 1998.
Mullaney, *Place of the Stage*	Steven Mullaney, *The Place of the Stage: License, Play and Power in Renaissance England*. Chicago: University of Chicago Press, 1988.

Rappaport, *Worlds Within Worlds*	Steven Rappaport, *Worlds Within Worlds: Structures of Life in Sixteenth-century London*. Cambridge: Cambridge University Press, 1989.
Riggs, *Ben Jonson*	David Riggs, *Ben Jonson: A Life*. Cambridge, MA: Harvard University Press, 1989.
Scott-Warren, *Early Modern English Literature*.	Jason Scott-Warren, *Early Modern English Literature* Cambridge: Polity Press, 2005.

List of Illustrations

Tables

1 Lexical Items in Selected Plays	12-13
2 Rhymed Couplets in Selected Plays (Excluding Prologue and Epilogue)	28-29
3 Vocabularies Deployed in Selected Plays	35
4 Speech Acts of *Dramatis Personae*	66
5 Descriptive Statistics of Debt Cases in Lower Norfolk County Court, 1637-46	110
6 Descriptive Statistics of Debt Cases in Accomack/Northampton County Court, 1633-40	110
7 Descriptive Statistics of Debt Cases in Northampton County Court, 1645-51	110
8 Numbers of Testators in "Leeds and District" Described as of "The Parishing"	133
9 Distribution of "Brought Home" and "Brought Forth", 1528-46, in Lichfield Diocese	134

Figures

1 Example of Concordance Analysis of *Shoemaker's Holiday*	72
2 Firk's Self-referential Use of Firk	72
3 Margery Eyre's Idiomatic "Let that pass"	73
4 Viola's Speech Referring to Candido's Patience	73
5 Simon Eyre's Deployment of "Peace!"	74
6 Colonial Virginia: Particular Counties	100
7 "Parishing" and "(Be)wit" in Northern Wills	135
8 "Brought Forth" in Wills, 1528-46, in Lichfield Diocese	136

All Tables and Figures have been generated by the author

Acknowledgments

During the time I have been interested in the potential use of literature, in particular drama, to illuminate the mundane, quotidian aspects of social relationships, I have incurred so many debts. The inauguration of the M.A. Humanities at the University of Leicester involved me in a genuine interdisciplinary approach from which I benefited so much from conversation with my colleagues and the participants. That course provided space for me to reflect on many issues. Although he is not responsible for any of the shortcomings here, Greg Walker has been a constant encouragement. All too infrequent discussion with Sarah Knight and Kate Loveman, of the School of English at the University of Leicester, has always been to my advantage. Exactly the same benefit has accrued to me from even more intermittent exchanges with Paul Griffiths and Keith Wrightson. The annual meeting of the North American Conference on British Studies has been ever stimulating. The Early Modern Seminar at the University of Leicester has consistently provided a stimulus and real enjoyment. Finally, I extend my thanks to all my colleagues in the School of English at the University of Leicester who accepted me amongst them as a University Fellow when I retired in 2005.

Chapter 2 is reprinted from *Literature and History* 17 (2008), 1-13, with the kind permission of Manchester University Press and the editors, of whom Roger Richardson gave much valued advice. Two chapters were read in some form at conferences of the Social History Society: chapter 4 ("Money Matters") and Chapter 7 ("The Drama of the Cockfight"), the former also presented at the research seminar of the School of English at the University of Leicester. Comments on Chapter 3 have been gratefully received from Bernard Capp and Keith Wrightson. Nigel Goose commented on part of the manuscript.

My wife, Suella, has patiently allowed me time and space to conduct this research. Our cat, Fred, has faithfully supervised the production, and I blame him for any inaccuracies which remain.

Introduction

> For he knows poet never credit gained
>   By writing truths, but things (like truths) well feigned.
> If any yet will (with particular sleight
>   Of application) wrest what he doth write,
> And that he meant or him or her will say:
>   They make a libel which he made a play.[1]

> I account this world a tedious theatre,
>   For I do play a part in't 'gainst my will.[2]

> The world's a stage on which all parts are played:[3]

One of the intriguing questions about dramatic representation is how far it corresponds to contemporary social mores and action and, especially, how far we can retrieve from it aspects of "low" dialogue. The issue is particularly germane for speech in the texts. The complications are undeniably difficult. At all times, even in collaborative enterprise, competition (critical or benign) about poetic prowess obtained between the dramatists. When composing works as individuals rather than collaboratively, the playwrights had a self-awareness which extended to self-referential allusion to their other works. This display of their intellectual ability extended to comments on the poets generically and even, by implication, individually.[4]

During the war of the poets, that disputation was especially enhanced. Jonson in particular had an immense desire to denounce his critics as inferior, with a lower understanding of the Aristotelian unities.⁵ His self-representation as Horace in *Poetaster*, in a classical context, was designed to humiliate the other "poets", Homer's adversaries (especially Crispinus, that is, Marston) in the play.⁶ He was also, nonetheless, playfully self-referential too, particularly in the several *Intermeans* in *The Staple of News*, in which the "audience" criticized the dullness of the main play, despising the author as a "paltry poet".⁷ Undoubtedly, Jonson's device here was multi-faceted, critiquing popular expectations of plays, with a fool and devil, perhaps defensively protecting his deviation from the popular form, or alluding in circumlocution to his own erudition. So at all times, we must be cautious less about poetic license than poetic self-fashioning.⁸

In Chapter 3, below, are addressed some of the other sources for social dialogue, such as court records, and their imperfections. The alternative material in life-writing is generally unavailable before the middle of the seventeenth century, although there is a limited number of texts for the early seventeenth century. The conundrum of this source is well rehearsed: the concealed rhetoric of the form; issues of self-presentation; self-revelation; personal judgment of self-worth; evolving identities; conformity to convention; biblical reflection and appropriation; the impact of office-holding on the sense of propriety; the influence of conduct books on self-consciousness; and, perhaps, an imagined readership.⁹

Plays were composed, moreover, in response to other plays, as allusion or counter. Inter-textuality involved cross reference between plays by the same and different authors.¹⁰ Some plays were produced as parodies of other dramas. Several plays acquired the basis of their narratives from popular literature, as in the main plot of *Witch of Edmonton*, which was assumed from the pamphlet composed by Henry Goodcole, *The Wonderful Discovery of Elizabeth Sawyer a Witch, Late of Edmonton* (1621).¹¹ Several allusions are made by the collaborative authors to earlier (*Gammer Gurton's Nedle*) and contemporary (*Moll Cutpurse* [by Dekker and Middleton, c.1611], *Bartholomew Fair* [by Jonson, 1614]) plays.¹² Dekker was directly involved in the production of the pamphlet literature, including, of interest here, *The Gull's Handbook* (1609).¹³ One commentator has described some of these texts as "journalistic plays", reflecting on recent real events.¹⁴ Irascible as ever, Jonson disdained Greene, a scholar-poet, educated at Cambridge, through a less than complimentary reference in *Epicoene*. When Haughty refers to cures through the *Sick Man's Salve* and *Greene's Groats Worth of Wit*, Truewit responds: "A very cheap cure, madam".[15]

The problem which pervades any discussion of audience response is "distance", the subjective "balancing of stage and other worlds".[16] Whilst that issue remains, for early-modern theater, something of an insoluble issue, some sensitive playwrights, through meta-theatrical devices, such as intermeans and interludes, partially addressed the "distance" between and external reality, and between performance and expectations, for which, see further below.[17]

Much literature has been produced about the theaters and their relationship to the liberties of the City.[18] We are then disposed to consider the plays as performed exclusively in the theaters from the 1570s. The plays examined here were, indeed, enacted in the theaters in the City and the liberties. Before the establishment of the theaters, players were itinerant and performed in households. An interesting sidelight is the continued reference to plays in households in the comedies. Thus, Sir La Foole is derided for his exuberant social display, which included shouting from the window of his house in The Strand inviting passers-by in their coaches to dinner and plays in this house which he retained for this purpose.[19] One of the mischievous strategies of Follywit with his band of never-do-wells is to arrive at the country house of Sir Bounteous pretending to be the itinerant players of Lord Owemuch.[20] The gentry house of Sir Bounteous was located in the Midlands, according to his pronouncements about the merits of Lincolnshire as against Bedfordshire thieves. The improvised masque or comedy created by the Poet in *The Jovial Crew* was performed in a gentry household in Nottinghamshire.[21]

The foundation of the essays below are the dramatic ventures of three playwrights in particular who collaborated and contended with each other in productions for the theater in the City and who engaged directly and unequivocally with social commentary.

Thomas Dekker (ca.1572-1632)
Ben Jonson (1572-1637)
Thomas Middleton (ca.1570-1623)

Intermittently, allusions are made to their other main contemporaries: Francis Beaumont; John Fletcher; Thomas Heywood (ca.1570-1641); John Marston (1576-1634); and William Rowley (ca.1585-1637). When other playwrights are mentioned (Richard Brome, for example), some biographical details are provided in that place.

The discussion below is based on plays which were (intended to be) performed in public venues, in the open theaters which were established from the foundation of *The Theater* in 1576 and the closure of these venues in 1642. Although some public places existed previously, in inn yards for example, and whilst there was some continuation of playing after 1642, the concern is with the openly accessible material which the official public theaters provided.[22] The epithets of the "popular stage" and "popular drama" have been applied to these venues and performances.[23] The plays considered comprise all of comedy, tragi-comedy and tragedy. The preponderance of the plays performed by the boys' companies comprised comedy, some eighty-five percent, mostly satires expounding social critiques. The City comedies can, nonetheless, be divided into those which were satires and those (mainly by Dekker) which were celebrations. Those plays–cautiously appraised–reveal much about social attitudes.[24] For some purposes, however, it is important to consider also the other two sub-genre, not least for the evaluation of vocabulary (as above). One of the complications is the potential change which occurred in the composition of audiences. Whilst initially the audiences at the public theaters were mixed, composed of all social groups, there was later a tendency to some extent for the withdrawal of some of the gentry into private theaters, which had a greater social cachet associated with more expensive prices for admission.[25]

As a matter of necessity, Chapter 1 engages with the deployment of poetic devices in the plays to explain the caution which should be borne in mind when extracting from the stage aspects of social existence. Secondly, a close analysis is undertaken of the use of specific words in the texts which illuminate social attitudes. Finally, estimates are produced of the wider vocabulary of playwrights (Jonson, and Beaumont and Fletcher) for comparative purposes and to illuminate how the poets' language related to "ordinary" language.

A particular aspect of language use is considered in Chapter 2, which analyses in more detail the meanings of "to fashion" and "fashion". The discussion here is, however, mainly concerned with the symbolic importance of the flat cap for the citizens of London. Anachronistically, Jonson used the symbol of the flat cap in *Poetaster*, when Chloë, of gentle birth, complains "'twere my fortune to marry a flat-cap", although the ostensible setting of the play is classical Rome.[26] This difference between spouses leads on to the question of conjugal conversations.

In Chapter 3, marital relationships are dissected from the material in the City Comedies. One of the many conundrums in the discussion is the relative influences on the patience of Candido in *Honest Whore*. It is possible that there was a combination of Stoicism and Puritanism, the latter informed by the former. Jonson divulges this possible connection in *New Inn*, when Tipto remarks to Fly: "thou art an exact professor, Lipsius Fly". In defining Fly further, Tipto comments that Fly is "a rare bird in his profession", with a "tall and growing gravity", and his "own Dictamen and genius".[27] It is Fly, indeed, described by Beaufort as "vicar-general", who performs the marriage ceremony between Beaufort and Frank (actually Laetitia) in the stable of the *New Inn*.[28] The association is also established by Clerimont declaring: "and leave this Stoicity alone till thou mak'st sermons".[29] Similarly, when Rabbi Busy is condemned to the stocks, Quarlous rhetorically asks: "What's here? A Stoic i' the stocks?" "Rabbi" referred, of course, to Busy's Puritanism, as did his moniker, and his speeches are mostly concerned with his "sigh and groan for the reformation of these abuses" of the heathens.[30] The connection with contemporary Stoicism is established, perhaps, by Lollio's question to Isabella whether she has read Lipsius.[31] One treatise of Lipsius at issue is *On Constancy*, published in 1584 by Plantin, expressing a "Christianized neostoicism".[32]

The social metaphors of money are considered in Chapter 4, aligned around the bimetallic coinage. When Cokes loses his first purse to a cut-purse, he is offended by the crime, but puts it down to simple experience of Bartholomew Fair. The loss was of no consequence to him, since "'Twas but a little scurvy white money."[33] Silver coin–low denomination–did not matter too much to him. He resolved to tempt the cut-purses with his other purse, containing gold, by which he hoped to catch the culprits. In such a manner, social distinction is demarcated in the City Comedies.

The interest in monetary matters is continued in Chapter 5, which commences with the expectations in *Eastward Ho* about the rewards which would accrue from the Virginian venture of Sir Petronel, urged on by Quicksilver. Jonson's main plot concentrates on their aspirations which went awry. In fact, their vision of Virginian society and credit arrangements were complete delusions.

In chapter 6, the language of the North is considered. The dramatists attempted to represent language and dialect in their plays, especially the comedies, which were occasionally set in the "provinces" or involved characters who had recently migrated to the City. When Ferret recited a hackneyed verse, the Host decried "your scurril dialect".[34] Dialect was, then, to some extent associated with social group as much as regionalism.[35] Perhaps we assume that dialects had become levelled and comprehensible by the evolution of Chancery Standard and the dominance of East Midlands dialect in the later middle ages.[36]

Finally, drama is extended to include the cockfight (Chapter 7), but in the context of the assertion of Sir Bounteous that he is still the cock of the heap with his spurs. The cockfight was another "popular" spectacle, which all "sorts" of people attended. The cockfight has also been conceived as communicating cultural significance to the actors, representing either an homologous culture of a whole society or confirming masculinity. In fact, of course, the cockfight had multiple meanings, depending on situations and circumstances.

> Be of myself in keeping this Light Heart,
> Where I imagine all the world's a play;
> The state of men's affairs, all passages,
> Of life to spring new scenes, come in, go out,
> And shift and vanish; ...[37]

Notes

[1] *Epicoene, Another Prologue*, lines 9-14.
[2] *Duchess of Malfi*, Act IV, scene i, lines 81-2.
[3] *Game at Chess*, Act V, scene ii, line 19.

Introduction 7

⁴ Some of the analytical content here was stimulated by Crystal, *"Think on My Words"*.

⁵ Scott-Warren, *Early Modern English Literature*, 121-4 on the exemplary unity of action, time and place in Jonson's *Alchemist*; Gordon Williams, "Mediation and Contestation: English Classicism from Sidney to Jonson", in *Renaissance Poetry*, ed. Christine Malcolmson (Harlow: Longman, 1998), 178-202.

⁶ *Poetaster*: Jonson's satirical retort to Marston and Dekker in 1601; Bruster, *Shakespeare and the Question of Culture*, 69.

⁷ *Staple of News*, Second Intermean, line 44.

⁸ For the fool, Robert Wilcher, "The Art of the Comic Duologue in Three Plays by Shakespeare", in *Shakespeare and Language*, ed. Catherine M. S. Alexander (Cambridge: Cambridge University Press, 2004).

⁹ Michelle M. Dowd and Julie A. Eckerlie, "Recent Studies in Early Modern English Life Writing", *English Literary Renaissance* 40 (2010): 132-62. In fact, in *Volpone*, Jonson satirizes the journal keeping by Sir Politic: Act IV, scene ii, lines 133-46.

¹⁰ Bruster, *Shakespeare and the Question of Culture*, 167-90 (chapter 7).

¹¹ *Witch of Edmonton*, 3-4.

¹² *Gammer Gurton's Nedle*, 207-89.

¹³ Goodman, *British Drama before 1660*, 182; Anna Bayman, "Rogues, Conycatching and the Scribbling Crew", *History Workshop Journal* 63 (2007): 1-17; McLuskie, *Dekker & Heywood*, 71.

¹⁴ Clarke, *Renaissance Drama*, 63-83 (chapter 4).

¹⁵ *Epicoene*, Act IV, scene iv, lines 95-7.

¹⁶ Susan Bennett, *Theatre Audiences: A Theory of Production and Reception* (2nd edn., New York: Routledge, 2001), 15, critiquing Chaim and Grotowski.

¹⁷ Scott-Warren, *Early Modern English Literature*, 110-12 for the metatheatricality of *Knight of the Burning Pestle*, which had the purpose of both blurring fiction and reality, but in the process criticizing that very reality.

¹⁸ Mullaney, *Place of the Stage*.

¹⁹ *Epicoene*, Act I, scene iii, lines 33-5.

²⁰ *Mad World*, Act V, scene i.

²¹ *Jovial Crew*, Act IV, scene ii, lines 170-220; Act V, scene i, lines 250-391.

²² Goodman, *British Drama before 1660*, 9, for continuity after 1642, and 156 for the opening in 1576; Mullaney, *Place of the Stage*, 27, for 1576 and public playhouses; Goodman, *Renaissance Drama*, 1, for 1576; Dillon, *Cambridge Introduction to Early English Theatre*, 44-6, for "fixed" theater from 1576. For courtyards as permanent play stages in the 1560s and 1570s, Scott-Warren, *Early Modern English Literature*, 103.

8   Introduction

[23] Mullaney, *The Place of the Stage*, vii, 8-9.

[24] Mullaney, *The Place of the Stage*, 53; for comic modes, Daryl W. Palmer, *Hospitable Performances: Dramatic Genre and Cultural Practices in Early Modern England* (West Lafayette, IN: Purdue University Press, 1992), 89-93.

[25] Gurr, *Shakespearean Stage*. For women in the audience, and how they might react or be addressed, Kathleen McLuskie, *Renaissance Dramatists* (Hemel Hempstead: Harvester Wheatsheaf, 1989), 87-99.

[26] *Poetaster*, Act II, scene i, lines 88-9.

[27] *New Inn*, Act III, scene i, lines 33, 45-53.

[28] *New Inn*, Act V, scene iv, lines 41-2.

[29] *Epicoene*, Act I, scene i, lines 59-60.

[30] *Bartholomew Fair*, Act IV, scene vi, lines 74-109.

[31] *Changeling*, Act III, scene iii, lines 183-4.

[32] Perez Zagorin, *Ways of Lying: Dissimulation, Persecution and Conformity in Early Modern Europe* (Cambridge: MA: Harvard University Press, 1990), 123; Scott-Warren, *Early Modern English Literature*, 234-6, for Lipsius and Neo-Stoic emphasis on constancy and patience as virtues.

[33] *Bartholomew Fair*, Act II, scene vi, line 125.

[34] *New Inn*, Act I, scene iii, line 13.

[35] Jonathan Hope, "Shakespeare and Language: An Introduction", in *Shakespeare and Language*, ed. Alexander, 6-7.

[36] Laura Wright, ed., *The Development of Standard English 1300-1800* (Cambridge: Cambridge University Press, 2000). For an overview of the tension between Standard English and dialect and between dialects, Adam Fox, *Oral and Literate Culture in England 1500-1700* (Oxford: Oxford University Press, 2000), 51-111.

[37] *New Inn*, Act I, scene iii, lines 127-32; for the quotation from Shakespeare which has become a cliché, Jonathan Bate, *Soul of the Age: The Life, Mind and World of William Shakespeare* (London: Penguin, 2008), 1.

1
Language, Literature and Life

My mere fools,
   Eloquent burgesses, and then my poets,
   The same that writ so subtly of the fart,[1]

Allowing for Jonson's scatological imperative, to what extent, then, can we discover the speech, actions and attitudes of contemporary society in the plays?[2] Characterization is here a double-edged sword. On the one hand, the development of characters was one dramatic device, somewhat artificial in its application. Characterization was surely also, however, established through the quotidian social encounters of the playwrights. So it may be entirely legitimate if, with discretion, we seek contemporary speech in the texts. Two elements will be of concern here: phrases (idiomatic speech); and vocabulary (lexis and lexical items). There are without doubt other sources from which some of these patterns can be recovered: ballads; cheap print and popular literature; and ecclesiastical court causes (in particular defamation causes in instance–*ex parte*–actions). To one extent or another, all have their deficiencies: ballads and print from similar problems as the plays–hyperbole, exaggeration, stereotyping, sensationalism; court records from their mediation through a clerical institution and the narrative strategies of the litigants.[3] What is suggested here is that the plays are another resource which cannot be ignored and that they do allow another valuable insight into contemporary speech and speech acts.

In particular, we can detect something about idiomatic speech, by gender and social group. In contrast to the causes in ecclesiastical courts, these words can be extracted from contexts which are not *always* conflictual. We are brought into contact with language use in non-libelous and non-slanderous situations. We have something approaching "normal" exchanges, if mediated through the hands of the dramatist. How far, however, does the imagination of the playwright interfere with the dialog and monologue? We cannot be certain, of course. The development of a character might depend on the dramatic device of repetitive use of a phrase or exclamation. The point remains, however, that the language use had to be credible to the diverse constituencies in the audience–to be realist to some degree, particularly if repeated by a character.[4] We rely here on the frequency of repetition of some phrases to indicate that they were understood and accepted by the diverse constituencies in the audience. Where, in particular, phrases and lexical items are used repetitively to the exclusion of different or optional forms, we may take them as conventional in the "real" world (a particular example is *dull,* below). Part of this chapter is concerned with these aspects of particular language use: recurrent phrases and lexical items.

Idiomatic Speech

In chapter 3 below, idiomatic speech of individuals (stereotypically representing their social group) receives particular attention. The language of Simon Eyre, the ebullient master shoemaker, and his wife, are examined, the former with his brusque language of "Peace!" and the latter with her self-effacing utterance of "let that pass". In *Eastward Ho,* the goldsmith, Touchstone, has constant recourse to the refrain: "Work upon that now", mimicked by Quicksilver when he rebelled against Touchstone, his master, and then commended by Quicksilver in song after his reformation and redemption.[5]

Important complications are parody, bathos and burlesque. When Bunch, the English chapman in exile on the continent through his inability to find the means to return home, utters his malapropisms, do we have an authentic representation of "low" speech of this social group? "Condemnations" instead of commendations suggests dramatic license rather than realism, although more credence might be attached to "petticessor" for predecessor.[6]

Language use: vocabulary
Certain reflexive use of words can be taken to represent some contemporary language use, not merely the literary fabrications of the poets/dramatists. Here, we must be aware of the differences of dramatic genre. Some language is expected in tragedy, but not in comedy, and vice-versa, with tragi-comedy occupying an interstitial literary space. In general, tragedies concerned upper social echelons: if set in Italian contexts, the nobility, but in an English context, the landed gentry. One of the most constant terms of reference in tragedy, tragi-comedy and melodrama was thus "honor". So in *Women Beware Women*, honor in some form (noun, adjective, verb, adverb) occurs thirty-six times, in *Revenger's Tragedy* fifty-three, *Changeling* twenty-three, *Duchess of Malfi* nineteen, *White Devil* seventeen, and *Woman Killed with Kindness* sixteen (several, of course, in a combination of gentry honor and female honor).[7] *Game at Chess*, which defies categorization by genre except as political satire, is also concerned with political and sexual honor, with twenty-two references. The tragedies were predicated, of course, on the inevitable transgression of honor, so that in comedic sub-plots in tragi-comedies, fools comment about its ephemeral nature. Lollio accepts the metaphor of Tony's foolish dance.

> [LOLLIO] Very proper; for honour is but a caper, rises fast and high, has a knee or two, and falls to the ground again.[8]

Here we are not concerned with honor, perhaps a term more redolent of the higher register of tragedy and higher social groups (although other types of honor preoccupied women and lower social groups), but with common language which (seemingly) traversed social groups, inclusive of the citizens of London and the lower social groups of the City which inhabited the City Comedies, including migrants from the provinces to London.

Sorts
During the early seventeenth century, social status was increasingly defined by reference to "sorts" of people: the poorer sort; the middling sort; and the better sort.[9] This more precise definition into three sorts of people evolved only slowly from more imprecise terminology.

12 Social Dramas

Some of the inchoate aspects are visible in contemporary plays. In *Eastward Ho*, the collaborating playwrights allude several times to sorts of people. Slitgut remarks, for example: "what a sort of people cluster about the gallows".[10] The jailer, Wolf, declares: "yet I have all sorts of men I' the kingdom under my keys".[11] At a higher social level, Touchstone, the goldsmith, and Sir Petronel, the impoverished

Table 1 Lexical Items in Selected Plays

Text	Company	Dissemble	Dull	Cunning(ly)	Fashion	Cozen(ed)	Shift	Gull	Honest
Jonson									
Every Man in His Humour	12	1	2	1	7	0	1	7	18
Staple of News	8	1	5	4	7	7	3	0	9
Poetaster	13	0	1	5	9	0	2	4	15
Sejanus	5	3	2	3	0	1	4	0	12
Every Man Out of His Humour	15	1	7	2	20	0	2	5	10
Volpone	1	3	7	2	6	6	5	8	6
Cynthia's Revels	8	0	3	5	16	1	5	4	2
Epicoene	14	1	4	4	8	2	1	0	8
Alchemist	6	1	3	3	6	20	2	13	16
Bartholomew Fair	27	1	5	6	6	2	2	0	21
Devil is an Ass	5	0	8	2	12	12	2	3	14
New Inn	15	4	4	0	7	4	4	0	8
Jonson et al.									
Eastward Ho	11	1	3	4	7	1	6	2	18
Middleton									
Michaelmas Term	9	1	0	1	11	15	7	5	22
Mad World	17	5	2	9	15	0	2	9¶	7
Trick...Old One	4	3	0	4	6	5	7	2	12
No Wit...	8	7	0	5	3	4	4	4	19
Chaste Maid	7	2	4	5	3	2	6	3	19
Women Beware Women	11	3	4	8	11	0	12	0	11
Revenger's Tragedy	3	7	1	1	5	2	1	0	16
Game at Chess	3	5	0	4	3	7	3	1	1
Middleton (and Rowley)									
Changeling	5	0	3	6	2	3	0	0	9
Middleton/Dekker									
Roaring Girl	12	1	0	3	7	4	13	8*	26
Dekker									
Honest Whore I	6	0	1	3	9	1	1	19	31

Language, Literature and Life 13

Text	Company	Dissemble	Dull	Cunning(ly)	Fashion	Cozen(ed)	Shift	Gull	Honest
Dekker									
Honest Whore II	10	0	1	1	4	0	2	0	22
Dekker, Rowley, Ford									
Witch of Edmonton	8	4	1	1	2	3	1	0	24
Marston									
Malcontent	4	4	6	4	14	1	3	0	17
Webster									
White Devil	3	5	2	13	7	4	1	3	8
Heywood									
Woman Killed with Kindness	4	1	1	1	3	0	2	0	7
Webster									
Duchess of Malfi	3	2	0	8	15	1	1	0	12
Beaumont and Fletcher									
Fourteen plays	87	21	58	45	36	59	18	7	288

* Additionally, the character *Gull*. ¶ Additionally, the character Frank Gullman, and the comment on the Courtesan as "Lady Gullman": Act II, scene v, line 2 (see also Act III, scene I, lines 21-2). **Note:** the sequence in which these lexical items is discussed below is in order of (personal) interest.

knight and Touchstone's prospective son-in-law, have a discussion about the "two sorts of gentlemen".[12] At the same social level, Edward dignifies Stephen as "[a] gentleman of your sort, parts, carriage, and estimation".[13] Self-referentially, Bobadill remarks on "a sort of gallants".[14] At completely the opposite end of the spectrum, "[a] sort of lewd rake-hells" were denounced by Downright.[15] The bluff Captain Tucca refers to "a sort of poor starved rascals".[16] When he reveals himself as Lord Frampul, the Host of *New Inn*, describes his previous itinerant life amongst "all the sorts of canters".[17] Condell in the Induction to *The Malcontent* decries "a sort of discontented creatures" whose disposition was always bitter.[18] In the asylum for the mad and foolish, Lollio, the servant of the proprietor, Alibius, observes that there are "but two sorts of people" there, fools and madmen.[19] Later, Lollio informs Isabella, the wife of Alibius, who is confined to the house and its attached institution, that Alibius contends that she has enough company if she would be "sociable", "of all sorts of people", to which Isabella responds that "all sorts" consists of only fools and madmen.[20] Complaining to the Duchess of Malfi, Bosola condemned the "sort of flattering rogues."[21]

[GRATIANA] Poor people, ignorant people:
The better sort, I'm sure, cannot abide it.
And by what rule should we square out our lives,
But by our betters' actions?[22]

Honesty

Oh, what is a man but his honesty, Master Easy.[23]

[FATHER to COUNTRY WENCH, his daughter] Though I be poor, 'tis my glory to live honest.[24]
[COUNTRY WENCH to her FATHER] Do not all trades live by their ware, and yet called honest livers?[25]
[PENNYBOY CANTER] Virtue and honesty, hang 'em; poor thin membranes
Of honour, who respects them?

The preoccupation with honesty in the City comedies is, of course, well considered in the literature on, for example, Middleton.[26] There is little need to elaborate further here. The tabulation above illustrates how dominant that trope was in the plays, in the playwrights' minds, and in contemporary society.

One complication can be addressed and discarded: honest was used as a form of address, just like good: so, "honest waterman" or "good waterman" as forms of amiable address or in gratitude. So Humil commends the watermen: "Well said honest knaves".[27] Another complexity, however, is more critical, that is, the intentional irony in its attribution in the texts. Responding to his courtesan, Witgood congratulates her: "Spoke like an honest drab i'faith".[28] The deceitful Host reflected: "I was never brought up with so little honesty to refuse any man's money, never".[29] The violently scheming Mendoza must have tongue in cheek when he utters: "we dull honest souls" and "Alas, I am too honest for this age".[30]

There is also a sense of honest as authentic or veritable, so Tucca bids farewell to Histrio as "my honest penny-biter", later to "an honest sycophant-like slave" and "mine honest pitiful stinkards".[31] The abruptness accords with Tucca's character as a tough gallant. Perhaps a modern analogy would be the description of someone as "a right so-an-so". In this sense, it seems, Malevole contends that

"Maquerelle is a cunning bawd, I am an honest villain, thy wife is a close drab, and thou art a notorious cuckold".[32]

Honesty and dissembling were conjoined and not necessarily antithetical, so that Maquerelle, the bawd, asks: "Have you the art to seem honest?"[33] More directly, she categorically states that "Honesty is but an art to seem so".[34]

The idea of dissimulation and dissembling was, to some contemporaries, inherent in the theater and players–the very noun (player) itself suggesting conceit and trickery. Thus, Philip Stubbes condemned players (actors) as "dissembling hypocrites", because of their unstable identity and impersonation.[35] For dissembling, see further below.

Fashion

[LITTLEWIT] Win, you see 'tis in fashion to go to the Fair.[36]

...in the sixteenth century there were both selves and a sense that they could be fashioned...an increased self-consciousness about the fashioning of human identity as a manipulable, artful process.[37]

The concern with fashion is reflected in the tabulation above, but receives extended consideration in Chapter 2 below on "flat caps". The varied senses of its usage in the plays, especially the comedies, included manner, custom or way (both collective and individual), new modes (especially civility and foreign influences) and, as an active verb, to make, to fashion (someone). In the chapter on flat caps, the concept of fashion addressed is the one about manners and modes. So, Sir Onesiphrous dispatched his niece to London to stay with his brother "to learn fashions".[38]

Fashion also featured as a verb, however. The verbal form of fashion sometimes also contained more sinister and cynical connotations. When discussing how Penitent could deceive Mistress Harebrain even further, the Courtesan remarked that "she's wax of your own fashioning".[39]

The art of fashioning was also associated with the creative practise of tailors. Pennyboy Junior, in *Staple of News*, refers to his tailor as Master Fashioner. Thomas accordingly remarked that "Master Fashioner" "Has hit your measures, sir. H'has moulded you/ And made you, as they say".[40] The tailor, Nick Stuff, was described as fashioner. Commissioned to make a gown for Lady Frampul, he, in his customary manner, dressed his wife, Pinnacia, in the gown and took her around the countryside outside the City to display her and fornicate with her in the gown in various country inns. Unfortunately for them, they happened to visit the *New Inn*, whilst Lady Frampul was also in residence.[41] A servant proclaimed to the Duchess of Malfi:

> an English tailor crazed I' th' brain
>   With the study of new fashion[42]

Company

> [STUFF] And wear them, too, sweetheart, but this wild company -
>   [PINNACIA] Why do you bring me in wild company?
>   You'd ha' me tame and civil in wild company?
>   I hope I know wild company are fine company,
>   And in fine company, where I am fine myself,
>   A lady may do anything, deny nothing
>   To a fine party, I have heard you say't.
>   *[Enter Pierce]*
>   [PIERCE] There are a company of ladies above
>   Desire your ladyship's company,[43]

> [OLDRENTS] Hear me for all then. Here are no beggars (you are but one, Patrico), no rogues, no players: but a select company to fill this house with mirth[44]

Recently, Withington has argued, mainly from court records, that company constitutes "a category of analysis through which the particularity of social practice...can be considered and interpreted".[45] Defined as "habitual and irregular moments of sociability, company existed between social structure and individual agency, both a structural element within society *and* an expression of individual intention".[46] In the records of ecclesiastical courts, company was closely associated with drinking, privately in houses and publicly in alehouses.[47] The term was employed regularly in contemporary drama and that literary source allows further illumination of its meanings and usage.

The notion of company was also understood in several contexts as a collective noun rather than social company and companionship: in a military context; as companies of players (or, quite humorously, "like a company of puppets"); as City companies; and, but not in the plays, as the whole company of heaven.[48] Some of these entities are represented in the plays, but more importantly they provide a metaphor for the aggregates of characters in the drama, most frequently through the military metaphor.

Two of the categories of company appear in *Shoemaker's Holiday*: the military company and the City company. Lincoln arranges that Lacy should be colonel-in-chief of "all those companies" mustered in London and some Home Counties (at Mile End, Tothill Fields, and Finsbury, the mustering points).[49] The Lord Mayor, Oatley, excuses his departure: "To the Guildhall I must hie/ I know my brethren stay in company" (his livery company) and Eyre refers to all those in "the livery of my company" (the Shoemakers).[50]

In exuberant admiration for Moll, Laxton reflected to himself:

Methinks a brave captain might get all his soldiers upon her, and ne'er be beholding to a company of Mile End milksops'[51]

In *Mad World*, the collective meanings are extended, including through metaphor. The principal character, Follywit, commands a gang of misfits who commit all the devious misdemeanors in the comedy. He refers to his associates in his intention "to maintain a company of villains, whom I love in my very soul and conscience". In return, they refer to him as their captain, and he to his mainstays, Mawworm and Hoboy as his lieutenants, through the military metaphor.[52] When the crew of miscreants, under Follywit's leadership, pretend to be a band of players, Sir Bounteous alludes to them as a "company".[53] After robbing the audience at their play, Follywit and his accomplices are arrested by the constable, who denounces the band as a "company of auspicious fellows".[54] Earlier in the play, Follywit impersonates Lord Owemuch, dispatching ahead a "footman" to alert Sir Bounteous of Owemuch's imminent arrival to request hospitality with Bounteous. The footman, punning on the collective noun, declares that Owemuch does not lack for company when he is in London, for he is free of the Mercers' [Company].[55]

The military metaphor is repeated in *Staple of News*, for Pennyboy Junior alludes to his barber, tailor, linen-man, spurrier, hatter, and shoemaker as his "company", "a brave troupe", and, punning, as "all bill-men", ordering them all to present arms before Canter.[56]

Company did not always imply honest sociability, as Formal, in self-defense, protested that he "happened into ill company by chance".[57] When confronting his current predicament as itinerant and impoverished, having left his family behind in order to seek some way to redress their ill fortune, Lod'wick explains his poverty to Sir Nicholas, from whom he supplicated alms: "I fear by keeping riotous company".[58]

Occasionally–very sporadically–a cognate was employed for company. Society is used as something of an alternative. Advising his nephew, Knowell professed:

> I would not have you to invade each place
>   Nor thrust yourself on all societies,
>   Till men's affections, or your own desert,
>   Should worthily invite you to their rank.[59]

Somewhat ironically, Shortyard remarks to Easy "but I began to affect your society very speedily", the absurdity residing in Shortyard's intention in collaboration with others to divest the gentleman, Easy, of his Essex estate through insinuating himself into the trust of Easy, naïve in the ways of the City.[60]

> [EASY] Methinks I have no being without his [Blastfield's] company; 'tis so full of kindness and delight, I hold him to be the only companion in earth.[61]

Society has the intimations also of social status as well as company. Commenting on his brother, Wellbred, Kitely remarks how

Wellbred has become "Forgetful of his friends and not content/ To stale himself in all societies".[62]

Although the association between company and alehouses does not particularly feature in the plays as much as in other sources, Sly exclaims that: "He will be laughed out of a tavern or an ordinary shall seldom feed well or be drunk in good company".[63]

Shift

> [SHORTYARD] let our wives make shift for children[64]
>
> [TUTCH] come sir, Ile shift with them, and now I must shift with you.[65]
> [BUNCH] Fie, fie, down with my stall, up with my wares, shift for myself.[66]

In historical literature, the most well-known context of "make shift" is the economy of makeshifts of the poor: the fragmented way in which a livelihood was made at the bottom of the social and economic scale. Pauperization and immiseration meant making ends meet through a variety of short-time and intermittent work in a condition of under-employment.[67] Shortyard, however, was invoking the gender division of labor, in which he (and men like him) engaged in controversial gullery out and about in the City, whilst his wife was charged with the domestic responsibilities. In early-modern drama, shift was not socially specific; its meaning was more concentrated on action and doing. We then encounter "to make shift" in the context of devising some means.

> [WITGOOD] my friends should ne'er have known on't; I meant to make shift for that myself.[68]

When Lucre, deceived by Witgood, offers to defray the latter's debts, Witgood professes that he had intended to redeem them himself. Later, Lucre, again manipulated by Witgood, offers advice about the betrothal of Witgood and the (fictitious) widow (who was Witgood's courtesan). To allay the fears of a failed contract, Lucre contends that "you can make shift to bring her to three hundred a year, sir".[69] When deluding his creditors, Witgood requests some more leniency from them about his terms of indebtedness: "do but make shift for me this once".[70] Colluding with his courtesan, as she herself impersonates a rich widow, Witgood wishes to involve her in redeeming his debts, but receives her rebuke: "you might have made some shift to discharge this yourself".[71]

> [FIRST LIVERYMAN] Who, Quomodo? Merely enriched by shifts
> And cozenages, believe it.[72]

> [JUDGE to QUOMODO] But setting these thy odious shifts apart[73]

Middleton's works in particular contain numerous incidences of shift, none moreso perhaps than *Women Beware Women*. Mother (Leantio's mother) recapitulates to him how their modest means have restricted his marriage prospects.

> And hitherto your own means has but made shift
> To keep you single, and that hardly too.[74]

Isabella explains to her aunt, Livia, how it is possible to "make good shift" in marrying the Ward, as he is so naïve.[75] To that end, Livia advises her how to "make shift here to taste your happiness".[76] Bianca alludes to how gentlewomen have "made shift" to convey their love.[77] A circumlocutory exchange between the Duke and Bianca returns again to making shift.

> [DUKE] This thing will make shift, sirs, to make a husband,
> For ought I see in him; how think'st Bianca?
> [BIANCA] 'Faith an ill-favoured shift, my lord, methinks;
> Once in nine year together, a wife then
> Might make indifferent shift to be content with him.[78]

When the Ward, with the counsel of his servant (and the fool of the play), Sordido, attempts to discover the qualities of Isabella to decide whether she is suitable to marry, according to his exacting standards, one of the absurd concerns is whether her feet are splayed, so they concoct a ruse so that Sordido can inspect them.

[WARD] But I have bethought a cleanly shift to find it [out];[79]

When danger and complication threaten, Livia condemns Hippolito, her brother, to "Shift for thyself".[80] To Isabella, Guardiano remarks that in the masque, "Your pages, madam, will make shift for Cupids".[81] Ultimately, in the tragic denouement, the Lord Cardinal proclaims: "See my lord/ What shift sh' has made to be her own destruction".[82]

These examples reveal the range of nuance of "shift" and "to make shift", from effort (noun) and to make an effort, to the more pernicious aspects of trick and to trick. When reduced to straitened circumstances, with only his inherited land which he and his sister have to work themselves, Sir Charles Mountford remarks to his sister, Susan, that they are "driven to hard shift/ To keep this poor house we have left unsold", repeating to Shafton, who attempts to divest him: "You see what hard shift we have made to keep it."[83]

Cozen

Adore me, all you students at the Inns of Cozenage.[84]

In John Lyly's *Mother Bombie*, the eponymous cunning woman, consulted by Riso and halfpenny, both servants, about their futures, responds:

You shall all thrive like coosners,
    That is, to bee cosned by coosners;
    All shall ende well, and you bee found coosners.[85]

Indeed, whilst the action of most plays centered on tricking and tricksters, *Mother Bombie* features cozenage in profusion. The players constantly refer to "exquisite coosnage", "coosnage", and "cosned".[86] In the brief exchanges between Gilthead and Plutarchus in Act III, scene i, of *Devil is an Ass*, there is a concentration on cozenage. Within the space of twenty-two lines, cozen or cozened are reiterated six times.[87] Gilthead explains the predicament: citizens never trust, they cozen; they cozen their debtors; if they fail to deceive their debtors, they cozen themselves. The whole of *Alchemist*, like most of the comedies of Jonson (and also Middleton), is predicated on gulleries, gulling, cozeners and cozenage: dupes and the dupers, deceived and deceivers, tricked and tricksters. Jonson attempts some alliterative humor with "cozening Captain", "chemical cozener", and "cave of coz'nage".[88]

Cunning

[SAVOURWIT] The age is cunning, sir;[89]

[TRUEWIT] Let cunning be above cost.[90]

With the exception of the more benign Dekker, the playwrights depicted metropolitan (and, indeed, provincial) life as hazardous, in which it was absolutely vital to be alert and have your wits about you. Cunning imputed wisdom in the ways of the world, sharpness and mental agility.

Dissemble

[PHILIP] I'll learn then to dissemble.[91]

[AMBITIOSO to SUPERVACU] 'Twill teach thee to dissemble.[92]

No doubt concealing one's true feelings is a constant feature of human behavior, but the political and religious circumstances of the sixteenth century lent a heightened significance.[93] Dissembling thus entered into the common vocabulary of the plays, comedies and tragedies alike.[94]

The political conditions are very well attested in *Game at Chess*. In this play, dissimulation features alongside dissembling, encountered first with the Black Knight's commendation to the Black Bishop's Pawn: "Honour's dissimulation be your due, sir".[95] It is the Black Knight again who contends that: "This whiteness upon him is but pure leprosy/ Of pure dissimulation."[96] So later, the Black Knight complains of a kingdom beggared by dissimulation.[97] It is in the endgame, however, that the dissembling reaches a sublime climax, for the victory by White is achieved by a sacrifice and discovered checkmate. In the manoeuvres, the White Knight confesses that he is an "arch-dissembler", clarifying in his next statement:

'Tis my nature's brand; turn from me, sir.
   The time is yet to come that e'er I spoke
   What my heart meant!

On that confession, the Black Knight congratulates him: "Now you're a brother to us; what we have done/ Has been dissemblance ever". The White Duke (castle/rook) can only exclaim in collusion: "Dissembler includes all".[98]

Here, in *Game at Chess*, we are brought into direct encounter with the political-religious context which intensified concerns about mental reservation, dissembling and dissimulation in the sixteenth and seventeenth centuries. The play engages directly with Jesuit casuistry, with the "Induction" consisting of a dialogue with Ignatius Loyola, and some of the black pieces belonging to the Order.[99]

Equivocation–mental reservation or ambiguous speech–was, of course, not a direct line to dissembling, which equated more with outright lying. Zagorin has explained the context of some playwrights' "deep fascination with the powerful effects of deceit and hypocrisy". His enumeration of Marlowe, Webster, Chapman, and Shakespeare, could easily be extended to all the playwrights, in comedies, tragi-comedies and tragedies alike. "Whether in relation to public or private affairs, the idea that people commonly went masked and habitually dissimulated their true beliefs came readily to contemporary minds." The combination of circumstances (matters of state and diplomacy, religious controversy, occultism [secret knowledge]) "all served to confirm the notion that dissimulation and lying had reached new heights and were more prevalent than ever before."[100] The prevalence of casuistry is reflected by Malevole: "From the public place of much dissimulation, the church".[101] The closest association of occultism and dissemblance occurs, of course, in Jonson's *Alchemist*.[102]

> [DAUPHINE] Run out o'door in's nightcaps to talk with a casuist about his divorce.[103]

In the Court of Love in *New Inn*, presided over by Prudence, in which Lovel, as appellant, appeals against Lady Frampul, as defendant, about her insinuation of the properties of love, the lady professes to be overwhelmed by Lovel's argument, but Lovel and the other witnesses cannot quite convince themselves that the lady is not dissembling, as is remarked on several occasions.[104]

Dull

> Bear with our willing pains, if dull or witty -
> We can only dedicate it to the City.

As remarked further below, the Prologue and the Epilogue to plays were usually constructed in rhyming couplets, the only elements in the plays to be consistently in rhymed meter. The Prologue to *Eastward Ho* finishes with this, perhaps falsely modest, apology to the audience. On initial reflection, we might assume that *dull* is merely poetic language. The word is, however, one of those repetitive lexical items which occurs frequently throughout plays, without any alternative adjective, which suggests that it was a conventional term in daily use.

The exposition of *Chaste Maid* is almost completely concerned with the opinion of Yellowhammer and his wife Maudline that their daughter, Moll, is dull-eyed and dull. That description of her resonates through the first exchanges in the play, establishing both her reticence to accede to her parents' wishes, but also that, ironically, she will eventually outwit them.[105]

More pertinently, perhaps, is the declamation by Mistress FitzDottrel in *Devil is an Ass*, that Wittipol, who has wooed her, will conceive her really "that dull stupid creature", adjectives in apposition.[106] Apposition also defines the adverb when Haughty proclaims that some merely "love flat and dully".[107]

Canting

"Low" dialog is not complete without some reference to canting or argot, although so much attention has been directed to it that not much more need be added here. It is well understood that most of the playwrights assumed their canting vocabulary from Thomas Harman rather than from intimate, personal knowledge.[108] In *Roaring Girl*, Dekker and Middleton include an exposition of the argot of the City underground, through the "maundering" of Tearcat and Trapdoor. Moll interprets for Jack Dapper and Sir Beauteous, explaining individual words. The nod to Harman is recited by Moll and Tearcat in a chorus:

> O, I would lib all the lightmans.
> > O, I would lib all the darkmans,
> > By the solomon, under the ruffmans,
> > By the solomon, in the harmans.[109]

"All the sorts of canters", according to the Host of the *New Inn*, comprised the "wilder nations" of the Peak and Lancashire, their pipers, fiddlers, rushers, puppet-masters, jugglers, gypsies, colonies of beggars, tumblers, and ape-carriers.[110] Undoubtedly, Jonson himself had a benign attitude towards these traditional recreational customs, an affinity imputed to the Host.

Jonson extended "canting" to include any obscure language or jargon. Oxford and Cambridge were thus denounced as the "canting universities", although we might detect there some personal animosity from this poet whose personal situation had denied him access to those institutions and whose career had commenced in context of competition with the "scholar-poets" such as Nash and Greene.[111] So, although very learned himself and inclined to recite Latin, Jonson has Fly dismiss Master Goodstock who "cants in Latin comely".[112]

Appropriately then, Jonson regarded the pseudo-sciences of the age as mere canting. Surly, naively impressed by the mystical conversations of Face and Subtle in *Alchemist*, bursts out: "What a brave language here is, next to canting", incantation as canting.[113] Astrologers receive the same treatment: "you shall cant alone".[114]

Perhaps the most satirical denunciation of canting is reserved for heraldry and heralds in *Staple of News*. The object of its disdain was the obscure language of heralds. As Piedmantle recounts descents and armorial bearings and charges, Pennyboy Canter ironically interrupts: "Is not this canting? Do you understand him?"[115] The subsequent interchanges are littered with the word "canter", culminating in Pennyboy Junior's project of establishing Canter's College.[116]

There are probably only two conclusions at which we can arrive about canting and argot in the plays: the knowledge was derivative, an excellent example of inter-textuality between the popular print media and drama; second, Jonson regarded jargon or any obscurantist language as equivalent to canting. The "lexical underworld" of the plays simply repeats Harman's lexicography, which itself borrowed heavily from earlier compendia.[117]

Metaphor, metonymy, simile, and synecdoche
Below, in chapter 4, considerable reference is made to coinage as a metaphor or metonymy. Our conversation is constantly peppered with metaphor and the playwrights fully reflected that characteristic.[118] On many occasions, they resort to contemporary adages to illuminate points. This usage was a conscious device, especially in the case of Jonson, who, as in all matters, reflected deeply and perhaps self-consciously on his texts. Likewise, Middleton and Rowley hazarded having Lollio discern that Franciscus had deteriorated into madness partly because he had been a poet: "he was a pretty poet too, and that set him forwards first;"[119]

> And he, this man, so graced, gilded or–to use a more fit metaphor–so tinfoiled by nature, as not ten housewives' pewter again' a good time, shows more bright to the world than he![120]

> WELLBRED Is a fit simile, a toy? Will he be poisoned with a simile?[121]

In similar vein, Marston signaled his use of simile three times in *The Malcontent*.[122]

Rhymed Couplets

The suggestion has been advanced that verse has a special significance in the plays.[123] Conventionally, verse is associated with a higher register, the speech of the social elite, whilst prose represents a "low" style of inferior social groups. Romantic passages are also conducted in verse. So discourse analysis may assist in divining social characteristics in the plays. Here, however, we are specifically concerned with the deployment of rhymed verse, not merely all meter (i.e. blank verse). Rhymed verse occurs in plays of all sub-genres, most typically as the final rhymed couplet closing a longer speech. The employment of rhymed couplets varied, however, by playwright and by play. Within plays, rhymed couplets often expressed some particular purposes.

In the analysis below (Table 2), songs and ditties within plays are omitted, since they were popularly rhymed. That very association with popular balladry might have influenced their use or non-use, their inclusion or their omission, their expectation and their dismissal, and their punctuation of the plays according to genre.

In *Eastward Ho*, indeed, rhymed couplets are deployed very sparingly, but to specific purpose. In five instances, the couplets consist entirely of quotations by the characters, not uttering their own words. Three other couplets are contained in the final announcement in the denouement of the play by Touchstone, the very last six lines of the play.[124] In the single-authored *Every Man in His Humour*, Jonson hardly employed rhymed couplets; indeed, he occasionally engaged in more sophisticated rhyming, alternate lines or even fourth line. There is a distinct possibility that he regarded rhyme with some disdain. In the penultimate speech in the play, Kitely addresses his wife in six lines, the last four consisting of rhymed couplets. He follows those rhymed lines with the declaration: "I ha' learned so much verse out of a jealous man's part in a play".[125] Most of the other rhymed lines consist of quotations read out by characters. One of the rhymed utterances by one of the characters suggests a large degree of bathos; Cob, the water carrier, responded to his wife, Tib (Isabel): "Tut, sweet or sour, thou art a flower,/Keep close thy door, I ask no more".[126] The lines contain no didactic significance whatsoever, although they marginally indicate a future crisis and reflect Cob's lowly status, although most of

Table 2 Rhymed Couplets in Selected Plays (Excluding Prologue and Epilogue)

Text	Rhymed Couplets	Total Lines	Comment
Jonson			
Every Man in His Humour (1598)	16	2869	Disdainful use?
Poetaster (1601)	114	2938	Disparaging?
Sejanus (1603)	165	3252	Purposeful?
Volpone (1606)	56	2970	Sparse
Epicoene (1609)	2	3130	Almost absent: prose
Alchemist (1610)	39	3061	Sparse
Devils is an Ass (1616)	37	3006	Purposeful
Staple of News (1626)	5	2927	Rare
Bartholomew Fair (1614)	0	3596	All prose, but the songs and puppet show are rhymed verse
New Inn (1629)	26	2549	Sparse
Jonson et al.			
Eastward Ho (1605)	13	2518	Specific usage
Middleton			
Michaelmas Term	100	2329	Copious
Mad World	88	2213	Copious
Trick ... Old One	41	2164	Concentrated in final scene
Chaste Maid	10	2136	Sparing usage
No Wit...	84	2959	Copious at end of long speeches
Women Beware Women	111	2899	Fairly copious
Revenger's Tragedy	229	2463	Extensive
Game at Chess	71	2073	Sparing

his speech was in prose. Jonson, then, might have considered that, rather than imparting significance, rhyme was a degenerate form.

Jonson's diffidence towards rhyming may perhaps be exemplified in *Staple of News*, in which there are barely half a dozen rhyming couplets, and in which Pennyboy senior utters with ennui: "Not Richard, but old Harry Pennyboy,/ And (to make rhyme) close,

Middleton (and Rowley)			
The Changeling	26	2192	Sparse
Middleton/Dekker			
Roaring Girl	110	2760	Consolidated usage
Dekker			
Honest Whore I	173	*	Plethora
Honest Whore II	278	*	Plethora
Dekker, Rowley, Ford			
Witch of Edmonton	48	2317	Sparse
Marston			
Malcontent	108	2399	Profuse
Webster			
White Devil	117	2902	Frequent
Heywood			
Woman Killed with Kindness	190	1959	Copious
Webster			
Duchess of Malfi	51	2853	Purposeful

* Lines not numbered in the Globe Quartos Edition
Note: There is a slight difference between my line counts and those of Bruster, *Shakespeare and the Question of Culture*, 113, since mine excludes the Prologue and Epilogue; Bruster's analysis is concerned with the number of props per thousand lines.

wary Pennyboy"[127] Superficially, Jonson appears to introduce more rhyme in *Poetaster*, but a detailed analysis reveals that he was probably employing it to disparage. A large proportion of the rhymed verse is contained in the poems read out by Ovid and Virgil and in the songs of Crispinus, perhaps indicating that these verses constituted a debased form of poetry, since, first, they were composed by rivals to Horace (Jonson) and, second, song was a "popular" (i.e. not erudite) form of poesy.

In *Volpone*, Jonson's deployment of rhyming is minimal, merely fifty-six or so couplets, but it is also deliberately confined to the opening of the second scene, the "dramatic presentation" by Nano and Androgino to Volpone. Nano, indeed, explicitly refers to the "false pace of the verse".[128] More than thirty of the rhymed couplets are concentrated here. If the songs are omitted, rhymed verse rarely appears elsewhere in the play. Writing a few years later, Jonson composed *Epicoene* almost completely in prose, although a couple of rhymed couplets occur. A minimal number of rhymed couplets are inserted in *Alchemist*, but with a sequence of seven in the first exchanges in Act III, scene v, in which Subtle and Face delude the blindfolded Dapper that the Fairy Queen has appeared to him. The recitation in the rhymed couplets affords an incantation.[129] In *Bartholomew Fair*, rhymed verse is restricted to the songs and the puppet show. Purposefully, in *Devil is an Ass*, Iniquity recites two-thirds of the rhymed verses (excluding the songs); since all his speech is rhymed in this manner, it defines his character. Iniquity engages in a display of bravado in verse to impress the novice Pug, but the Devil dismisses Iniquity's juvenile gusto.[130] More importantly, as the Devil clarifies in no uncertain terms, Iniquity is behind the times; he is antiquated and no longer useful. No longer sufficiently subtle for the mischief of the times, Iniquity is ordered by the Devil to return to his "rope and sand", toiling away laboriously behind the scenes. "Old" Iniquity belongs to a past, eclipsed generation, as does, Jonson suggested, rhymed verse: unsubtle, pointless, and lacking in wit.[131]

One of the reasons that *New Inn* was so critically received might have been its paucity of rhymed verse, as well as the somewhat inconceivable plot. Jonson also, perhaps disdainfully, included a fair number of couplets in which exactly the same word finished the succeeding line: "purposh...purposh"; "horse...horse"; "him...him"; "horses...horses"; "it...it"; "love...love"; for example.[132] A sequence of five lines each completed with the name "Pru" was no doubt intended to convey the estimable qualities of Prudence, the confidante of Lady Frampul, as admired by the Host, but one wonders about the audience's reaction.[133] Perhaps the audience did not have the same perception of the Poet in *Jovial Crew* that: "There's as good poetry in blank verse, as metre."[134]

By contrast, Middleton and Dekker use rhyming effusively in *Roaring Girl*, but with strategic effect: to break up long disquisitions and maintain the audience's concentration. So the long passages of speech by Sebastian, Sir Alexander, Laxton and Openwork, for example, contain intermittent rhyming couplets.

Webster, in *Duchess of Malfi*, distributes the rhymed couplets sparingly, to make an impact. The couplets are usually located to complete longer speeches. Most have some moral value or wider perception, represented, perhaps, by the couplet which concludes the play:

> Integrity of life is fame's best friend,
> Which nobly, beyond death, shall crown the end.[135]

One of the purposes of rhyming was to make connections with the audience through the rehearsal of conventional stereotypes, re-iteration of well-known aphorisms, or the construction of new adages. Some examples may perhaps suffice.[136]

> [SEBASTIAN] By opposite policies, courses indirect:
> Plain dealing in this world takes no effect.[137]

This general observation about the current condition of the reverse side of City life reiterates a commonly-held opinion, but also establishes the motives of some of the actors in the play.

> [GALLIPOT] Gods-so, our friends! Come, come! Smooth your cheek -
> After a storm the face of heaven looks sleek.[138]

A common aphorism establishes contact with the audience.

> [LAXTON] The money being paid, sir, I am gone.
> Farewell. O, women, happy's he trusts none.[139]

> [LAXTON]... Rarely!
> That while,
> By which the serpent did the first woman beguile,
> Did ever since all women's bosoms fill:
> You're apple-eaters all, deceivers still.[140]

Whilst reinforcing stereotypes, the aphorisms were also critical to understanding the plot, which was established on conventionally-understood actions. So, Sir Alexander comments about the value of his furniture which "Cost many a fair grey groat ere it came here/ But good things are most cheap when they're most dear".[141] The rhymed adage about value and social distinction resonates with part of the audience as well as communicating the nature of his character.[142]

The rhymed couplets of Middleton and Dekker also re-connected with the audience by either recapitulating the action or signaling future developments.

> [MOLL] Rescue? A pox on 'em, Trapdoor, let's away!
>   I'm glad I have done perfect one good work to day:
>   If any gentleman be in scrivener's bands [sc. Bonds],
>   Send but for Moll, she'll bail him by these hands![143]

The rhyming re-establishes Moll's previous actions in the audience's mind and also presages her future deeds, fore-grounding the future direction of the play.

> [SIR ALEXANDER] Thou shalt come closely in and filch away,
>   And all the weight upon her back I'll lay.[144]

The audience's attention is brought back to the sub-plot which had been established in the exposition, by which Sir Alexander hatched a plan to trap Moll through using Trapdoor as his agent to insinuate himself as Moll's servant and report back to Sir Alexander. So now Sir Alexander directs Trapdoor again to make progress with the trap.

After the several crises and moving towards the climax, Laxton recapitulates the whole of a sub-plot in which he had endeavored to win Moll, for the audience's benefit. His two speeches here amount to thirty-one lines, consisting mostly of rhyming couplets (fourteen couplets). The rhyming serves not only to break up the long speeches (of eleven and twenty lines), with the intention of keeping the audience's attention, but also to remind the audience of one of the sub-plots as it has developed and been resolved through the entire action.[145]

Middleton copiously employs rhymed couplets in *A Mad World*, but the verse is mostly concentrated in the long conversations between Penitent and the Courtesan, Penitent and the hypochondriac Mistress Harebrain, the Courtesan and her Mother, and Penitent with the Succubus. Those dialogs constitute almost half of the rhymed couplets. The rhyming heightens the comedic effect, breaks the long speeches, but also quickens the pace.[146]

More sparingly, in *A Trick to Catch the Old One*, Middleton's rhymed couplets are concentrated in the close of the play, Act V, scene ii, in the final speeches, uttered by the Courtesan and Witgood, the two principal characters. Half of the rhymed couplets are contained here.

Other poetic devices obviously pervade the texts, but they do not have too much impact on the social implications.[147] We might just note the incidence of chiasmus and antithesis. *A Mad World* has numerous examples.

[FOLLYWIT] I shall have all when he has nothing; but now he has all I shall have nothing.[148]

[FOLLYWIT] Though guilt condemns, 'tis gilt must make us glad.[149]

The introduction of these devices serves a purpose, signaling, perhaps more than rhymed couplets, some salient matters to the audience. In the former, the essence of Follywit's position is emphatically indicated to the audience. The second quotation illustrates the ambivalent position of Follywit in deceiving his relative, Sir Bounteous.

Audiences, nonetheless, had their expectations which sometimes had to be appeased. Middleton undoubtedly catered to those demands in *Women Beware Women* by the introduction of Sordido, the servant of the Ward, who acted also as the fool in the play, a role traditionally expected. Sordido, therefore, engages in rhyme to explicate to the Ward the qualities that the Ward should expect in a potential bed-mate: "I have 'em all in rhyme", adumbrating the fifteen criteria in nine sequential rhymed couplets.[150] The gratification of the audience with rhymed couplets is most completely illustrated in *Knight of the Burning Pestle*. Satirically, Beaumont's play within the play consists almost entirely of rhymed couplets, mostly absurd. The constant repetition of the rhyming reduces the speeches to illogicality. So Humphrey proclaimed, for example:

> Let no game,
>   Or anything that tendeth to the same,
>   Be evermore remembered, thou fair killer,
>   For whom I sat me down and broke my tiller.[151]

A satire on the "low" cultural expectations of the citizens of London, in this case the grocer and his wife, authored by one of gentry status, Beaumont, the trenchant criticism is not entirely misdirected.

Rhymed couplets could therefore be employed with purpose. The pace of exchanges could be quickened by the device. In Jonson's case, rhymed verse might insinuate inferiority, another device in his armory of irony and satire. We should not strive, however, to detect some point behind every passage of rhymed verse. Audiences expected certain features in plays and their demands were satisfied. In Jonson's self-references and pointed remarks about poets in his plays, in his "Intermeans", and in Beaumont's *Knight of the Burning Pestle*, the expectations of audiences are revealed as traditional and customary. In satirizing those popular expectations, both playwrights still acceded to the audience's wishes. Jonson learned that disappointment with the failure of *New Inn*, about which he composed a rejoinder: "The just indignation the author took at the vulgar censure of his play by some malicious spectators begat this following ode to himself". In short, he had failed to compromise with his audience, despite his admission in the Epilogue that: "Plays in themselves have neither hopes nor fears/ Their fate is only in their hearers' ears". Another perspective on audience critique of plays occurs in the Induction to *The Malcontent*.

Poetic Vocabularies

Dramatists' language differed, of course, from quotidian speech in the extent of the vocabulary.[152] Their language use incorporated popular speech, but also consisted of a much wider thesaurus. We can make some effort to recover the expanse of their vocabulary by a corpus analysis of the plays. It has recently been suggested that Shakespeare's vocabulary consisted of about 20,000 words, although previous estimates had extended to as much as 50,000.[153] Table 3 below indicates the potential vocabulary deployed by dramatists in various plays. The analysis is based on a selection of plays by each dramatist, not their entire corpus.

Beaumont and Fletcher employed about seven percent fewer different words than Jonson. We should, however, consider the impact of the different genre. Jonson's texts contain comedy, tragicomedy, and tragedy, whilst those of Beaumont and Fletcher contain no tragic forms and have a preponderance of comedy. Since

Table 3 Vocabularies Deployed in Selected Plays

Dramatist/Play	N of unique words (raw count)	[Number of plays]
Jonson: *Sejanus*; *Poetaster*; *Volpone*; *Epicoene*; *Alchemist*; *Every Man in His Humour*; *Everyman Out of His Humour*; *Cynthia's Revels*	11, 713	[8]
Beaumont/Fletcher: *Maid's Tragedy*; *Philaster*; *Custom of the Country*; *Humorous Lieutenant*; *Scornful Lady*; *Spanish Curate*; *Beggars Bush*; *Faithful Shepherdess*; *King and No King*; *Wit Without Money*; *Laws of Candy*; *Rule a Wife*; *False One*; *Little French Lawyer*	10, 939	[14]

Jonson also situated his tragi-comedies and tragedies in classical environments, usually Rome, his vocabulary accordingly contains specialized and archaic terms. There is no doubt, however, that Jonson endeavored to present a more literate and sophisticated vocabulary–and image of his intellectual prowess. Circumspection has to be exercised in deducing ordinary language from the plays.

Throughout the subsequent chapters, the meanings of words constantly arises. Throughout, attention to the context is vital, but with sufficient discretion, the plays can be used to illuminate social life and attitudes as it (by representation) occurred in "normal" activities, not through the mediation of a forum like courts or in pathological circumstances. In the following Chapter, further discussion is devoted to one of the lexical items considered above, "fashion" and "fashioning".

Notes

[1] *Alchemist*, Act II, scene ii, lines 61-63.

[2] Riggs, *Ben Jonson*, 30.

[3] Discussed further below in Chapter 3.

[4] For the composition of audiences, we still depend heavily on Gurr, *Shakespearean Stage*.

[5] *Eastward Ho*, Act I, scene i, lines 11-12, 16, 19, 89; Act I, scene ii, lines 90, 124, 148, 155, 168; Act II, scene i, lines 78, 113, 135-6; Act III, scene ii, lines 124-5, 136; Act IV, scene ii, line 126; Act V, scene ii, lines 4-5, 10; Act V, scene v, line 45.

[6] *Weakest Goeth to the Wall*, scene xviii, lines 13, 15.

[7] For sexual connotations of honor, Gordon Williams, *A Glossary of Shakespeare's Sexual Language* (London: Athlone Press, 1997), 160-1.

[8] *Changeling*, Act IV, scene iii, lines 99-100.

[9] Keith Wrightson, "'Sorts of People' in Tudor and Stuart England", in *The Middling Sort of People: Culture, Society and Politics in England, 1550-1800*, ed. Jonathan Barry and Christopher Brooks (Basingstoke: Palgrave, 1994), 28-51; Henry French, *The Middle Sort of People in Provincial England 1600-1750* (Oxford: Oxford University Press, 2007).

[10] *Eastward Ho*, Act IV, scene i, line 97.

[11] *Eastward Ho*, Act V, scene ii, lines 26-7.

[12] *Eastward Ho*, Act III, scene ii, lines 116-25.

[13] *Every Man in His Humour*, Act I, scene ii, lines 87-8.

[14] *Every man in His Humour*, Act I, scene iv, lines 17-18.
[15] *Every Man in His Humour*, Act IV, scene i, line 158.
[16] *Poetaster*, Act I, scene ii, line 152.
[17] *New Inn*, Act V, scene v, line 97; *Honest Whore II*, 161 (Matheo: "a sort of rascals").
[18] *Malcontent*, Induction, line 52.
[19] *Changeling*, Act I, scene ii, lines 44-5.
[20] *Changeling*, Act III, scene iii, lines 12-14.
[21] *Duchess of Malfi*, Act III, scene ii, line 233.
[22] *Revenger's Tragedy*, Act II, scene i, lines 145-8.
[23] *Michaelmas Term*, Act III, scene iv, line 130 (Quomodo)
[24] *Michaelmas Term*, Act IV, scene ii, line 1.
[25] *Michaelmas Term*, Act IV, scene ii, lines 10-11.
[26] Chakravorty, Society and Politics.
[27] Robert Armin, *The History of the Two Maids of More-Clacke* ed. Alexander S, Liddle (New York: Garland Publishing Inc., 1979), Act I, scene ii, line 45. This play was first produced in 1609.
[28] *A Trick...Old One*, Act I, scene i, line 51.
[29] *A Trick...Old One*, Act III, scene i, lines 133-4.
[30] *Malcontent*, Act II, scene v, lines 61, 65.
[31] *Poetaster*, Act III, scene iv, line 300; Act V, scene iii, lines 93, 349.
[32] *Malcontent*, Act I, scene iii, lines 83-5.
[33] *Malcontent*, Act II, scene iv, line 24.
[34] *Malcontent*, Act V, scene ii, line 12.
[35] Scott-Warren, *Early Modern English Literature*, 109.
[36] *Bartholomew Fair*, Act I, scene v, line 127.
[37] Greenblatt, *Renaissance Self-fashioning*, 1, 2.
[38] *Trick...Old One*, Act I, scene i, line 131.
[39] *Mad World*, Act I, scene i, lines 111-12.
[40] *Staple of News*, Act I, scene i, line 34; Act I, scene ii, lines 93-5, 108-18, and throughout the scene.
[41] *New Inn*, Act IV, scene iii, lines 33-5.
[42] *Duchess of Malfi*, Act IV, scene ii, lines 50-1.
[43] *New Inn*, Act IV, scene ii, lines 91-9.
[44] *Jovial Crew*, Act V, scene i, lines 469-71.
[45] Phil Withington, "Company and Sociability in Early Modern England", *Social History* 32 (2007): 291-307, at p. 306.
[46] Withington, "Company and Sociability", 300.
[47] Withington, "Company and Sociability", 293.
[48] For the "company of puppets", Thomasine in *Michaelmas Term*, Act II, scene iii, lines 58-9.
[49] *Shoemaker's Holiday*, scene i, lines 45-50.

[50] *Shoemaker's Holiday*, scene ix, lines 104-5; scene xx, line 4.
[51] *Roaring Girl*, scene iii, lines 171-3.
[52] *Mad World*, Act I, scene i, lines 1-76; Act III, scene iii, lines 85-136.
[53] *Mad World*, Act V, scene i, line 57.
[54] *Mad World*, Act V, scene ii, line 79.
[55] *Mad World*, Act II, scene i, lines 17-18.
[56] *Staple of News*, Act I, scene iii, lines 11-20.
[57] *Every Man in His Humour*, Act V, scene i, lines 189-90.
[58] *The Weakest Goeth to the Wall*, scene viii, line 66.
[59] *Every Man in His Humour*, Act I, scene i, lines 65-8.
[60] *Michaelmas Term*, Act III, scene i, lines 20-1. See also *Poetaster*, Act I, scene ii, line 94; Act V, scene iii, line 420; *Devil is an Ass*, Act I, scene vi, line 101; *New Inn*, Act I, scene vi, line 37.
[61] *Michaelmas Term*, Act III, scene ii, lines 6-8.
[62] *Every Man in His Humour*, Act II, scene i, lines 55-6.
[63] *Malcontent*, Act I, scene i, lines 9-11.
[64] *Michaelmas Term*, Act IV, scene i, line 35.
[65] Armin, *The History of the Two Maids of More-Clacke*, scene xvi, lines 222-3.
[66] *Weakest Goeth to the Wall*, scene ii, lines 108-9.
[67] Olwen H. Hufton, *The Poor in Eighteenth-century France, 1750-1789* (Oxford: Oxford University Press, 1974).
[68] *Trick...Old One*, Act II, scene i, lines 251-2.
[69] *Trick...Old One*, Act IV, scene ii, lines 40-1.
[70] *Trick...Old One*, Act IV, scene iii, line 50.
[71] *Trick...Old One*, Act IV, scene iv, line 162.
[72] *Michaelmas Term*, Act IV, scene iv, lines 15-16.
[73] *Michaelmas Term*, Act V, scene iii, line 34.
[74] *Women Beware Women*, Act I, scene i, lines 63-4.
[75] *Women Beware Women*, Act II, scene i, lines 80-1.
[76] *Women Beware Women*, Act II, scene i, line 121.
[77] *Women Beware Women*, Act III, scene i, lines 17-18.
[78] *Women Beware Women*, Act III, scene iii, lines 228-33.
[79] *Women Beware Women*, Act III, scene iv, lines 114-15.
[80] *Women Beware Women*, Act IV, scene ii, line 48.
[81] *Women Beware Women*, Act IV, scene ii, line 214.
[82] *Women Beware Women*, Act V, scene ii, lines 216-17.
[83] *Woman Killed with Kindness*, scene vii, lines 1-2, 38.
[84] Quomodo in *Michaelmas Term*, Act II, scene iii, lines 432-3.
[85] John Lyly, *Mother Bombie* (London, 1594), Act IV, scene i, lines 1320-1.
[86] *Mother Bombie*, Act I, scene i, line 113; Act II, scene i, lines 449, 489, 588, 601; Act II, scene iv, lines 808, 855; Act III, scene ii, lines 1033, 1063; Act

III, scene iii, line 1103; Act IV, scene ii, line 1630; Act V, scene iii, lines 1942, 2021, 2051, 2170, 2176-7, 2245.

[87] *Devil is an Ass*, Act III, scene i, lines 22-42.

[88] *Alchemist*, Act V, scene iii, line 38; Act V, scene v, line 18; Act V, scene v, line 115.

[89] *No Wit...*, Act I, scene iii, line 172.

[90] *Epicoene*, Act IV, scene i, line 102.

[91] *No Wit...*, Act IV, scene iii, line 27.

[92] *Revenger's Tragedy*, Act III, scene v, line 37.

[93] Perez Zagorin, *Ways of Lying: Dissimulation, Persecution and Conformity in Early Modern Europe* (Cambridge: MA: Harvard University Press, 1990), 1.

[94] Jean-Christophe Agnew, *Worlds Apart: The Market and the Theater in Anglo-American Thought, 1550-1570* (Cambridge: Cambridge University Press, 1986), 79-82 (especially concerning the permission for dissimulation in William Scott's *An Essay of Drapery*, 1635).

[95] *Game at Chess*, Act I, scene i, line 272.

[96] *Game at Chess*, Act III, scene i, lines 259-60.

[97] *Game at Chess*, Act IV, scene ii, line 24.

[98] *Game at Chess*, Act V, scene iii, lines 145-64.

[99] For the "introduction" of concepts of Catholic equivocation from Douai-Rheims, Zagorin, *Ways of Lying*, 122-4, 186-220.

[100] Zagorin, *Ways of Lying*, 255.

[101] *Malcontent*, Act I, scene iii, line 4.

[102] For this relationship between alchemy and dissemblance, Zagorin, *Ways of Lying*, 255-88.

[103] *Epicoene*, Act IV, scene v, lines 2-3.

[104] *New Inn*, Act III, scene ii, line 277; Act IV, scene iv, lines 144, 308.

[105] *Chaste Maid*, Act I, scene i, lines 1-20.

[106] *Devil is an Ass*, Act II, scene ii, line 28.

[107] *Epicoene*, Act V, scene ii, lines 16-17.

[108] Haaker's introduction to *Jovial Crew*, pp. xii-xiii, reciting, in particular, Dekker's *English Villainies* and *Bellman of London* and Middleton and Rowley's *The Spanish Gipsy*—and, indeed, the borrowing of plots.

[109] *Roaring Girl*, scene 10; quotation from lines 199-202.

[110] *New Inn*, Act V, scene v, lines 94-9.

[111] *New Inn*, Act I, scene v, line 39.

[112] *New Inn*, Act II, scene v, line 42.

[113] *Alchemist*, Act II, scene iii, line 42.

[114] *Staple of News*, Act II, scene iv, line 78.

[115] *Staple of News*, Act IV, scene iv, line 27.

[116] *Staple of News*, Act IV, scene iv, passim.

[117] Geoffrey Hughes, *A History of English Words* (Oxford: Blackwell, 2000), 248-51; Lee Beier, "Anti-language or Jargon? Canting in the English Underworld in the Sixteenth and Seventeenth Centuries", in *Languages and Jargons: Contributions to a Social History of Language*, ed. Peter Burke and Roy Porter (Cambridge: Polity Press, 1995), 64-101, but Robert Jűtte, *Poverty and Deviance in Early Modern Europe* (Cambridge: Cambridge University Press, 1994), 178-85; Julie Coleman, *A History of Cant and Slang Dictionaries Volume I 1567-1784* (Oxford: Oxford University Press, 2004).

[118] Lakoff and Johnson, *Metaphors*.

[119] *Changeling*, Act III, scene iii, lines 47-8.

[120] *Every Man in His Humour*, Act I, scene iii, lines 91-4. See also *New Inn*, Act II, scene v, line 21 ("mend you metaphor") and Act II, scene vi, line 6 ("lose your house metaphor").

[121] *Every Man in His Humour*, Act IV, scene vi, line 32.

[122] *Malcontent*, Act I, scene vi, line 39; III, scene i, line 10; Act III, scene iii, line 61.

[123] Crystal, *"Think on My Words"*, 208-11.

[124] *Eastward Ho*, Act V, scene v, lines 189-94.

[125] *Every Man in His Humour*, Act V, scene i, lines 274-80.

[126] *Every Man in His Humour*, Act IV, scene ii, lines 34-5.

[127] *Staple of News*, Act II, scene v, lines 201-2.

[128] *Volpone*, Act I, scene ii, line 4.

[129] *Alchemist*, Act III, scene v, lines 1-14.

[130] *Devil is an Ass*, Act I, scene i, lines 44-75; Act V, scene vi, lines 12-28.

[131] *Devil is an Ass*, Act I, scene i, lines 116-20.

[132] *New Inn*, Act II, scene vi, lines 267-8, for the first example ("purposh").

[133] *New Inn*, Act II, scene vi, lines 223-7.

[134] *Jovial Crew*, Act IV, scene ii, line 156.

[135] *Duchess of Malfi*, Act V, scene v, lines 119-20.

[136] In general, Adam Fox, *Oral and Literate Culture in Early Modern England, 1500-1700* (Oxford: Oxford University Press, 2000), 112-72.

[137] *Roaring Girl*, scene iv, lines 187-8.

[138] *Roaring Girl*, scene vi, lines 155-6.

[139] *Roaring Girl*, scene vi, lines 249-50.

[140] *Roaring Girl*, scene vi, lines 254-7.

[141] *Roaring Girl*, scene ii, lines 12-13.

[142] Pierre Bourdieu, *Distinction: A Social Critique of the Judgement of Taste*, translated by Richard Nice (London: Routledge, 1986), 260-1, 268-9, 284-5.

[143] *Roaring Girl*, scene vii, lines 212-15.

[144] *Roaring Girl*, scene viii, lines 22-3.

[145] *Roaring Girl*, scene ix, lines 296-306, 309-28.

[146] *Mad World,* Act I, scene i, lines 136-65; Act I, scene ii, lines 75-96; Act IV, scene i, lines 1-71; Act IV, scene iv, lines 40-82.

[147] Hattaway, *Renaissance and Reformation,* 7-37 (Chapter 1: "Speaking and writing"–techniques and devices).

[148] *Mad World*, Act I, scene i, lines 39-40.

[149] *Mad World*, Act II, scene ii, line 28.

[150] *Women Beware Women*, Act II, scene ii, lines 100-17.

[151] *Knight of the Burning Pestle*, Act I, scene I, lines 133-6.

[152] Methodological note. The analysis was performed as follows. The text was retrieved from Project Gutenberg. The external (editorial) apparatus was deleted from each text. The files for each text were then combined into a single file for all the plays. That composite file was then interrogated from the command line interface (CLI) in Linux: tr ' ' ' <return> [at the prompt >] ' < filename.txt | sort | uniq -c | wc -l. The occurrences of words were then reduced manually to remove ambiguities. There remains, of course, the methodological issue of "What is a word?": Hope, "Shakespeare and Language: An Introduction", pp. 11-15.

[153] Crystal, *"Think on My Words,* pp. 2-10.

2
Flatcaps, Fashioning and Civility

> And sooner may a gulling weather spy
>   By drawing forth heaven's scheme tell certainly
>   What fashioned hats, or ruffs, or suits next year
>   Our subtle-witted antic youths will wear[1]

Whether self-fashioning was a newly Renaissance phenomenon or not, there is considerable evidence to support its existence, regardless of how we perceive such major individuals as More or Shakespeare. Self-fashioning has usually been approached from the perspective of how individuals attempted to define themselves, to represent themselves outwardly to the external world. Much attention has therefore been directed to the sumptuary laws as an attempt to restrain those who desired to dress above their station.[2] The concern with how people could outwardly re-define themselves had become by the late sixteenth century a matter of much discussion in the public realm, illustrated by constant comment in the City comedies.[3] Whatever attitude the dramatists adopted towards attire to impress, the common debate about clothing and self-representation featured strongly in their plays.[4]

The *locus* of their dramatic representations was the City of London, whilst the *dramatis personae* were constituted of all levels of London society, including all elements of the working population, but mostly excluding the very lowest echelon of the rogues and vagabonds of contemporary description.[5] Predominant in these plays was the encounter between the citizens and gentle society. The citizenry of the plays consisted of the masters who were craftsmen and tradesmen, but encompassed also the moneylenders and usurers.[6] These encounters occurred on several planes: younger sons of gentle folk apprenticed to citizens; gentlemen from the country gulled by moneylenders and sharp citizens; marriages between the daughters of citizens and the sons of rural gentry; and the distracted activities of gallants and wayward sons of gentry in the metropolis. During the sixteenth century, as has been demonstrated, London had developed into a centre of conspicuous consumption, frequented by gentle society, bringing into contact in the City these different social and cultural elements.[7]

Accordingly, the material about the dramatic representation of this debate about headgear is derived from the works principally of three authors: Thomas Dekker (ca.1572–1632); Thomas Middleton (1580–1627); and Ben Jonson (ca.1572–1637). All three had an intimate acquaintance with the City, but their attitudes towards civic culture diverged. Although little is known about Dekker's origins, he was perhaps closest to the "citizen values" of the City and his dramatic representations most sympathetic to the "low life realism" of this milieu.[8] Dekker's attitude to the City was expressed in one of his earliest major plays, *Shoemaker's Holiday* (composed in 1599) and he repeated this eulogy of the City in *The Seven Deadly Sins of London* (1606). In his cony-catching pamphlets, he professed a great comprehension of the whole life of the City.[9] Perhaps because of his immigrant (Dutch) extraction he felt a greater indebtedness to and affinity with the City where he spent his whole life. Although more critical of aspects of the excesses of bourgeois morality, Middleton was in fact a son of the City, born to a master "bricklayer" (builder) who belonged to the Tilers' and Bricklayers' Company. His early life was much influenced, however, by the death of his father when the son was aged only six and the unfortunate remarriage of his mother which resulted in the destruction by his step-father of all that his father had constructed and the dissipation of the family's fortunes. Those events probably influenced Thomas's attitude towards the litigiousness and acquisitiveness often evident in the City and citizens' dealings.[10] His plays thus contain a jaundiced perspective of lawyers, moneylenders, and "cozenage" (deception) but also of the foolishness of citizens in the marriage "market" and their presumptions of status.[11]

Jonson was a rather different kettle of fish, for, although also of City origins, he had a more "conservative" mindset and different education. Attendance at Westminster School furnished him with a classical education in a highly traditional environment. After that experience, he was apprenticed as a bricklayer, but abandoned that occupation first to venture to the Low Countries to serve as a soldier and then to enter upon the uncertain life of a jobbing actor and writer. In his youth, his misadventures were reckless, including escaping, through benefit of clergy, execution for homicide, and licentious sexual encounters. Like Dekker he also sustained indebtedness which incurred spells in prison, the Counter. The difference between Jonson and the others consisted in his aspirations to status, in social position and intellectual recognition. Some have asserted that Jonson adopted a rather moderate social and political position in the early-sevententh-century context, whilst others have asserted that he had a more profound political agendum.[12] Looking backwards to an earlier golden age of nobility and honor, he did not, however, reserve his acerbic wit to any one object in his plays, but scattered it liberally against all hypocrisies that he perceived (except, perhaps, his own).[13]

All three thus had intimate knowledge of the metropolis, its customs, and environments, Dekker and Jonson in particular participating in the routines of drink, debt and incarceration. Their works thus provide an element of "dramatic realism" of City life, but from different perceptions of that reality.[14] The issue of fashioning was directly addressed, probably acerbically, by Jonson in *Staple of News*.

> [FASHIONER]
> Believe it sir
> That clothes do much upon the wit as weather
> Does on the brain, and thence comes your proverb:
> 'The tailor makes the man'. I speak by experience
> Of my own customers. I have had gallants,
> Both court and country, would ha' fooled you up
> In a new suit with the best wits in being,
> And kept their speed as long as their clothes lasted
> han'some and neat; but then as they grew out
> At the elbows again, or had a stain or spot,
> They have sunk most wretchedly.[15]

Both Thomas and Pennyboy Junior are compelled to agree with this logic. Thomas commended the tailor (fashioner) for "moulding" Pennyboy Junior and "making him", "as they say".[16] Afterwards, Pennyboy Junior, the object of this dressing, equates fashion with wit, for men out of fashion were out of countenance and out of countenance was out of wit.[17] In *Michaelmas Term*, Hellgill explained the aphorism: "What base birth does raiment not make glorious? And what glorious births do rags not make infamous?" The context was the re-fashioning of the country wench from Northamptonshire by Lethe as a prospective courtesan.[18] In *New Inn*, Prudence, the servant and temporary Lady of Misrule, elicited the name of Pinnacia's tailor, upon which her question is rephrased by her mistress, Lady Frampul: "Pray you, your fashioner's name!" Pinnacia responded in terms of her fashioner.[19]

As Greenblatt asserts, although the sixteenth century did not herald a completely new departure for "fashion" in attire, what was different was the self-consciousness of fashioning (one)self and being fashioned. The frequency of the verb "to fashion" (in both active and passive indicative) was categorical.[20]

As intimated in the dramatists' words, self-fashioning did not just depend on re-defining oneself, but also in the rhetorical representation of others as unfashionable and unrefined. This piece is not, then, an essay in Geertzian hermeneutics through "thick description" of a cultural item to elicit a cultural milieu, for it acknowledges the politics as well as the poetics of cultural situations. New Historicists such as Greenblatt originally derived something from Geertz, perhaps the conflation of culture and text.[21] Here an attempt is made to acknowledge the politics and "hard surfaces" of culture adumbrated by Roseberry, Sewell and Asad.[22]

Two strategies were available to implement the social othering of representation. In line with self-presentation through costume, one calculation was the derogation of ordinary or common clothing. The defining and labelling of common clothes as "base" separated and elevated oneself from most others, although not entirely as an individual but as belonging to an elite group, such as gallants. The other means of social critique to demean others was metaphor, in particular the equation of the commonalty with silver coin–by contrast with gold coin–in the bimetallic currency. The metaphor of coin provided a ready-made and existing dualism to demarcate people and society (see Chapter 4 below).

Categorizing clothing concentrated on appearance. Blue coats and clothing, for example, became associated metaphorically with lowly status: servants or confined prostitutes. The blue gown worn by prostitutes in the workhouse had metaphorical resonance.[23] To interpret expensive clothing as containing "symbolic capital", after Bourdieu, has some resonance, but is not then the entire story; Bourdieu's epistemology of structuration depends very much on class difference as (symbolic) distinction.[24] One problem is that, as has recently been elucidated, gender cuts across late medieval sumptuary laws, if not the Elizabethan proclamations.[25] The second issue is pursued below: that restraint in dress also had its "symbolic capital" in another milieu. The head and hats were immediately visible, and not only readily seen, but worn on the apex of the upper half of the body. The lower half of the body had already been appropriated for characterizing baseness in general.[26] Hats offered a better prospect for social critique. In *Mad World*, the etiquette of headgear is explained by Sir Bounteous, who bids Follywit put on his hat. Only social inferiors were required to stand bareheaded before their wealthier superiors. Conduct was not the only aspect addressed by Bounteous, however, for he commented also on the difference of hats by social position: "Go to, wealth must be respected; let those that have least feathers stand bare".[27] The number of feathers in the hat defined social position.

Feathers in caps defined fine social gradations, levels of affluence amongst the wealthy. To differentiate social groups, hats were again seized upon as symbols of difference. The fixing of identity through hats was expressed in the depiction of social groups in the *tableaux* in Speed's map of the kingdom of England printed in 1610.

Amongst them, we can compare and contrast the tall hat of the gentleman and the flat cap of the citizen (and the headgear of the others fixes their identity too).[28] Accordingly, when he became irritated, the Essex gentleman Easy referred to the City woollen draper, Quomodo, as goodman goosecap (see further below for goosecap). Although confused and overawed by the complexity of the City, young Easy, when nervous and anxious, reverted to type in attempting to put Quomodo in his place by reference to, derogation of, his clothing, the cap associated with a City tradesman. Although out of place himself, Easy responded to the situation by the social metaphor of headgear.[29]

Self-consciously, then, the City merchant, Kitely, complained that Wellbred and his associates, who entertained ideas of elevated status as gallants, "mock me all over,/ From my flat cap unto my shining shoes".[30] They asserted their presumption of superior status by disparaging the normal headgear associated with merchant society. Flat cap then became the metaphor by which those with superior aspirations decried the nascent urban "middling sort".[31] The use is epitomized in *Eastward Ho.*

Although of a gentle family, Quicksilver, as a younger son, was apprenticed to the goldsmith, Touchstone.[32] Disdaining his situation and embroiled with a company of gallants, Quicksilver acted quixotically, demanding to be released. Responding to Touchstone and Golding, he demurred: "Marry, foh, goodman flatcap".[33] Worse than that, Quicksilver condemned Touchstone as "dull flat-cap", despising the industry and industriousness of the City craftsman, insipid by the standard of the inebriated, oath-swearing gallant.[34] The epithet was repeated, despairingly rather than artlessly, by Gertrude, one of Touchstone's three daughters, who aspired to become a lady, "though my father be a low-capped tradesman".[35]

The flat cap had been traditional headgear, particularly in the City of London. As the sixteenth century progressed, however, more exotic headgear became fashionable–and competitive. Whereas the flat cap had been symbolically illustrative of "commonweal", new fashions in headgear epitomized social division. The flat cap thus became the metaphor for the unfashionable and the unmodish, and by association, tradesmen and merchants.[36]

An equivalent metaphor was that of goose-cap. The Portuguese merchant domiciled in London, Pisaro, had three daughters, the Dutch merchant Vandalle being suitor to one. His conversation was so monotonously concerned with trade that Laurentia decried him as "good-man Goose-cap", a term also applied by another of the daughters, Mathea.[37] The young, naïve, Essex (landed) gentleman, Easy, in a pique of anger, addressed the usurious Quomodo as "goodman goosecap" (as noted above).[38]

In the competitive world of honor and status of the late sixteenth and early seventeenth century, fine distinctions of degree acquired heightened significance. Although the later description of the middling sort would be an extensive category, in the late sixteenth and early seventeenth century reference to industry and trade could be asserted disparagingly. It was thus with some consciousness of this common deployment of social critique that the leading burgesses of Stafford felt compelled to regulate this language of insult in the early seventeenth century:

> If anye of these by his honest meanes & indeavours have attayned to an estate of 2 or 300li and carry the reputacion of an honest and sencible person we esteeme worthye upon occasion to bear Rule a mongest us higher dignitye our Spheare affourdes not Soe that the difference of orders in pollicie referres not to the differences of professions as if some were of more honour amongest us then others But to that distinction which wealth and discretion putes betwixt us And therefore yf anye one shall throwe the woord mechannicke or trades man upon us in contempt he shall but show himselfe to be ashamed of his Auncestours.[39]

The intention was to proscribe the sort of choleric eruption in which the country gull, Master Stephen, exclaimed: "Whoreson base fellow! A mechanical serving man!"[40]

Metaphors of disparagement extended to habits of social groups, so that Justice Clement could berate the poor, downtrodden, water-bearer Cob for bringing a complaint against Captain Bobadill's smoking of tobacco in Cob's house: "A slave that never drunk out of better than piss-pot metal".[41] Clement objected not to Cob's suit against Bobadill, but to Cob's denunciation of tobacco. This commodity was the preserve and custom of a social elite and was considered a refinement illustrative of social status. Clement's retort, in committing Cob to gaol, was to deprecate Cob's lowly social position by allusion to his unrefined drinking vessels, denoting Cob's lower status. Dramatists turned naturally, of course, to metaphor and the City comedies are replete with metaphorical allusions. The language of the laity is, nonetheless, pervaded by metaphor, metonym, and synecdoche.⁴² We find that on occasion contrarians resorted to the metaphor of the flat cap to disparage and denounce their adversaries:

> That in one of the monethes of Januarie or Februarie nowe laste paste he this deponent beinge in the Church of Arnold articulate uppon a workedaye & standing at the communion table by the articulate Saunder Barnes did see heere the articulate Roger Sullie beinge angrie at the said Saunder uppon somme occasion of speeches which passed betweene them saye to the said Saunder these words or the like in effecte videlicet Them that wold tell anye such flatt capps as thou art anye thinge have little to doe & presentlie uppon the same words did violentlie pull or plucke the hatte of the said Saunder over his eyes addinge other threatninge speeches.⁴³

This cause in the archdeaconry court of Nottingham in the early seventeenth century indicates that the abusive term flat-cap had extended outside London. Its interest lies also in Sullie's actions, since he not only verbally abused Barnes as a flat-cap, but physically and symbolically tugged on Barnes' hat, emphasizing his point about Barnes, and perhaps even re-shaping Barnes' hat into a flat cap. In addressing Barnes and his ilk as flat-caps, Sullie's implication was that they were dullards and inconsequential. It is interesting to unravel the genealogy of the term. In its first incarnation, flat-cap was associated in dramatic contexts with dullness–"dull" is the recurring adjacent adjective. Eventually, the intent was transformed from dull to dullard, from lacking flamboyance to wanting in consequence.

The first context–dullness–is contained within Kitely's remorseful complaint that the gallants mocked him from his flat cap to his shiny shoes. Kitely's lamentation concerned the activities of Wellbred whom Kitely had received into his house. Wellbred, mesmerized by gallants, had rejected all notions of urban civility: "a stranger to all due respect".⁴⁴ The mark of the citizen of London was self-restraint and modesty, exhibited not only in etiquette but also in dress. Sobriety of dress and manners remained the characteristics of the urban elite which even regalia and aldermanic coloured gowns on civic occasions did not entirely obliterate.[45] This modesty and politic character were exemplified in Golding, one of the two apprentices of Touchstone, who, although gentle, accepted with grace his position as a City tradesman.[46] The flatcap was a signal symbol of this self-restraint and modesty of attire and manners. In *Knight of the Burning Pestle*, the citizen-grocer and his wife, George and Nell, demand that the players refrain from performing yet another play critical of the commons of the City. At their instigation, their servant, Rafe, adopts the role of the hero who confronts the giant, Barbaroso. On the stage, Rafe becomes responsible, through the personage of the knight but still servant of a grocer, for maintaining the honor and dignity of the craft. The text contained, of course, all of satire, parody and burlesque. The couple are enthusiastic, but naïve. It is in keeping with this tenor that, when asked by Nell if Rafe would defeat the giant, George exclaimed: "I hold my cap to a farthing he does".[47] The cap symbolizes the heroism and modesty of the calling of the citizen-grocer.

Dekker, with his empathy for the City, proffered an eloquent defence of the flat cap. Although *Honest Whore* is ostensibly set in Milan, the context replicates the City of London. In the *Second Part* of the play, Dekker devoted half a scene to a favourable discussion of the citizen's headwear. Each status, it was conceded, had its own headgear: seamen; gallants with their high hats and feathers; and soldiers. This prelude precedes the justification for the citizen's particular headwear:

> One should be laid by for the citizen;
>   And that's the cap, which you see swells not high,
>   For caps are emblems of humility.
>   It is a citizen's badge.[48]

The dialogue maintains that the cap is appropriate to the denizen of the City: "Flat caps as proper are to city gowns".[49] The assertion is followed by a long proposition about the integrity and the utility of the flat cap, the genealogy purportedly extending back to the freemen of Rome. The flat cap conforms to one of the two geometric figures of simple beauty and proportion, the circle and the square, the latter represented in the scholar's square cap associated with learning, and the former with the round City cap signifying good governance. The flat cap, moreover, did not obscure the face and thus obviated dissembling–or that shame of cuckoldry which could be obfuscated by wearing a brimmed hat "ore their eye-browes".[50] Finally, its utility was its lightness in summer and its warm closeness to the head in winter.

Perhaps it was Dekker too who addressed the issue in *Westward Hoe*, on which he collaborated with John Webster. Even the bawd Birdlime could be moved to express consternation at the new fashion. When visited by gentlemen, Birdlime took exception to them since, although they passed as civil gentlemen without beards, she objected to their wearing cloaks, rapiers, boots and spurs. She demurred: "I protest to you, those that be your Ancientes in the house would have come to my house in their Caps and Gownes, civilly and modestly".[51]

Despite his strenuous efforts, Dekker nonetheless conceded other perceptions of the flat cap and acknowledged that some regarded it as an object of derision: "Let then the city cap by none be scorn'd".[52] He recognized too that it was derided in some quarters. In the first part of the drama he had himself employed the motif, allowing two apprentices to be denounced (abused) as flat caps.[53] The irony of Dekker's extolling the virtue of the flat cap was, of course, the Milanese location and setting of the two parts of *Honest Whore*, for it was precisely from the "Italian" states that the fashion for exotic headgear originated. The English gallants' and aristocracy's penchant for high hats and feathers aped a "civility" associated with southern Europe. The restrained "civility" of the round, flat cap was diminished by Italianate gallants, but the civic culture persisted.[54]

That situation introduces another context for the flat cap, that of its indigenous quality. The new Italianate fashion did not appeal to all and some objected precisely because of its foreign origin. In some cases, that exogenous lineage was regarded as devilish. In *Like Will to Like*, the dramatist Ulpian Fulwell associated the introduction of new fashions in apparel with Nichol Newfangle. The implication was not only that the new clothing was uselessly newfangled, promoting misplaced pride, but also the work of the devil, since Nichol was the Devil's apprentice in the play.[55]

Thomas Creede extended the criticism in 1595: "All the naughtie fashions in the world at this day" were, he maintained, imported, so that the Mother in *Pedlar's Prophecy* denounced all aliens and their fashions as a dilution of "English plaine maners and good state".[56] We should not then assume that the Elizabethan proclamations about apparel contained only empty rhetoric against foreign influences.

In particular, City and urban tradesmen might well have been sensitive to the erosion of domestic trade and industry. Flat cap production had been an integral part of urban economies, not least in Coventry where at least eighty-four cappers made their living in the 1520s.[57] One of the last really affluent cappers of Coventry was John Lawghton, whose inventory on his death in 1543 amounted to over £70 of personal estate.[58] Denizens might well have remembered this economic foundation. Certainly Parliament busied itself during Elizabeth's reign with bills about the proper production of caps, the wearing of caps not hats on holidays and Sundays, and prohibiting fulling by mills in the manufacture of caps. Such bills were designed to regenerate domestic production, not only to regulate apparel, and also to sustain internal goods and native customs of dress against foreign intrusions.[59]

Therein, however, resided another potential cause of condescending scoffing by the gallants. The coarse woollen cloth employed in the making of flat caps, native as it might be, perhaps also equated with and symbolized in gallants' eyes the coarse disposition of the caps' bearers. High hats, by comparison, were composed of more exotic materials. Although the finery of high hats was exogenous and foreign, yet it had associations of a transmitted "Italianate" culture admired from some perspectives even if without eroding some of the ambivalence towards the perceived social habits of Mediterranean cousins. So many English plays superficially situated in "Italy" testify to this perplexed (and perplexing) admiration. This complex approach is perhaps best orchestrated in John Webster's *Duchess of Malfi*.[60]

The flatcap was, thus, ridiculed by English gallants as the symbol of dullness. An external perception directly contradicted the internal one, in a contrast of different concepts of virtue and "civility". So Quicksilver, younger son of a gentle family, rejoiced when released from his apprenticeship to a London goldsmith: "Avaunt dull flat-cap", metaphorically rejecting the status of City tradesman.[61] Quicksilver also deployed dull, however, in its other sense of dullard: those who have wit (intelligence and quickness of mind) should take advantage of their astuteness, whilst those without this faculty should be satisfied with being tradesmen; to which Security responded that it would be regrettable if any trade should dull Quicksilver's quickness of thought.[62] The abnegation of sober dress is contained in Follywit's first utterances in the opening scene of *Mad World*. His dissembling and humorous complaint to his company of never-do-wells is that under their influence he has been transformed from an upstanding civic state of sober dress ("went all in black") to exuberant attire ("blown into light colours").[63]

There was no imperative for citizens to retain the flat cap. The Elizabethan sumptuary laws (Statutes of Apparel) and proclamations between 1562 and 1597–repeating earlier iterations–made few restrictions on headwear, apart from prohibiting trimming with gold, silver or pearl in 1574. Those injunctions about these precious materials might indeed have been directed only at hatbands, which, of course, were not appropriate to flat caps, but only the higher headwear of the new fashions. The issue of flat caps seems to have been identity rather than coercion. Flat caps, moreover, were not entirely bereft of fashionable modes. So Wil Cricket set his cap "oth to side" as was the current fashion.[64]

The retention of the flat cap was one aspect of the social and cultural identity of the City's governing elite. The "relative homogeneity" of the City elite who composed its government has been proposed, and it might well have been around such lowly symbols–like the flat cap–that the elite cohered, as well as the higher-status symbols of mace, civic processions and magistrates' formal dress.[65] The flat cap, for example, extended outside the ruling caucus to the whole of the citizenry, reminding them of their common status and origins, especially against the interlopers and intermittent visitors who propelled their higher status. Comment on the cohesion of the City elite has frequently been related to the social pressures from below, but the dramatists clearly identify the importance of exogenous social groups.[66] Civic identity could be formulated against another elite as well as against the deprived and disadvantaged in London society. The flat cap and the high hat epitomized that difference.

We have then, it seems, two contemporary perceptions of the intention behind the metaphor of flat cap. Although Dekker attempted to elucidate the integrity represented in the flat cap, out of his esteem for and closeness to the citizens of London, Jonson and Middleton had no such propensity.[67] The last two dramatists had no compunction about consistently associating their allusions to the flat cap with derision. In their deployment of the metaphor, both Jonson and Middleton employed bathos, favouring neither gallants nor citizens. If the gallants' denunciation of citizens as flat caps emphasized the dullness of trade and tradespeople, in their utterances nonetheless simply reverberated their own false sense of superiority and haughtiness, comic self-delusion, and crassness. In Jonson's and Middleton's hands, the metaphor was, to use another metaphor, a two-edged sword.

Dekker's affinity with the City is well understood; his celebration of the citizens was refracted clearly in, most emphatically, *Shoemaker's Holiday*. Here he combined perspectives of "citizen values and low life realism".[68] *Shoemaker's Holiday* (1599) can be read as a critical exposition of the contest between aristocratic and citizen values in its own exposition which leads on to its crisis and denouement: the conscription of Rafe dramatizes the contest between Lord Lincoln and the future Lord Mayor, Simon Eyre, a conflict of two concepts of honor, those of the gallant (but not the mock gallant) and those of the citizen.[69] That contest can be reduced to the emblematic difference in styles of head-wear. Decidedly more cynical than Dekker, Jonson indeed became an adversary of his former collaborator, Dekker.[70] By the time of the height of Jonson's powers of authorship in 1614–16, commerce in London had become tainted by the corruption of money-lending. Jonson's spleen was thus directed equally at false gallants and dissembling citizens. The high hats of the one represented falsity and the low caps of the others low morality. Although the son of a citizen-bricklayer, Middleton too came to perceive corrosiveness in the City. He too coruscated hypocrisy wherever and in whomsoever it occurred.[71]

Dramatic reference to the flat cap thus illustrates, as we are well aware, the frequent resort to metaphor in the theater of the late sixteenth and seventeenth centuries. Apparel became in the playwrights' hands a synecdoche for the person, in this case the male persona. As we might expect, the use of the metaphor reflected authorial intention: Dekker's closeness to City life contrasted with Jonson and Middleton, who, although sons of the City, having been engaged in the City's quotidian social and cultural negotiations, had a disinterested regard. These last two set a plague on all houses of self-regard and pomposity, even if Jonson had his own internal ambiguities. The flat cap signifies more, however: a conflict of customs and cultures of social groups in the urban environment of the time, revolving around civic restraint and dignity in opposition to aristocratic and gallants' exoticisms; one form of self-fashioning counterpoised by another; and a commemoration of the good, old values of English urban civility which were still in the process of formation and development confronting a newly introduced, foreign, excretion. In the meanings of the flat cap, then, there was a brusque dialogue of two different notions of civility.

Notes

[1] John Donne, "Satire 1", lines 59–62 (1593 or 1598?). I am grateful to Professor Roger Richardson for helpful comments and advice.

[2] For a recent discussion of the sumptuary laws from the perspective of gender rather than social hierarchy, Kim M. Phillips, "Masculinities and the Medieval English Sumptuary Laws", *Gender and History* 19 (2007): 22–42, which considers the laws up to and including 1509/10, and has a comprehensive bibliographical note at pp. 37–8.

[3] In general, for classic studies, Ann R. Jones and Peter Stallybrass, *Renaissance Clothing and the Materials of Memory* (Cambridge: Cambridge University Press, 2000); Daniel Roche, *A History of Everyday Things: The Birth of Consumption in France, 1600–1800* (Cambridge: Cambridge University Press, 2000), chapter 8.

[4] For the wider social contests, Jean E. Howard, *The Stage and Social Struggle in Early Modern England* (London: Routledge, 1994).

[5] Approaches to the City are divergent: Rappaport, *Worlds within Worlds*, adopts the most optimistic view of stability; Ian Archer, *The Pursuit of Stability: Social Relations in Elizabethan London* (Cambridge: Cambridge University Press, 1991), attends to the problems and how they were managed; more recently, Paul Griffiths, *Lost Londons: Change, Crime and Control in the Capital City, 1550-1660* (Cambridge: Cambridge University Press, 2008).

[6] For their context, Joseph P. Ward, *Metropolitan Communities: Trades, Guilds, Identity and Change in Early Modern London* (Stanford, CA: Stanford University Press, 1997).

[7] F. J. (Jack) Fisher, "The Development of London as a Centre of Conspicuous Consumption in the Sixteenth and Seventeenth Centuries", repr. in *London and the English Economy 1500–1700*, ed. Penny J. Corfield and Negley B. Harte (London, 1990) (being Fisher's collected essays).

[8] McLuskie, *Dekker & Heywood*, 14; Kinney, *Renaissance Drama*, 245.

[9] Ann Bayman, "Rogues, Conycatching and the Scribbling Crew", History Workshop Journal 63 (2007): 1–17.

[10] J. Jowett, "Thomas Middleton", in *Companion to Renaissance Drama*, ed. Kinney, 34–5; and Margot Heinemann, *Puritanism and Theatre: Thomas Middleton and Opposition Drama under the Early Stuarts* (Cambridge: Cambridge University Press, 1980).

[11] Chakravorty, *Society and Politics*.

[12] Blair Worden, "Ben Jonson Among the Historians", in *Culture and Politics in Early Stuart England*, ed. Kevin Sharpe and Peter Lake (Basingstoke: Macmillan Press, 1994), 67–89; David Norbrook, *Poetry and Politics in the English Renaissance* (Oxford: Oxford University Press, 2002), 135–72.

[13] Riggs, *Ben Jonson*, 2–10 and passim.

[14] S. Mukherji, "Women, Law and Dramatic Realism in Early Modern England", *English Literary Renaissance* 35 (2005): 248–72.

[15] *Staple of News*, Act I, scene ii, lines 108–18.

[16] *Staple of News*, Act I, scene ii, lines 92–4.

[17] *Staple of News*, Act I, scene ii, lines 125–9.

[18] *Michaelmas Term*, Act II, scene i, lines 1–5.

[19] *New Inn*, Act IV, scene iii, lines 32–5.

[20] Greenblatt, *Renaissance Self-Fashioning*, 1–3. See also, for the vocabulary of the self, Scott-Warren, *Early Modern English Literature*, 226.

[21] Clifford Geertz, "Deep Play: Notes on the Balinese Cockfight", in Geertz, *The Interpretation of Cultures* (New York: Basic Books, 1973), 412–5 and Fred Inglis, *Clifford Geertz: Culture, Custom and Ethics* (Cambridge: Polity Press, 2000), 84–9; Vincent Pecora, "The Limits of Local Knowledge", in *The New Historicism*, ed. H. Aram Veeser (London: Routledge, 1989), 243–76.

[22] William Roseberry, "Balinese Cockfights and the Seduction of Anthropology", *Social Research* 49 (1982): 1013–28, but compare Geertz, *Available Light: Anthropological Reflections on Philosophical Topics* (Princeton: Princeton University Press, 2000), xi-xiii; A. Biersack, "Local Knowledge, Local History: Geertz and Beyond", in *The New Cultural History*, ed. Lynn Hunt (Berkeley: University of California Press, 1989), 72–96; Talad Asad, "Anthropological Conceptions of Religion: Reflections on Geertz", *Man* new series 18 (1983): 237–59; and William Sewell, "Geertz, Cultural Systems, and History: from Synchrony to Transformation", in *The Fate of Culture: Geertz and Beyond*, ed. Sherry Ortner (Berkeley: University of California

58   Social Dramas

Press, 1999).

[23] *Honest Whore II*, Act V, scene i, line 11 and scene ii, line 398; blue coats of servants, Act IV, scene i, line 100; "smell-smocks", Act IV, scene i, line 129.

[24] John Parker, *Structuration* (Buckingham: Open University Press, 2000); Pierre Bourdieu, *Distinction: A Social Critique of the Judgment of Taste*, trans. Richard Nice (London: Routledge, 1984).

[25] See Phillips, "Masculinities and the Medieval English Sumptuary Laws", 22–42.

[26] See Anthony Synnott, *The Body Social: Symbolism, Self and Society* (London: Routledge, 1993), 20–1.

[27] *Mad World*, Act V, scene i, lines 41–4.

[28] *The Counties of Britain. A Tudor Atlas by John Speed*, with an introduction by Nigel Nicolson (London, 1988), 26–8.

[29] *Michaelmas Term*, Act II, scene iii, lines 263–4.

[30] *Every Man in His Humour*, Act II, scene i, lines 103–4.

[31] Jonathan Barry and Christopher Brooks, eds., *The Middling Sort of People. Culture, Society and Politics in England, 1550–1800* (Basingstoke: Macmillan Press, 1994).

[32] For apprentices of gentle status see Rappaport, *Worlds Within Worlds*, 81–3.

[33] *Eastward Ho*, Act I, scene i, line 90; at line 102 "this flat-cap Touchstone"; and at line 29 "dull flat-cap".

[34] *Eastward Ho*, Act II, scene ii, line 29.

[35] *Eastward Ho*, Act I, scene ii, lines 3–4.

[36] For the use of the term, Eric Partridge, *Dictionary of Historical Slang* (Harmondsworth: Penguin, 1972), s.v. Flat-cap; A. Lee Beier, "Engine of Manufacture: the Trades of London", in *The Making of Metropolitan London 1500–1700*, ed. Beier and R. Finlay (Harlow: Longman, 1986), 141–67.

[37] *Englishman for my Money*, lines 969, 1842.

[38] *Michaelmas Term*, Act II, scene iii, line 263.

[39] Staffordshire Record Office, D1721/1/4, fol. 52r.

[40] *Every Man in his Humour*, Act I, scene i, line 108.

[41] *Every Man in his Humour*, Act III, scene iii, line 112.

[42] Lakoff and Johnson, *Metaphors We Live By*.

[43] University of Nottingham Dept. of MSS AN/LB 222/1/2/1 (1612).

[44] *Everyman in his Humour*, Act II, scene i, line 55.

[45] Robert Tittler, "Freemen's Gloves and Civic Authority: the Evidence from Post-Reformation Portraiture", *Costume* 40 (2006): 13–20, and "Civic Portraiture and Political Culture in English Provincial Towns, ca. 1560–1640", *Journal of British Studies* 37 (1998): 306–29, esp. 315–16.

[46] *Eastward Ho*, Act IV, scene ii, lines 55–61, 88.

⁴⁷ *Knight of the Burning Pestle*, Act III, line 287.
⁴⁸ *Honest Whore II*, Act, I, scene ii, lines 42–5.
⁴⁹ *Honest Whore II*, Act I, scene ii, line 70.
⁵⁰ *Westward Hoe*, Act I, scene i, line 154.
⁵¹ *Westward Hoe*, Act IV, scene i, lines 12–19.
⁵² *Honest Whore II*, Act I, scene ii, line 72.
⁵³ *Honest Whore II*, Act III, scene i, line 174.
⁵⁴ Jonathan Barry, "Civility and Civic Culture in Early Modern England: the Meanings of Urban Freedom", in *Civil Histories. Essays Presented to Sir Keith Thomas*, ed. Peter Burke, Brian Harrison and Paul Slack (Oxford: Oxford University Press, 2000), 181–96; Phil Withington, *The Politics of Commonwealth: Citizens and Freemen in Early Modern England* (Cambridge: Cambridge University Press, 2005), esp. 137–49.
⁵⁵ *Like Will to Like*, lines 80–99.
⁵⁶ Thomas Creede, *The Pedlar's Prophecy* (1595) ed. W. W. Greg (Malone Society Reprints, Oxford, 1914), lines 341–52.
⁵⁷ M. Hulton, *Coventry and its People in the 1520s* (Dugdale Society 38, 1999), 30 (Table 2).
⁵⁸ Lichfield Record Office BC/2/11 John Lawghton, Coventry, 1543.
⁵⁹ See, for example, the repetitive bills 1559–81: The Journals of all the Parliaments during the Reign of Queen Elizabeth (1682), 44–53, 69–72, 110–13, 127–35, 145–54, 290–301, 361–74 <http://www.british-history.ac.uk/report.asp?compid=43698&strquery=caps. Date accessed: 22 May 2007>.
⁶⁰ *Duchess of Malfi*. I owe most of this paragraph to Professors Roger Richardson and Greg Walker.
⁶¹ *Eastward Ho*, Act II, scene ii, line 29.
⁶² *Eastward Ho*, Act II, scene ii, lines 115–20.
⁶³ *Mad World*, Act I, scene i, lines 13–18. For the "light colours" of the late sixteenth century in London, J. Schneider, "Fantastical Colors in Foggy London. The New Fashion Potential of the Late Sixteenth Century", in *Material London, ca. 1600*, ed. Lena C. Orlin (Philadelphia: University of Pennsylvania Press, 2000), 109–27.
⁶⁴ *Wily Beguilde*, line 440.
⁶⁵ For the "relative homogeneity" of the City elite see Archer, *Pursuit of Stability*, 39–49.
⁶⁶ Archer, *Pursuit of Stability*, 49–57 ("Elite and People"); the elite issue was really identified by Fisher, "Development of London as a Centre of Conspicuous Consumption".
⁶⁷ Riggs, *Ben Jonson*; McLuskie, *Dekker & Heywood*; Manley, *Literature and Culture in Early Modern London*.
⁶⁸ McLuskie, *Dekker & Heywood*, 14.

[69] McLuskie, *Dekker & Heywood*, 67. For the date, Dillon, *Cambridge Introduction to Early English Theatre*, 218.

[70] W. D. Kay, "Ben Jonson", *Companion to Renaissance Drama*, ed. Kinney, 469–70.

[71] Chakravorty, *Society and Politics*.

3
Conjugal relations

> Be dumb, you beggars of the rhyming trade,
>   Geld your loose wits, and let your muse be spayed.[1]

INTRODUCTION

How do we arrive at an understanding of marital relationships and household authority in early-modern England?[2] We know that ideology and experience could be very different, but that discourse arose out of and re-defined social relationships and expectations.[3] There has recently been substantial recourse to speech patterns to elucidate the position of women in medieval and early-modern England, addressing questions of conformity, agency, and disorderliness.[4] We have to be extremely critical in our interpretation of source material.[5] Courtesy texts and conduct manuals were prescriptive, but there are issues about their reach, audience, and adoption, particularly by social group. Court records largely depend on the pathological breakdown of domestic arrangements, but can be read backwards or "reverse engineered" to speculate on the normative. Cheap print–ballads–no doubt had an audience which traversed social groups, but which, by their consumerist intention, were largely sensational, with the emphasis on conflict.[6] These problems of genre have been explicated.[7]

What of the theater? It might seem perverse to invoke the comedies of the period to attempt to focus a spotlight on gendered relationships in a domestic context. What about authorial intention? Isn't the dramatic all about representation? Doesn't drama necessarily also assume the heightening of sensation? In the context of the *dramatis personae*, isn't characterization inextricably intertwined with emplotment? There are some counter-arguments to these questions: drama presents the imaginable, not the unimaginable; and the impact of drama depends upon audience reception as well as authorial intention. The content of the drama had to be in some way familiar to audiences, whatever their composition.[8] In the case of Dekker, we can also be fairly confident that he is replicating the idiomatic speech of the London citizenry.[9] Two of the most critical points derive directly from the format and production of drama: first, the composition by exclusively male dramatists; and secondly, the (almost) exclusively male company of actors, in which boys or men acted the parts of the female *dramatis personae*; in particular, the playing of young women by boys who might be challenged by long soliloquies or interchanges.[10]

It might seem rather paradoxical to seek the nature of everyday communication and verbal exchange in drama, but that is exactly the intention below. It will be argued that the dramatic also contained the mundane. The examination is based on the City comedies, which has an advantage and a disadvantage.[11] First, the advantage is that comedy avoids the dramatic devices of tragedy which invoke conflict or dissatisfaction in its outcomes. Comedy is more likely to portray the everyday, if sometimes in the form of burlesque, comedy of manners, farce, or comedy of characters, which are likely to be exaggerations rather than total inaccuracies. On the other hand, the material is focused on the societies of the City of London, and thus not necessarily representative of the wider social organization of early-modern England. What the City comedies do permit, however, is an insight into the normal marital relationships of the emerging urban "middling sort" of the City. The analysis is thus formed around a detailed dissection of the conversation in the plays between married couples in their various contexts and circumstances.[12]

One of the issues with drama is that it involves representation and, more particularly, that it might depend on stereotyping.

> Public representations have the power to select, arrange, and prioritise certain assumptions and ideas about different kinds of people, bringing some to the fore, *dramatising* and idealising or demonising them, while casting others into the

social margins, so that they have little public presence or only a narrow and negative public image. These practices are central to the politics of representation...The politics of representation cover both the power to speak of and for others, whether in news narratives, social documentaries, feature films or advertising, all of which follow their own rules and conventions. The consequences of providing accounts and images of others for structures and relations of social power are central to the analysis of any study of symbolic representations, where questions of under-representation, over-representation and misrepresentation are necessarily high on the critical agenda.[13]

Dramatists, of course, indulged in the over-determination of characters, particularly for satirical purposes and in comedy of characters. What will be demonstrated below, however, is that the playwrights were also sensitive to status and situation/context, which allowed them to engage with complexity as well as with ordering and closure.[14] One might, indeed, contend that the authorial intention of the City comedies was purposely to allow disorder and openness to and inconclusiveness of interpretation.

There remain a couple of caveats which should be explained here. The concern here is not primarily with questions about the *transition* to an affective family (Stone and his discontents), late companionate marriage, or questions of separate spheres, private and public. The examination relates to questions of conjugal relationships and intimacy (without consideration of whether they were novel or otherwise).

'PEACE'! AND PEACE: DEKKER'S TWO CONCEPTS OF DOMESTIC PATRIARCHY, 1599-1604[15]

[EYRE] Peace, you cracked groats, you mustard tokens ...[16]

[CANDIDO] Let the world say what it can,
   Nothing can drive me from a patient man.[17]

Perhaps the best point of departure is to investigate the relative use of the term peace. In *Shoemaker's Holiday*, there are thirty-one occurrences of Eyre's exclamation of "Peace!". Each usage introduces his speech. Each time the declamation is an injunction. On each occasion, he interrupts or negates another character. His deployment of 'Peace!' is an utterance in the sense of a speech act, performative and imperative.[18] Extending the analysis further, a high proportion of his speeches are comprehensively imperative: eighty-four (44 percent) of his sentences can be classified as imperative, whilst 107 (56 percent) can be categorized as non-imperative. His speeches are thus significantly ordering and commanding. His interventions are assertive, abruptly curtailing, exhibiting his dominance, and impose his own propositions.

If we consider the distribution of his exclamation and imperative sentences, they occur in the first action within the play. These portions contain the inter-action within the household and his workshop. In the later acts, when he is in different, often superior company, his speech is moderated. So his deployment of "Peace!" and his imperative sentences define his relationship with his wife and his journeymen and maids. Here, however, we have to take into account also that Dekker intended to establish Eyre's character and status at the earliest opportunity in the play–the predisposition of the most important, central character–which happen to be the interactions within his household *cum* workshop. So there is a complication, a dual strategy.

So, to return to his injunction of "Peace!", he was principally addressing his wife, Madge (Margery) in seven instances, his senior journeyman Hodge in three, and his second journeyman, Firk in ten. Those specifically directed injunctions comprise twenty of thirty-one usages: two-thirds. The remainder are directed to the whole ensemble of his household collectively.[19]

Here, it's important to interject a comment on Firk. Firk is essential to the comedic content of the play, the principal comic character. One of his main purposes is to utter the self-referential "firk", which he insists on fourteen times. He constantly accompanies Eyre, Madge and Hodge, consistently foregrounded. That situation explains why he is the receiver of the injunction "Peace!" and the preponderance of his speech occasions (to which we shall return). We shall not completely dismiss his presence as merely a dramatic device, however, for his inclusion reveals how Eyre's patriarchal authority extends over his workshop and extended household. So although we cannot rely unequivocally on the quantity of the speech acts of each individual character as an indication of their social importance, there is again a dual aspect here.

Now we can compare the language of Candido in *Honest Whore I*. For dramatic purposes, he is self-referential, to expose his character. Seven times he employed the noun patience and six times the adjective patient. He renounces the noun anger three times and the adjective angry five. In a complementary way, his wife, Viola, despairs of him as a patient man eight times and expressed her intention to vex him seven. The difference, of course, is that he regards his patience as a virtue and she his excessive impassivity as a negative trait. So, by contrast with Eyre, when Candido employs peace it is to express inner contentment.

It is important to recognize that both characters are validated in the denouement of the two plays. Both are authenticated by the same *deus ex machina*, the king and the duke, both sovereign figures. The king confirms Eyre through a physical act, by attending his mayoral feast; the duke validates Candido through a speech act, a performative utterance:

> Come, therefore, you shall teach our court to shine;
> So calm a spirit is worth a golden mine.[20]

> Thou hast taught the city patience, now our court
> Shall be thy sphere, where, from good report,
> Rumours this truth unto the world shall sing:
> A patient man's a pattern for a king.[21]

So the concordance of speech reveals the characters of the two protagonists in their patriarchal contexts of household *cum* workshop or shop. We can explore the intra-familial relationships further by examining the extent of their speech acts, as in Table 4.

The "contributions" of Simon Eyre dominate his household. As interestingly, the interventions of the two journeymen, Ralph and Firk, exceed those of Eyre's wife, Margery. Firk's prominence can be explained, as above, by his indispensability to the humor of the comedy. Even the fairly restrained foreman, Hodge, has more voice

Table 4 Speech Acts of *Dramatis Personae*

Character	Total number of words
Shoemaker's Holiday	
Simon Eyre (master)	3178
Margery (Madge) Eyre (wife of SM)	1040
Hodge (Roger) (foreman)	1164
Firk (journeyman)	2883
Honest Whore I[23]	
Candido (draper)	2300
Viola (wife of C)	1873

In these numbers, only Part I of *The Honest Whore* has been analysed, as that was first printed in 1604, whereas Part I was not printed until 1630. Although Part I was technically a joint composition of Dekker and Middleton, the prevailing opinion is that Dekker was the predominant contributor.

than Margery. Despite her presence, Margery is allowed only a third of Eyre's voice. When we compare the respective speech patterns of Candido and Viola, husband and wife, the contrast is apparent. Viola's exchanges consist of four-fifths of Candido's. Margery Eyre's recalcitrance is matched by Viola's volubility. Again, of course, we have to take into account the dramatic intention. Eyre is the principal character and his social advance constitutes the main plot. Candido and Viola can be assumed to be a sub-plot within *Honest Whore*, although ultimately Candido's personal attributes shine through. Still, our concern is with the relative contributions within the marital relationship. The submissiveness of Madge can be further demonstrated through her idiomatic speech, in particular her qualification or "hedging" language: "but let that pass"; she reiterates the phrase fourteen times, subverting her own suggestions.[22] Viola is much more secure and assertive, if ultimately unsuccessful.

Here we should introduce another complication into the dialogue of the marital relationship, which is important in assessing the patriarchal arrangements in households: the issues of hypergamy and hypogamy, the relative pre-marital status of the partners. Eyre has no compunction in reminding Margery of her inferior status.

> Have not I ta'en you from selling tripes in Eastcheap, and set you in my shop, and made you hail-fellow with Simon Eyre the shoemaker? And now do you deal thus with my journeymen? Look, you powder-beef quean, on the face of Hodge. Here's a face for a lord.[23]

The implications about Viola, on the other hand, are that her lineage is of a superior position to Candido's. In her first ruse to unsettle Candido, to disturb his patience, she enlists the assistance of her brother, Fustigo. Fustigo has experienced the fashionable life of a gallant, travelling in his youth before contemplating settling. Viola is disturbed to understand that Fustigo has "cast off all [his] old swaggering humours" which are vital to her scheme. She explains to Fustigo that Candido was already a wealthy merchant at their marriage.[24] We have the prospect then of a woman of superior status who has married a wealthy merchant. The conjugal relationship could then be affected by the original status of the partners.

We may need then to find that interaction between ideology and practise/experience which has been advocated.[25] Men's control of women's speech no doubt theoretically resided "at the heart of the early modern gender system", demanding a submissive use by women of language, and inculcating the centrality of the household in the enforcement of gender order, but the existence of socially exogamous marriages may have either reinforced or traduced that expectation.[26]

That adjustment alone will not, however, explain the full import of the differences between Eyre and Candido. It has been suggested that the characterization of Candido was influenced by the accession or impending accession of James I, the pacific king who entertained the notion of harmony throughout Christendom.[27] Perhaps there is a case, however, for placing the contrast between the two characters in a wider context: changing notions of the self and self-possession. In this scenario, Eyre represents the ancient and Candido the modern: the traditional versus the new. Eyre's exclamations within the household and workshop situation are invested with emotion, a certain thoughtlessness, and ebullience. In contrast, Candido's voiced reflections are, whatever the situation, restrained, disciplined, and exhibit constancy. Perhaps, in Charles Taylor's terminology, what is being represented is the traditional "porous" self, invested with emotional responses, and the inception of the "buffered" self, the disciplined, almost disembodied, mind. Behind this portrayal of Candido, the citizen draper, might be the influence of the Neo-Stoicism which obtained some currency in the last decades of the sixteenth century, the Christianized Stoicism of Justus Lipsius (1547-1606).[28] "The good man shows *constantia, patientia, firmitas*"; constancy was the consummate virtue, a *continentia* equivalent to self-control and self-discipline.[29] The *De Constantia* of Lipsius was printed in 1584, although he had already recovered works of Seneca and Tacitus. This re-discovery of Senecan Stoicism informed ideas of civility.[30] The perseverance of Candido–his constancy–is epitomized by the equanimity of his conduct when incarcerated in Bedlam at the instance of Viola. In fact, to our understanding, his endurance might appear as consummate folly and perhaps that was the reaction of some of the contemporary audience, but others would have appreciated the integrity of his Stoicism.[31]

George and Nell

Referring back to the traditional understanding, moreover, we can perceive in Beaumont's *Knight of the Burning Pestle*, how a citizen grocer's wife might wheedle and influence her husband to promote her desires, how the female might manipulate the male partner in a companionate marriage. Indeed, the play has been interpreted as a representation of female domestic influence. The insinuation of female desire is, however, somewhat oblique, particularly in the relationship between the grocer, George, and his wife, Nell. There is no doubt about the loquacity of Nell by comparison with the relative taciturnity of George: Nell's 3,318 words uttered against George's 1,601. Nell's speech consists of 1,174 different words, but, if we exclude the expected prepositions, articles and pronouns, the most frequent utterances are I (eighty-eight), Ralph (eighty), George (seventy-six), him (seventy-three, usually referring to Ralph), you (sixty-nine), so that her speech is more often directed to others. We can take this speech pattern a stage further. Of her 322 complete sentences, fifty-two are questions (sixteen percent). Another eight percent commence, furthermore, "Let...", with the implication "May...". Her speech is thus infused with "canonical" tag questions and hedges.[32] In his contributions, George, in uttering 1,601 words, used 682 different words. Omitting again the repetitive prepositions and articles normal in all speech, his most frequent lexical items were: Ralph (forty-eight), him (forty-six, Ralph), I (forty-four), you (twenty-two), and Nell (nineteen). Whilst Nell addressed him most frequently as George, George used a variety of terms of reference to Nell, including chicken, cony (thirteen times), duck, duckling, honey, honeysuckle, lamb, love, mouse, puppy, sweet and sweetheart.[33] As significantly, George exclaimed "peace", directed at Nell, on ten occasions. As interestingly too, fourteen of George's sentences were interrogative, but in the form consistently of "challenging" questions: rhetorically addressed to the boy assistant of the play.[34]

FORMALISM

In *Knight of the Burning Pestle*, Beaumont perhaps intended to satirize the mawkishness of the emergent "middling sort" of the City, here through the utterances of a citizen-grocer. With origins in the landed gentry of north-west Leicestershire, Beaumont's depiction was probably derisive. Other dramatists in other contexts envisaged, indeed, a more formal relationship between wife and husband.

In *Eastward Ho*, Chapman, Jonson and Marston construed a much more formal relationship between Touchstone and his wife, Mistress T. As a goldsmith, Touchstone was perhaps higher up the City's hierarchy than the grocer. Even in familiar and familial circumstances, they address each other as "wife" and "[gentle] husband".[35] The circumstances are, however, conversations in front of and with their children. We should here recapitulate that none of Simon/Margery, Candido/Viola, and George/Nell, ostensibly had any children, and none of their discussions were conducted before or with children. The forms of address between Touchstone and his wife may thus be influenced by the familial context, with the attendance of their daughters, Mildred and Gertrude.

Middleton's *Chaste Maid in Cheapside* exhibits both a similar and another context for the deployment of more formalism of address between husband and wife. The congruence is the superior position of the *dramatis personae*: Yellowhammer, the eponymous goldsmith, and his wife, Maudline; Touchwood Senior, the "decayed gentleman", and his wife (indicated only as "Wife"); Sir Oliver Kix and his wife ("Lady"); and Master Allwit and his conjugal companion ("Wife"), maintained by Sir Walter Whorehound. All, then, belong to a higher social echelon, if only just, some having aspirations for even higher social position. The other circumstance, however, is that one of the couples converses out of company; their conversations are always in the company of others, sometimes peers, sometimes subordinates, but not family. Their address to each other may thus be governed by these two influences: one socially conditioned, and the other socially situated. Thus, Yellowhammer addresses his wife six times as "wife", but only once as Maudline, whilst she titles him once "husband" and twice "sir". Touchwood addresses his wife twice as "wife" and she him twice as "sir", their only direct addresses. The Kixes, devoted but childless, still address each other as "(sweet) wife" (six times) and "(sweet) husband" (four), never by forename. The conjointly complicit Allwits refer to each other in direct speech as "wife" (four), "husband" and "sir" (twice each). By and large, no other epithets were employed by these actors.

In *Mad World*, the citizen Harebrain addresses his wife, Mistress H., simply as "wife" (seven occasions) and she returns only with the formality of "sir" (ten).[36] No companions, inferiors or kin are attendant. The sense conveyed by the formality is the undeserved suspicion of Harebrain towards his wife, an unwarranted jealousy, which she senses and is concerned to protect her virtue.

Reflections

What can we elicit then from these representations of gendered relationships in the households, workshops and shops of the citizenry of early-modern London? We can conclude, I think, that it was possible to imagine more than one marital situation. The stereotype of Simon and Margery Eyre was manifestly an influential discourse. Even so, in certain circumstances, where the marriage involved social exogamy, a more active female role might be countenanced, if only, ultimately, to be rejected. The social imaginary was not completely circumscribed or delimited. Old discourses could be partly tempered with new perceptions, traditional roles encounter newer transformations. "There is a consciousness in these plays that traditional patriarchy is at odds with the emerging notions of companionate marriage and the wife's role within it...", but, as they say, that's another story.[37]

72   *Social Dramas*

Figure 1 Example of Concordance Analysis of *Shoemaker's Holiday*

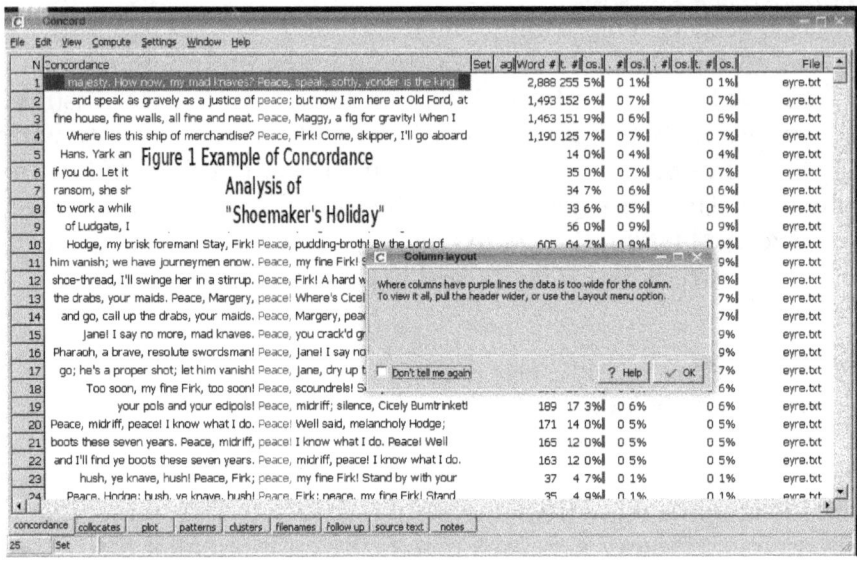

Figure 2 Firk's Self-referential Use of Firk

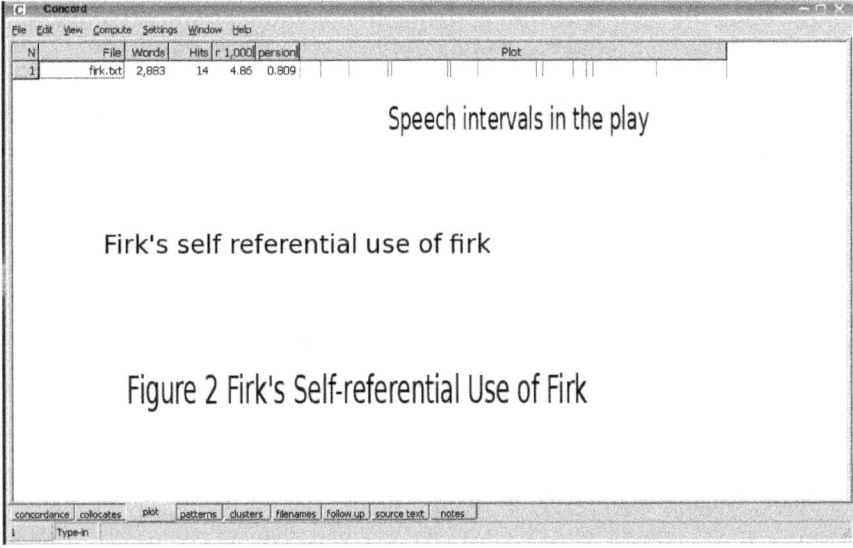

Conjugal Relations 73

Figure 3 Margery Eyre's Idiomatic "Let that pass"

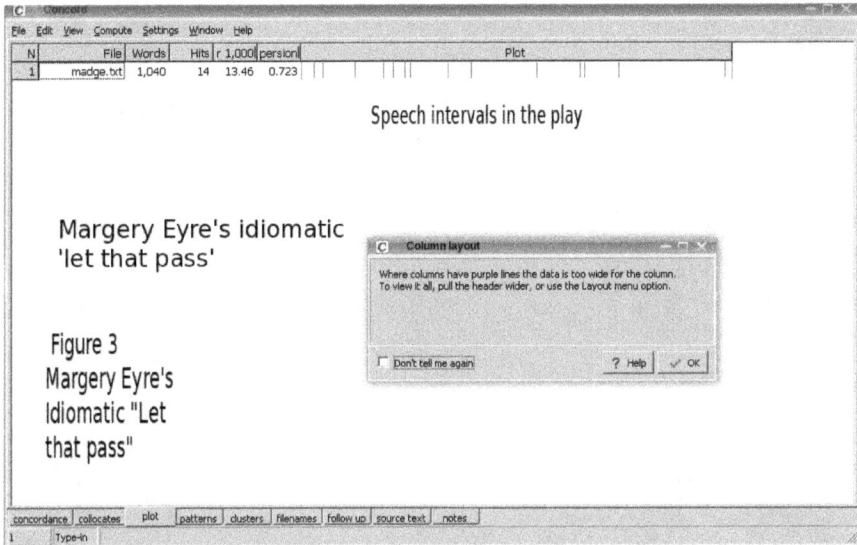

Figure 4 Viola's Speech Referring to Candido's Patience

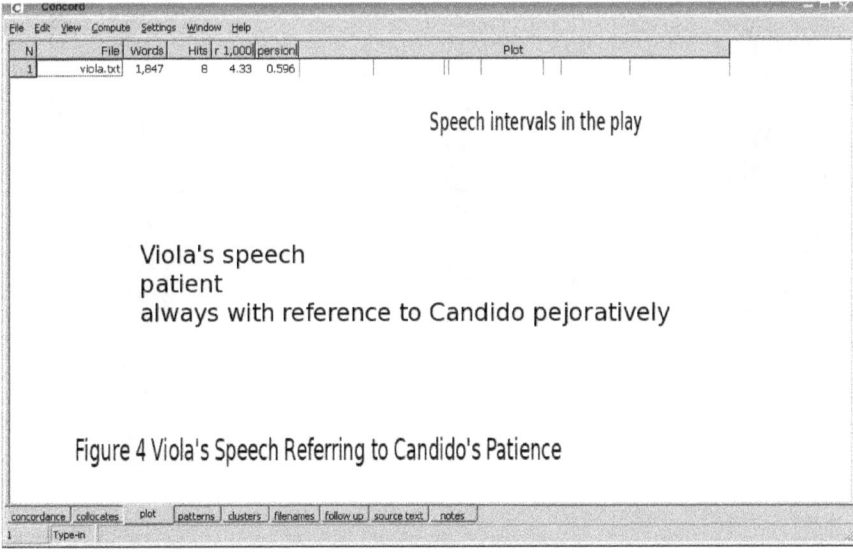

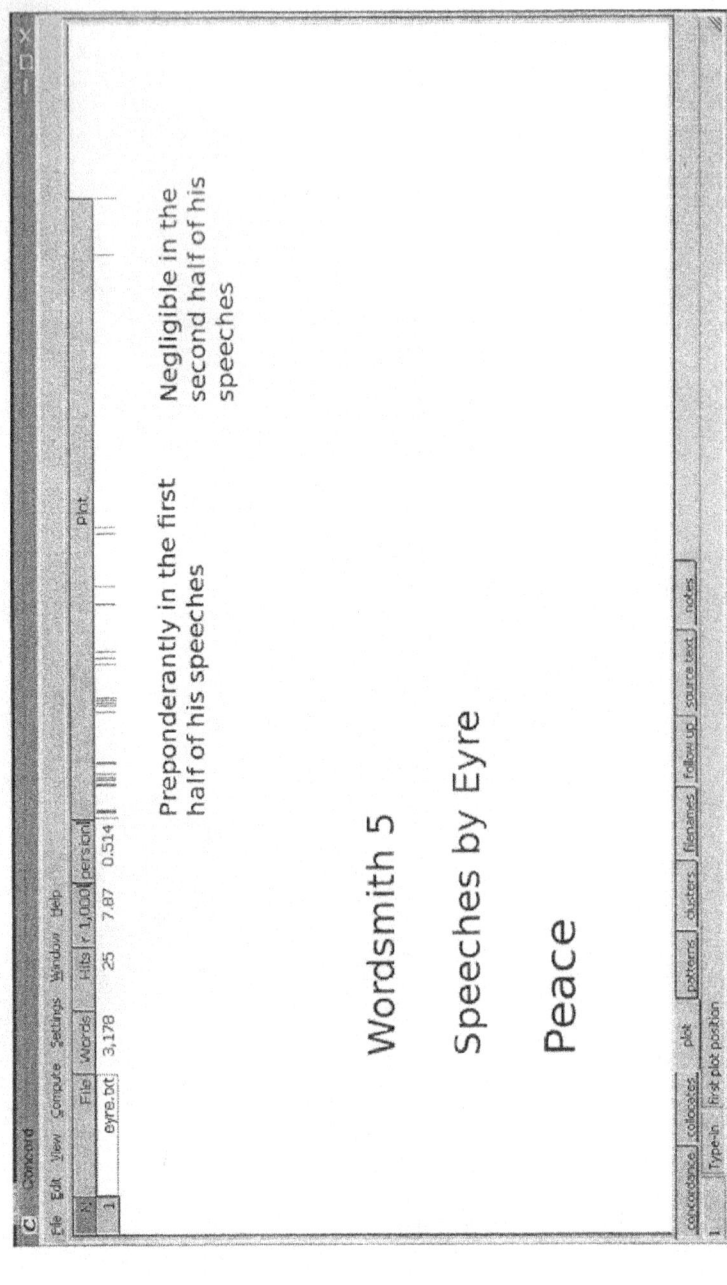

Figure 5 Simon Eyre's Deployment of "Peace!"

Notes

[1] John Cleveland, "The Hetacomb to his Mistress", in *Metaphysical Poetry*, edited by Colin Burrow (Harmondsworth: Penguin, 2006), 158 (lines 1-2 of the verse).

[2] "For historians, the relationship between husband and wife is a mystery for a different reason. It is, after all, mainly a private matter. Its most interesting aspects are hidden from us and we must make do with maddeningly contradictory hints": Beatrice Gottlieb, *The Family in the Western World: From the Black Death to the Industrial Age* (Oxford: Oxford University Press, 1993), 89; see also 92 for a brief notion of address between wife and husband.

[3] Susan Amussen, "Punishment, Discipline and Power: The Social Meanings of Violence in Early Modern England", *Journal of British Studies* 34 (1995), 1.

[4] More particularly, Laura Gowing, *Domestic Dangers: Women, Words, and Sex in Early Modern London* (Oxford: Oxford University Press, 1996); Sandy Bardsley, *Venomous Tongues: Speech and Gender in Late Medieval England* (Philadelphia, PA: University of Pennsylvania Press, 2006); Jane Kamensky, *Governing the Tongue: The Politics of Speech in Early New England* (Oxford: Oxford University Press, 1997); Bernard Capp, *When Gossips Meet: Women, Family, and Neighbourhood in Early Modern England* (Oxford: Oxford University Press, 2003).

[5] Anthony Fletcher, *Gender, Sex and Subordination in England 1500-1800* (New Haven and London: Yale University Press, 1995), xix-xxi, 112, 117-18. Fletcher concentrates on tragedy which arguably overemphasizes marital difficulties: Fletcher, *Gender, Sex and Subordination*, 21, is an illustration. It is probably necessary to return to an "Aristotelian" notion of genre, differentiating between tragedy and comedy, the former likely to heighten conflict and a discordant denouement, the latter a more harmonious outcome.

[6] Tessa Watt, *Cheap Print and Popular Piety, 1550-1640* (Cambridge: Cambridge University Press, 1991); Margaret Spufford, *Small Books and Pleasant Histories: Popular Fiction and Its Readership in Seventeenth Century England* (Cambridge: Cambridge University Press, 1985).

[7] Alistair Fowler. "Transformations of Genre", in *Modern Genre Theory*, ed. David Duff (Harlow: Pearson Educational Ltd., 2000), 232-49.

[8] S. Mukherji, 'Women, Law and Dramatic Realism in Early Modern England', *English Literary Renaissance* 35 (2005): 248-72; Manley, *Literature and Culture*; McLuskie, *Dekker & Heywood*, esp. 2, 14; Clark, *Renaissance Drama*, 63-83 ("Journalistic plays").

[9] For the social context of these plays, Rappaport, *Worlds within Worlds*; Joseph P. Ward, *Metropolitan Communities. Trades, Guilds, Identity and*

Change in Early Modern London (Stanford, CA: Stanford University Press, 1997).

[10] I am grateful to Kate Loveman for elucidating this issue of boy actors and female parts.

[11] Manley, *Literature and Culture*.

[12] Methodological note: in the discussion of Dekker's two plays, the investigation was conducted using WordSmith, but in the later discussion, the data were extracted using the command line (interface) (CLI) of Linux to compile word lists.

[13] Michael Pickering, *Stereotyping. The Politics of Representation* (Basingstoke: Palgrave Macmillan, 2001), xiii. There are many more passages from Pickering which I could cite in this regard. The italics are mine. Importantly, Pickering associates stereotyping with an attempt to maintain the status quo: 3.

[14] Pickering, *Stereotyping*, 3: "This is the dilemma which stereotyping faces: to resort to one-sided representations in the interests of order, security and dominance, or to allow for a more complex vision."

[15] There is no space to define patriarchy here; it is, indeed, a contested concept, depending on the various stages of femininist epistemology: Sylvia Walby, *Theorizing Patriarchy* (Oxford: Blackwell, 1990). I shall work here with the "radical feminist" perception "in which men as a group dominate women as a group and are the main beneficiaries of the subordination of women" (Walby, *Theorizing Patriarchy*, 3). I also, nonetheless, employ it in its familiar early-modern sense of authority over the household and workshop, as in Filmer's *Patriarcha*. Here, I confine myself to the analysis of language use, but there is much in the two plays concerning the sexual division of labour and spheres of action and authority in household and workshop in a stereotyped context, although, again, there are differences between the relative interventions of Madge Eyre and Viola, the latter more forceful in her presence in the drapery shop. The literature on all these aspects, even for just early-modern gender relationships, is so vast that it cannot be recited here. I take on board the critique that "[h]istorians have focused on the relationship between husband and wife at the expense of other relationships" (Patricia Crawford, *Blood, Bodies and Families in Early Modern England* [Harlow: Longman, 2004], 3-4). Below, I allude to the extended household that is the workshop and shop, although the married couples in these two plays were childless.

[16] *Shoemaker's Holiday*, scene i, line 204.

[17] *Honest Whore I*, scene 5.

[18] John L. Austin, *How to Do Things With Words* (Oxford: Oxford University Press, 1962); John R. Searle, *Mind, Language and Society. Philosophy in the Real World* (London: Weidenfeld and Nicholson, 1999), chapter 6;

Jenny Thomas, *Meaning in Interaction. An Introduction to Pragmatics* (Harlow: Longman Group Ltd., 1995).

[19] In the early exchanges, he also addresses Jane, his maid and the lover of his journeyman, Ralph, the latter conscripted to the army: *Shoemaker's Holiday*, scene i, lines 160-8.

[20] *Honest Whore I*, scene 15.

[21] *Honest Whore II*, scene 13.

[22] For "hedges" in female speech patterns, for example, Janet Holmes, *Women, Men and Politeness* (Harlow: Longman Group Ltd., 1995), 72-114. For challenges to the stereotyping of female language use, Deborah Cameron, *Feminism and Linguistic Theory* (Basingstoke: Palgrave, 1985), esp. 44.

[23] *Shoemaker's Holiday*, scene vii, lines 60-4.

[24] *Honest Whore I*, scene ii.

[25] Amussen, *An Ordered Society: Gender and Class in Early Modern England* (Oxford: Basil Blackwell, 1988).

[26] Fletcher, *Gender, Sex and Subordination*, 12, 121, 204ff.

[27] Nick de Somogyi, "Editor's Introduction" to Thomas Dekker: *The Honest Whore Parts One and Two* (London: Globe Quartos, 1988), ix; W. Brown Patterson, *King James VI and I and the Reunion of Christendom* (Cambridge: Cambridge University Press, 1997).

[28] I follow Charles Taylor, *A Secular Age* (Cambridge, MA, and London: Harvard University Press, 2007), 114-22; for the influence of Lipsius, Adriana McCrea, *Constant Minds: Political Virtue and the Lipsian Paradigm in England, 1584-1650* (Toronto and London: University of Toronto Press, 1997). See also, *Epicoene*, Act I, scene i, lines 38-60 for the circumspection of Truewit, attributed by Clerimont to "Stoicity" and the reading of Plutarch's Morals "or some such tedious fellow..."

[29] Taylor, *A Secular Age*, 116, 118; Lucy Gent, ed., *Albion's Classicism: Visual Art in Britain, 1550-1660* (New Haven: Yale University Press, 1995).

[30] For general contexts, without reference to Lipsius, Euan Cameron, "'Civilized Religion' from Renaissance to Reformation and Counter-Reformation" and Jonathan Barry, "Civility and Civic Culture in Early Modern England: The Meanings of Urban Freedom", both in *Civil Histories. Essays Presented to Sir Keith Thomas*, ed. Peter Burke, Brian Harrison and Paul Slack (Oxford: Oxford University Press, 2000), 49-66, 181-96; there are fertile ideas in Martin Ingram, 'Sexual Manners: The Other Face of Civility in Early Modern England", in *Civil Histories*, 91-4.

[31] For a different interpretation, based on the enmity between gallants and citizen merchants, and centered on the relationships of the market place, McLuskie, *Dekker & Heywood*, 72-4.

[32] Holmes, *Women, Men and Politeness*, 72-114.

[33] For William Gouge's strictures against such frivolities, Gottlieb, *Family in the Western World*, 99; see also James Casey, *The History of the Family* (Oxford: Blackwell, 1989), 109. In *Every Man in His Humour*, Jonson has Dame Kitely address her husband, the London merchant, affectionately as "good muss": Act II, scene i, lines 202, 205 and 209: intimately and not before children.

[34] Holmes, *Women, Men and Politeness*, 80-1.

[35] *Eastward Ho*, Act IV, scene ii, line 137; Act V, scene iv, lines 8, 27.

[36] *Mad World*, Act III, scene i, lines 81-125; scene ii, lines 235-40.

[37] Clark, *Renaissance Drama*, 62.

4
Money Matters

[SHORTYARD] Well said i'faith: hang money! Good jests are worth silver at all times.
[EASY] They're worth gold, Master Blastfield.[1]

[MAMMON] Silver I care not for.
[FACE] Yes, sir, a little to give to beggars.[2]

Punning references to and metaphorical use of coin pervade the Revels plays, the City comedies and also Jonson. Some contemporary playwrights like Middleton and Jonson exhibited concern about the seemingly excessive and intemperate desire for riches, in gold and gold coin, and deployed metaphors of gold and silver as the instrument of their satire.[3] In the City comedies, coin is thus frequently employed as a metaphorical representation (and critique) of contemporary social attitudes.[4] Gold coin and silver coin symbolize different social sectors. Through adopting this metaphor, society is inevitably presented as dichotomous. We might initially be troubled by how that dramatic representation of the binary division of society can relate to social reality, for we are accustomed to the introduction of fine gradations of social description in the late sixteenth century and early seventeenth century: the "sorts" of people with their attendant qualifying adjectives so clearly enunciated by Keith Wrightson.[5] Wrightson argues that the language of sorts provided a more flexible description than that of estates as social change advanced in early-modern England. More recently, in a rural context, Henry French has returned to a more structured hierarchical ordering of society constructed around principal or chief inhabitants.[6] (It is noticeable, however, that French's emphasis is on rural society whilst Wrightson regards the formulation of a language of sorts as evolving out of late-medieval urban social organization). We might therefore be tempted to conclude that the dichotomous relationship portrayed by the City comedies is an inadequate social description.[7] (The frequent resort by some writers to the epithet of "middle class" is surely an anachronism, for, as Wrightson has illustrated, even "middling sort" did not emerge until the middle of the seventeenth century).

We might be inclined to consider that the needs of sub-genre, literary conventions and modes, and dramatic devices ineluctably lead away from social realism. Jonson was perhaps more constrained by, because conscious of, the conventions of genre inherited from antiquity. Issues of genre (and the stability of genre) are complicated. Rigid distinctions were being traduced in England–not least in tragicomedy.[8] Although they had their prejudices, political and personal, all three authors–Dekker, Middleton and Jonson–had an intimate–sometimes too intimate –experience of most aspects of City life, fortunate and unfortunate. By adopting the metaphor of silver coin and gold coin as clear demarcations in social life on the stage, the authors were drawn to a false dichotomy, a dilemma resulting purely from literary production. Metaphor was not the only deceit in this respect.[9] The distinction in the latter between "live" and "dead" metaphors is important as the metaphor of coinage was distinctly "live", not yet "dead" (i.e. cliché). The constant use of antithesis as a poetic device, especially by Middleton, constrained social description in a similar way. Authors, by using this metaphor and also antithesis could not, in their treatment of social relationships and social organization, escape the bounds of a dichotomous description of social interaction.[10] We might illustrate this combination by a non-monetary passage from Middleton: "all that live in the world are but great fish and little fish, and feed upon one another".[11]

At issue here is how three playwrights in particular and from their own perspectives (Dekker, Middleton and Jonson) used in their comedies the metaphor of coin–in particular gold coin–and how that compared with social reality. (Here the concern is strictly with social organization, but one might equally consider: gold and gender relations; gold and "the gift"; and money and "xenophobia").

One of the purposes here is to illustrate one extent to which the cultural and the social in the past intersect and mutually inform each other.[12] In part, the issue is to reconcile representation and realism. In essence, the reconciliation involves the proposal of a (in this limited case, virtuous) hermeneutic circle, which is discussed more fully towards the end.

MONEY AS METAPHOR FOR SOCIAL STATUS

We can begin then with two episodes from Dekker's *Shoemaker's Holiday*.[13] When he becomes resigned to the conscription of Ralph to the muster to fight in France, Simon Eyre, the master shoemaker, decides that his only course is to support Ralph by giving him money: "Hold thee, Ralph, here's five sixpences for thee". After a flight of mock heroic encouragement about fighting for the honor of the gentle craft, the gentlemen shoemakers, the courageous cordwainers, the flower of St Martin's, and so on, Eyre urges Ralph to crack the crowns of the French knaves. Eyre's second journeyman, Firk, following the example of his master, proffers Ralph three tuppences with the encouragement that Ralph firk (salaciously punning on his name) the *baisez-mon-culs*. Likewise, the first journeyman, Hodge, furnishes Ralph with a shilling in the hope that Ralph will "cram thy steps" with French crowns.[14]

Significant here is the conferment of silver coin on Ralph: sixpences, tuppences and a shilling. Equally important is the relative equality of the donors: Eyre no less than his journeymen proffers silver coin. Master and servants are of the same social position symbolized by the metallic content of the coin. Perhaps as important is the comparison with the French whose crowns are not only heads but foreign gold coins in circulation in England: exotic and extrinsic.

Advancing forward, after Eyre is elected as sheriff of the City, he proclaims his status with his usual exuberance: "See here, my Maggy, a chain, a gold chain, for Simon Eyre".[15] When Oatley, the Lord Mayor and knight, visits Eyre and his journeymen, Oatley confers two angels for the journeymen to dispose on beer at Stratford Bow, to which Eyre adds another. The gold chain, but more particularly the gold coins, represent the transformation in Eyre's status. Like Oatley, he now engages with gold coin, angels. The transition from the employment of silver coin to the deployment of gold pieces indicates the transmutation of Eyre's status from ordinary citizen to successful citizen and member of the civic elite. Gold denominates success–benign achievement in this case.

We can agree with Joel Kaplan that Eyre's ebullience tends to mask the ethical issues contained within the events: "when Simon faces moral disparities which are inherent in the actions of others we are allowed a brief glimpse of these ambiguities before they are dissolved in his verbal euphoria".[16]

Getting rich quick

Unlike Dekker, Jonson (and his collaborator Marston) was more acerbic about what success gold coin represented.[17] (The events in *Eastward Ho* probably represent another aspect of Jonson's "satiric economy", that wealth cannot be created from nothing and that the most satisfactory form of wealth is inherited wealth). Throughout the collaborative *Eastward Ho* coin as a metaphor displays pejorative qualities. More especially, gold coin and aspiration to success are combined in the ambition of Quicksilver, the apprentice of gentle status who regards his social position as traduced by his trade. Quicksilver–as his moniker implies–desires a quick fix to success (as well as, perhaps, reflecting his mercurial temperament in the early stages of the play). When his adventurous (in contemporary as well as modern sense) scheme in Virginia collapses farcically, Quicksilver turns to another avenue to redeem himself from the usurers and his indebtedness: the counterfeiting of gold coins from copper and a second injudicious enterprise to debase angels: "I'll take you off twelve pence from every angel with a kind of aquafortis, and never deface any part of the image".[18]

The symbolism of coinage is profuse. Quicksilver's name also implies a limit to his capabilities: silver coin, not gold.[19] His character and attitudes are the equivalent of silver coin in a bimetallic coinage: distinctly lower in value.[20] With his ambitious schemes for gold coinage, like his Virginian adventure, he overreaches himself and his name. Jonson's acerbic wit is directed even more poignantly at the scheme to both counterfeit and debase gold coins, angels. The copper is to be transmuted into a simulacrum of gold with arsenic: "ratsbane". The angels will be denuded of their exterior content (without damaging the image, the angel symbolizing to a crypto-Catholic like Jonson a higher value) and then their weight deviously restored: "take your *sal alchyme* prepared, and your distilled urine, and let your angels lie in it but four and twenty hours, and they shall have their perfect weight again".[21] So the angels will be restored in weight by the absorption of piss.[22]

Our episode from Middleton exhibits a similar acerbity. In *Michaelmas Term*, the objective of Quomodo and his associates is to gull Easy, the young gentleman from Essex making his first visit to the metropolis. The intention is to cozen Easy out of his landed estate. The ruse involves several stages, initially to deprive Easy of his coin in hand. Quomodo's associate, Shortyard, is entrusted with inveigling Easy into this situation. The action takes place around a game of dice. Shortyard encourages Easy to contemplate his status through the metaphor of gold coin.

> Sir, you shall not give out so meanly of yourself in my company for a million. Make such privy to your disgrace? You're a gentleman of fair fortunes; keep me your reputation. Set 'em all; there's crowns for you.[23]

Easy consequently wagers all his coin, either crowns or angels– the later context suggests angels as Rearage exclaims: "The devil and his angels!", to which Lethe, the winner, retorts, "Welcome, dear angels, where y'are cursed, ne'er stay".[24]

In all scenarios, gold then is, as one might expect, used metaphorically as an attribute of success. Gold coin differentiated, marked off, the successful from the rest of society, silver coin. Differences existed, however, between the playwrights. Dekker's deployment of the metaphor is an affective use. In the elevation of Sim Eyre to a user of gold coin, there is admiration both for the success of the person and for the civic institution. Social honor is reinforced by the giving of gold; gold is used to furnish hospitality. It is neither hoarded nor used for nefarious purposes. The status of the people, Oatley and Eyre, is reflected in the ability to part with gold: to dispose of it without any necessity to keep it.

By contrast, Middleton and Jonson perceive no moral value in success and its representation as gold. Rather, success is amoral or, sometimes as the plot demands, tainted by immorality. In the hands of the successful, the purity of gold is traduced, even debased. The privileged owners of gold deploy it for iniquitous and morally dubious intent.

IDEAS ABOUT MONEY

In recent research, there has been a turn to the language of capitalism in early-modern England, the culture of capitalism in the City or agrarian capitalism in rural England.[25] There are senses in which the use of this term is both prescient, but premature. Macpherson's offering of "possessive individualism" has been challenged, at least in so far as it pertains to Hobbes.[26] There is a sense in which, however, we might rehabilitate Macpherson's description in a different context, not as a referent for political theory, but as distinctive of an upper echelon of City society as portrayed by Jonson and Middleton. Polanyi, in *The Great Transformation*, conceived of the monetization of social values. That phrase too feeds into what can be perceived in the City comedies. Partly following Polanyi, Deborah Valenze proposed the formation an "acquisitive self" or a "monetary self" in the eighteenth century. Again, we might perceive antecedents in the City comedies. We might express this earlier attitude as aggressive materialism.

It is interesting how, in the representations of Middleton and Jonson, this aggressive materialism coheres around the issue of gold coin. We might regard their reflections as acerbically satirical. Gold coin demarcates the successful from the lump of society, but not with any inherent moral value. Whilst Middleton and Jonson were not of the same cut, they critiqued and regretted the urgent acquisitiveness of the City.[27]

Of course, English people's attitude to coinage was also conditioned by fluctuations and vicissitudes through the sixteenth century: the assault on a coinage based on the intrinsic metallic content, by the influx of silver, official debasement and devaluation, and the issuing of new coinage. People's experience of holding coin was thus confusing and traumatic. Bimetallic ratios were disrupted. That last matter might seem of little instance, but, since high denomination coins consisted of gold, it was of some social importance. When people invested emotional significance in coins as symbolic tokens, the more affluent usually had in mind these high-value gold coins. High emotional value was often represented through high-value, scarce, coins.[28]

Silvered speech acts

Gold, then, was often embedded in the emplotment of the comedies, part of the narrative structure. In complete contrast, the dramatic narrative did not depend on silver. When silver was mentioned, it was in utterances, declamatory or exclamatory, performative utterances or speech acts with illocutionary force. The force was illocutionary and not perlocutionary because of the authorial intention in the utterance. The metaphor of silver was deployed to imply a character's lack of substance or as a scabrous denunciation, deprecation or personal insult. These speech acts are comparable with Austin's "You are a poltroon" in his explanation of the ambiguous illocutionary force of some speech acts: are they censure or insult or both? Following on from Austin, Searle commented on the propositional content of such speech acts and the intentionality of the speaker. He categorized these sorts of speech acts ("You are a poltroon") as assertive speech acts. More complexity was expected by Medina who referred to the complex inter-relationship of content, force and effect.[29] To all intents and purposes, however–and intents and purposes are fundamental to this matter–the use of the metaphor of silver coin to represent persons in comedic drama was a performative utterance, a speech act which did something rather than simply making a statement: it marginalized people, placed them lower in a binary hierarchy, and described them as characteristically inferior. Small coin–silver money–also had the imputations of baseness, associated with the poorer and meaner sort of people as well as having a minimal value.

> [1] [GERTRUDE] Marry, fist, o' your kindness. I thought as much. Come away, Sin, we shall as soon get a fart from a dead man, as a farthing of courtesy here.[30]

[2] [GOLDSTONE] How you rogue costly, out ath'house, you slip-shood, shamlegd, browne-thred, penny-skeand rascall.[31]

The insinuation was meanness of status and character.

Here too we should interject some comments about the condition of English silver coinage. Despite the evident pride exhibited by Eyre and Firk, the coinage was in terrible straits–an accumulation of minting of different reigns, some elderly and decrepit. For this reason, Middleton and Jonson could allude to the lower-denomination, silver coins–those in regular exchange–as metaphors for loss of male honor and disregard: "cracked" three-farthings and groats. So, in dismissive vein, Eyre chastises his wife and journeymen: "Peace you cracked groats..."[32] The straight-talking Downright exclaims: "He values me at a cracked three-farthings, for aught I see..."[33] The imputation here consists of all of new and not established, lacking the solidity of tradition, insubstantial, weak, and poorly constructed. The three-farthing coin had been introduced in the late sixteenth century and was notoriously thin. Previously, three farthings had been composed of the halfpenny and the farthing coins (*obulus quadrans*). Imputing disfavor, Edward Knowell compares the accomplished skill of some beggars to the smoothness of the "shove-groat shilling".[34] The arrogant Quicksilver thus defines the attitude of gentlemen to silver coin: "Why, do nothing, be like a gentleman...Wipe thy bum with testons, and make ducks and drakes with shillings".[35]

Small coin–silver money–thus had the imputations of baseness, associated with the poorer and meaner sort of people as well as having a minimal value.

[COKES] 'Twas but a little scurvy white money, hang it: it may hang the cutpurse one day. I ha' gold left to gi' thee a fairing, yet, ...[36]

In similar vein, in the exchange between Face the housekeeper and Epicure Mammon, the knight, although both gold and silver were the province of Mammon, he protests that he dislikes silver; Face retorts that a little silver is necessary to give to beggars.[37] The disdain of the more fortunate social groups for silver was enunciated and the association of silver with the poorer "sort" confirmed. The allusion of poverty and begging with silver was extended further.

> [JOYCE] ...his hat is off already, as if he were begging one poor pennyworth of kindness.[38]

The differentiation is illustrated by the complaint of Young Chartley gaming at dice in *The Wise-woman of Hogsdon*, one of Thomas Heywood's later concoctions (London, 1638). "Must you be set in gold, and/not a jot of silver in my purse". Later, however, his lament contains the golden pun: "Or hee that hath uncrown'd me,/ Ile take a speedie order with him".[39] So silver money was "ready money", but in particular it was coinage for lower social groups rather than young gallants and pups like Chartley.[40]

The demeaning aspect of silver coin recurs in the manner in which Tibet Talkapace, a poor maidservant, dismissively refers to not caring a groat.

> There it lieth; the worst is but a curried cote;
> Tut, I am used therto; I care not a grote![41]

GROATSWORTH

Let's briefly return to silver coin and its association with the poorer sort. That statement can be made because, as Muldrew has described to us, those with credit–social and material–could rely on "reckonings" and deferred payment.[42] The poor could not: they constantly needed low denomination coins, not least for oblations to the church associated with life-course events, tithe and Easter (which might have necessitated "earmarking" of small coin).[43] We can, indeed, perceive some associations of silver money: the familiarity with the groat. That coin/amount is dominant in bequests in wills to parish churches. When legacies of a lamb to a godchild declined, 4d. was a frequent substitute, especially amongst testators in the Leeds area and in Lincolnshire and Somerset.[44] In many ways, the groat seemed to be the minimally acceptable symbolic gift of the lower "middling sort". The symbolism of the groat is perhaps reflected in the benefaction under the will (1528) of Richard Clarke, gentleman of Lincoln, by which he assigned a hundred groats to a hundred people suffering from poverty or age in the City; if that number did not exist in Lincoln, then the impotent in the "next townes" were to be included, "so that every person may have on grote".[45] We might place significance too on the allegation against Joly and Balles that, in the hearing of the congregation, they had uttered to the vicar who was conducting a funeral ceremony: "Yf ye wolle demaunde or aske dirige grotes for sayeng dirige we will not offre".[46]

Accordingly, all the characters of lower social status in *Gammer Gurton's Nedle* talk about small silver coins: "I holle thee a grote" (Chat); "Chil hold the a peny" (Hodge); "chould give him a new grot" (Hodge); and "I chould a penny" (Cocke).[47] This observation obtains even if the comedy is a parody of lower social groups. When a resolution to the problem of the lost needle is discovered in the denouement, and harmony restored between neighbours, Gammer Gurton takes the assembled party off to drink, although she explains that "Cha but one halfpeny".[48]

We can explore further the social significance of small denomination coin. There was an ideology surrounding small coin. It was regarded as providing the liquidity of the commonwealth. Halfpennies and farthings were, in a patriarchal perception, viewed as a service to the poorer sort. Denouncing the forestallers of grain and counterfeiters of coin, Lord Richardson proclaimed in Star Chamber in the 1630s: "for the one would let them have noe bread, and the others noe small money to buy bread". Alluding to the production of small coin, he explained the meaning of the statutes for farthings from Edward III onwards, but went on to denounce how the purpose of those acts had been defeated by the inflated value of silver. The introduction of copper farthings by James I had, moreover, succumbed to the malfeasance of counterfeiters. At the heart of Richardson's *obiter dicta* was a patriarchal concern for the provision of small currency to the poor for their daily existence.[49]

[1] A penny pot, for that's the old man's gallon[50]
[2] I, Giue me a valiant Turke, though not worth ten pence[51]

[3] [COUNTRYWOMAN] I would have, sir,
A groatsworth of any news–I care not what–
To carry down this Saturday to our vicar.[52]

expound this understanding further.[53] The importance of silver coin at lower social levels is also demonstrated by the continual reference to the payment of legacies "in penny or pennyworthe".[54]

It was unlikely that this differentiation of the coinage did not attract attention and comment, and, indeed, Lodge and Greene, perhaps reflecting an intimate acquaintance with "popular" opinion in the City, voiced this concern through the mouth of the poor man, Alcon.

I hold my Cap to a noble that the Usurer hath given him some gold, and he, chawing it in his mouth, hath got the toothache that he cannot speake.[55]

Here, Alcon may be expressing a widespread dissatisfaction amongst the urban poorer sort with their lot by comparison with the unrestricted avarice which they witnessed around them, symbolized by gold coin.

Conclusion

The theater yet occupied an ambiguous position. Dramatists represented the "new world" of commercial consciousness from a vantage point, but were enmeshed in that same cosmology of coin. The theater engaged with commerce: in the livelihood of playwrights; in performance; and the publication.[56] Dramatic work had entered into the world of commerce. That ambivalence has been indicated by Tanya Pollard in her metaphor of early-modern English drama as narcotic: all of a social sedative, a cultural prism, and community therapy, but with unexpected side effects.[57] Dramatists launched a social critique against the commercial ethic, but remained within it. We might then adapt here the encapsulation of Leyshon and Thrift: these writers occupied a space for public discourse, but were themselves part of that discourse. Physically and materially, they belonged to money-space: the *locus* created and sustained by coin and commerce, constituted around the goldsmith-bankers: the City and its Liberties. Just as coin provided a metaphor for drama so it also produced space in which those writers acted.[58] Perhaps the dilettante William Cavendish, earl of Newcastle, recognized this dilemma when his Frenchman, Monsieur Device, expounds:

> there will be a new play/
>   shortly, a Pretty Comedy written by a profest scholler/
>   he scornes to take money for his witt as the/
> Poets doe.[59]

How do the representations of the dramatists, of the Revels plays, City comedies and Jonson, correlate with historians' perceptions of the rapid transformation and fluidity of social organization and description? There is some consistency. French's chief inhabitants consisted of a self-selecting elite in rural society. Their rhetorical self-representation constituted not a graduated hierarchy, but a pronounced demarcation between those with a self-evaluation of local worth and the remainder of local society. Wrightson's sorts of people superficially presents both a more dynamic and fluid description and a more graded hierarchy. Behind the fluidity of description, nonetheless, resided a marking off of the better sort from the poorer sort. In this interstitial time, between the dominance of a doctrine of estates and the formation of the middling sort in the middle of the seventeenth century, the language of sorts cohered around a division between the better sort and the poorer sort.[60] So consistently exhibited is the attempt of those who considered themselves superior to separate themselves off from those perceived by them as inferior.

Notwithstanding that division of society, Wrightson's and French's divisions differ from the implications of the dramatists. The distinctions in Wrightson's and French's delineations are as much moral as economic: the conviction of the elite of their moral authority which separated them from the remainder of society. Dekker, indeed, subscribed to this perception of an evolving middling sort in the City which had this moral assurance, qualities symbolized through the intrinsic value of gold.[61] This representation of the City elite resonates both in Rappaport's consideration of the harmony of civic society and Archer's suggestion of the pursuit of stability by the City's magistracy.[62] Those convergences did not cut ice with Jonson and Middleton, whose humor is contained within an engagement with serious and contentious issues.[63] In complete contrast–and although Middleton collaborated with Dekker on occasion[64]–these two playwrights conceived of a profound lack of any moral substance in the divisions of society, although for different reasons. Far from an honorable status symbolized through gold, these two acerbic critics employed the metaphor of the misuse and abuse of gold to signify an acquisitive and unscrupulous nexus within City society.[65]

> But Gold is sweete, and they deceive themselves,
>   For though I guild my Temple with a smile,
>   It is but Iudas-like to worke their endes.[66]

Many, like Manley, have remarked upon the erosion of the social order and the fluidity of social processes in late-sixteenth and early-seventeenth-century London.[67] This dislocation came from within successful social cadres as much as from without. It is epitomized in the derogation of gold as a symbol of success in some contemporary comedic drama.

The work of metaphor is important in the inter-relationship between social and cultural history. "But metaphor is never innocent".[68] We might reconfigure that *dictum* as the intentionality behind metaphor is never innocent.[69] Metaphor always performs work: it acts and is transformational. Through metaphor, abstract language becomes a language of action.[70] Metaphor works through prefiguration, configuration and transfiguration. By prefiguration is meant that the audience has some idea of the attributes of both the subject and the substitutive metaphorical object. The metaphorical use configures the relationship between subject and substitutive object. "Live" metaphor (but not "dead" metaphor) then transfigures the subject: creates a new understanding through compelling the audience to reconsider the subject in a new way.[71] That is the poetic work of metaphor.[72] More explicitly, then, playgoers have an inkling of what is happening in their society, but through the deployment of metaphor, the playwrights induce the audience to reconsider–perhaps brusquely to re-evaluate–the challenges occurring in society. It is demanded of the audience that it participate in this simple hermeneutic circle of interpretation: the audience has a vague familiarity with the social problem; the dramatic (cultural) voice heightens the issue; the cultural "take" on the dilemma feeds back into the social. Critical to this process is "live" metaphor, for "dead" metaphor cannot perform this work. The reception of "dead" metaphor would be laconic since the totally familiar does not excite the mind. The place of the dramatists is to produce "live" metaphor: to astound and force to reconsider through quick imagination and inventiveness. Even allowing for issues of reception and reader response, thought about the metaphor is provoked.[73]

Finally, it will be noticed that metaphor is not simply the substitution of words. Metaphor is constituted in whole dialogues and discourses, even in the emplotment or narrative organization of dramatic work. The actual composition of the metaphor–how its allusiveness is used–is important: gold is often embedded in a narrative and is discursively related, whilst silver is dismissively contained in brief declamations and exclamations. Form and function are combined.

Notes

[1] *Michaelmas Term*, Act III, scene i, lines 248-53; compare Robert Greene's autobiographical *A Groatsworth of Wit* (1592) for his criticism of the intellectual ability of contemporary authors. For the "structure" of credit in the early-modern economy, Muldrew, *The Economy of Obligation*, but which does not really reflect on the City's materialism as represented in the City comedies. For Greene's own contempt for contemporary acquisitiveness: "THRASYBULUS O miserable time, wherein gold is above God": Thomas Lodge and Greene, *A Looking Glasse for London and England* (London, 1594), line 849, in *The Life and Complete Works in Prose and Verse of Robert Greene M.A.*, ed. A. Grosart (15 vols, New York, 1964), vol. 14. (Thrasybulus, like so many *dramatis personae* in the Revels plays, is a young gentleman brought low to poverty–compare the Essex gentleman, Easy, below).

[2] *Alchemist*, Act IV, scene i, lines 3-4.

[3] Linda Woodbridge, ed., *Money in the Age of Shakespeare: Essays in New Economic Criticism* (Basingstoke: Palgrave Macmillan, 2004); Henry S. Turner, ed., *The Culture of Capital: Property, Cities, and Knowledge in Early*

Modern England (London: Routledge, 2002). See also, Matthew R. Martin, *Between Theater and Philosophy: Skepticism in the Major City Comedies of Ben Jonson and Thomas Middleton* (Newark, DE: University of Delaware Press, 2001). Patrick R. Williams, "Ben Jonson's Satiric Choreography', *Renaissance Drama* new series 9 (1978): 121-45.

⁴ Below, I refer indiscriminately to metaphor, metonym and synecdoche, but each has its own semantic composition: for a succinct discussion, Karl Simms, *Paul Ricoeur* (London: Routledge, 2003), 66.

⁵ Keith Wrightson, "'Sorts of people' in Tudor and Stuart England", in *The Middling Sort of People: Culture, Society and Politics in England, 1550-1800*, ed. Jonathan Barry and Christopher Brooks (Basingstoke: Palgrave, 1994), 28-51.

⁶ Henry French, "Social Status, Localism and the "Middle Sort of People" in England, 1620-1750", *Past and Present* 166 (2000): 66-99.

⁷ Perhaps the best description of the milieu of the City comedies is Rappaport, *Worlds within Worlds*.

⁸ For dramatic realism, S. Mukherji, 'Women, Law and Dramatic Realism in Early Modern England', *English Literary Renaissance* 35 (2005): 248-72 who argues for the "fictive component" being a "historically meaningful phenomenon". For Jonson, Riggs, *Ben Jonson*; Douglas A. Brooks, "Recent Studies in Ben Jonson (1991-mid-2001)", *English Literary Renaissance* 33 (2003): 110-52. Perhaps the best exposition of the issues of genre is Alistair Fowler, "Transformations of Genre', repr. in *Modern Genre Theory*, ed. David Duff (Harlow: Longman, 2000), 232-49; see also his "Georgic and Pastoral: Laws of Genre in the Seventeenth Century", in *Culture and Cultivation in Early Modern England: Writing and the Land*, ed. Michael Leslie and Timothy Raylor (London: University of Leicester Press, 1992), 81-8.

⁹ For the use of metaphor in quotidian speech, Lakoff and Johnson, *Metaphors*, but see also José Medina, *Language* (London: Continuum, 2005), 121-31.

¹⁰ The exploration of the social meaning of money owes a significant debt to Viviana Zelizer, *The Social Meaning of Money: Pin Money, Paychecks, Poor Relief and Other Currencies* (New York: Basic Books, 1994); I have used the 1994 edition although there have been several subsequent issues. Muldrew, "'Hard Food for Midas': Cash and Its Social Value in Early Modern England", *Past and Present* 170 (2001): 78-120, adopted Zelizer's insights to early-modern England without fully exploring the symbolic or semiotic significance of money. More successful in that regard is Deborah Valenze, *The Social Life of Money in the English Past* (Cambridge: Cambridge University Press, 2006), especially 11-28 and chapter 2 which addresses the "phantasm" of money, including its metaphorical use. At 42, she indicates, for example, the aristocratic notion of intrinsic value in the retention of a

traditional content of coinage in the Great Recoinage of 1696. Valenze's exegesis is mainly concerned with developments from the late seventeenth century and in particular in the eighteenth century. My own reflections on the earlier semiotic value of money began about the same time as Valenze's, but have not progressed as maturely. As well as a forceful and convincing exploration, Valenze's book has an extensive bibliography and historiography. My first inspiration was reading Zelizer.

[11] *Roaring Girl,* scene 7, lines 134-5.

[12] Peter Mandler, "The Problem with Cultural History'", *Cultural and Social History* 1 (2004): 94-117; Geoff Eley and Keith Nield, *The Future of Class in History: What's Left of the Social?* (Michigan: University of Michigan Press, 2007); Eley, *A Crooked Line: From Cultural History to the History of Society* (Michigan, University of Michigan Press, 2005).

[13] Drama was, of course, only one genre in which Dekker indulged: see Manley, *Literature and Culture,* 355-71, both for Dekker's "heterocosmic" description of London and his pamphlet output.

[14] *Shoemaker's Holiday,* scene 2, lines 210-21. See Marie-Madeleine Martinet, "Le vocabulaire de l'or dans les appelations satiriques au temps de la Renaissance anglaise", in *L'Or au Temps de la Renaissance: Du Mythe a l'Économie,* ed. M. T. Jones-Davies (1978), 99-104.

[15] *Shoemaker's Holiday,* scene 10, line 129.

[16] Joel L. Kaplan, "Virtue's Holiday: Thomas Dekker and Simon Eyre", *Renaissance Drama* new series 2 (1969): 103-22 (p. 104).

[17] Katharine Eisaman Maus, "Satiric and Ideal Economies in the Jonsonian Imagination", *English Literary Renaissance* 19 (1989): 42-64.

[18] *Eastward Ho,* Act IV, scene i, lines 206-7. For the general context of counterfeiting, Martin Gaskill, *Crime and Mentalities in Early Modern England* (Cambridge: Cambridge University Press, 2000). The respective contributions of the collaborators are still not fully unravelled: Suzanne Gossett, "Marston, Collaboration and *Eastward Ho!*', *Renaissance Drama* new series 33 (2004): 181-200.

[19] For "Aristotelian formalism" over the use of "speaking names", Anne Barton, "*The New Inn* and The Problem of Jonson's Late Style', *English Literary Renaissance* 9 (1979): 395-418, where it is suggested that Jonson abandoned such names on the realization that people *can* learn from experience: 399-404. Marston was probably more misanthropic and virulent than Jonson: Michael Scott, "Ill-mannered Marston", in *The Drama of John Marston: Critical Re-Visions,* ed. T. F. Wharton (Cambridge: Cambridge University Press, 2000), 212-30: in short, he was his own *Malcontent.*

[20] For bimetallism, Peter Spufford, *Money and its Uses in Medieval Europe* (Cambridge: Cambridge University Press, 1988); for England, the best explication is probably still Barry Supple, *Commercial Crisis and Change in*

England, 1600-1642: A Study in the Instability of a Mercantile Economy (Cambridge: Cambridge University Press, 1957); see also David H. Fischer, *The Great Wave: Price Revolutions and the Rhythm of History* (New York: Oxford University Press, 1996).

[21] *Eastward Ho*, Act IV, scene i, lines 210-12. For Jonson's (and others') more usual association of "created" wealth and excrement, E. Pearlman, "Ben Jonson: An Anatomy", *English Renaissance Literature* 9 (1979): 364-93 at p. 382.

[22] Jonson's critique is extended in *Staple of News*, Act IV, scene iii, lines 22-4: "[PENNYBOY SENIOR]: Noble? How, noble? Who hath made him noble? [PENNYBOY JUNIOR]: Why, my most noble money hath, or shall..." Here Jonson rails at the debasement of the nobility, employs the punning metaphor of the gold coin (the noble), and critiques the sale of honors.

[23] *Michaelmas Term*, Act II, scene i, lines 33-6. See the parallel emplotment in Middleton, *Your Five Gallants*, Act II, scene iv, lines 120-330.

[24] *Michaelmas Term*, Act II, scene i, lines 53-5.

[25] See, for example only, Manley, *Literature and Culture*, 17 ("urban beginnings of capitalistic accumulation"); Turner, ed., *Culture of Capitalism*. An original stimulus might have been Robert Brenner's idea of "agrarian capitalism": see Trevor H. Aston and C. H. E. Philbin, eds., *The Brenner Debate: Agrarian Class Structure and Economic Development in Pre-industrial Europe* (Cambridge: Cambridge University Press, 1985).

[26] C. B. Macpherson, *The Political Theory of Possessive Individualism* (Oxford: Oxford University Press, 1962). See also, Don E. Wayne, "*Drama and Society in the Age of Jonson*: An Alternative View", *Renaissance Drama* new series 13 (1982): 103-29.

[27] For Middleton, Chakravorty, *Society and Politics,* and Margot Heinemann, *Puritanism and Theatre: Thomas Middleton and Opposition Drama under the Early Stuarts* (Cambridge: Cambridge University Press, 1980), for different estimates of Middleton. For differing evaluations of Jonson, Blair Worden, "Jonson Among the Historians", in *Culture and Politics in Early Stuart England*, ed. Kevin Sharpe and Peter Lake (Basingstoke: Palgrave, 1994), 67-89, and David Norbrook, *Poetry and Politics in the English Renaissance* (revised edn., Oxford: Oxford University Press, 2002), 135-72.

[28] A succinct way into these "monetary" issues is now Fischer, *Great Wave*; the meanings of bimetallic ratios in seventeenth-century England are probably still best explained by Supple, *Commercial Crisis and Change.*

[29] John L. Austin, *Philosophical Papers* (3rd edn., Oxford: Oxford University Press, 1979), 233-53, esp. 245; John Searle, *Mind, Language and Society: Philosophy in the Real World* (London: Penguin, 1999), 135-61, esp. 148; Medina, *Language*, 21-38.

[30] *Eastward Ho*, Act IV, scene ii, lines 127-9.
[31] *Your Five Gallants*.
[32] *Shoemaker's Holiday*, scene i line 203.
[33] *Everyman in his Humour*, Act II, scene i, line 67.
[34] *Everyman in his Humour*, Act III, scene v, lines 11-13.
[35] *Eastward Ho*, Act I, scene i, lines 106-8
[36] *Bartholomew Fair*, Act II, scene vi, lines. 121-2.
[37] *The Alchemist*, Act IV, scene i, lines 1-4
[38] Cook, *Greenes Tu quoque*, in *Selected Collection* vol. 11, p. 204.
[39] *The Dramatic Works of Thomas Heywood now First Collected* (6 vols, London, 1874), vol. 5, p. 280.
[40] Record Office for Leicestershire, Leicester and Rutland (ROLLR) 1D41/4/428b (1588): it was deposed that Thomas Insley of Lutterworth had asserted before his death that he had distributed about his house £60 in coin; when the probate inventory was taken, a bag containing £20 or £30 was discovered in the "Bedstrawe" where his servant slept.
[41] Nicholas Udall, *Roister Doister*, Act I, scene iii, lines 356-7.
[42] Muldrew, *Economy of Obligation;* for fine illustrations, Robert Tittler, ed., *Accounts of the Roberts Family of Boarzell, Sussex, c. 1568-1582*, Sussex Record Society 71 (Lewes, 1979), 18, 65, 86, 112, 114, 136, 139, 143, but merely as examples in this account book.
[43] For example, ROLLR 1D41/4/438a: the tithing custom at Queniborough that if a sheep was sold between Candlemas and clipping a halfpenny was due for tithe and if a lamb was sold between weaning and Mary Magdalen another halfpenny; 1D41/4/252: "bread monie" of 1d. owed to the incumbent of Stockerston by tenants of two yardlands. For opposition to Easter pence (for communion), E. R. Brinkworth, ed., *The Archdeacon's Court:* Liber Actorum *1584 Volume 1*, Oxfordshire Record Society 23 (Oxford, 1942), 124. For the demands of secular taxation, Michael Braddick, *The Nerves of State: Taxation and the Financing of the English State, 1558-1714* (Manchester: Manchester University Press, 1996).
[44] The following are merely examples, not a complete listing. William Foster, ed., *Lincoln Wills Registered in the District Probate Registry at Lincoln, vol. 3, 1530 to 1532*, Lincoln Record Society 24 (London, 1930), 63, 108, 109, 116, 151, 156, 157, 158, 165, 167, 187, 207, 212, 222, 229, 233; David Hickman, ed., *Lincoln Wills 1532-1534*, Lincoln Record Society 89 (Lincoln, 2001), 3, 25, 38, 39, 43, 58, 59, 95, 137, 156, 160, 179, 184, 190, 217, 223, 230, 275, 350, 368, 372, 279.
[45] Foster, *Lincoln Wills ... vol. 2, 1505 to May, 1530*, 90.
[46] E. D. Stone and B. Cozens-Hardy, eds., *Norwich Consistory Court Depositions, 1499-1512 and 1518-1530*, Norfolk Record Society 10 (Norwich, 1938), no. 381.

⁴⁷ *Gammer Gurton's Needle*, Act I, scene v, line 175; Act III, scene iii, lines 625, 634; Act IV, scene i, line 717. See also *Roister Doister*, Act I, scene iv, line 530: "I will foote it for a grote" (Madge Mumblecrust).

⁴⁸ *Gammer Gurton's Nedle*, Act V, scene ii, lines 1269-1270.

⁴⁹ S. R. Gardiner, ed., *Reports of Cases in the Courts of Star Chamber and High Commission*, Camden Society new series 39 (London, 1886), 86-8.

⁵⁰ Henry Porter, *The Pleasant Historie of the two angrie women of Abington* ... in *Select Collection*, vol. 7, p. 300.

⁵¹ *Faire Quarrell*.

⁵² *Staple of News*, Act I, scene iv, lines 10-12. [See also Act III, scene ii, lines 122-5 and 140-1 for other news valued in terms of money–6d. and 9d.]

⁵³ At this point too, Porter repeats the common term for a miser: "penny-father".

⁵⁴ Lumb, *Testamenta Leodiensia*, 106, 167, 199, 203, 218, 252, 260, 273, 305.

⁵⁵ Lodge and Greene, *A Lookinge Glasse for London and England*, lines 810-14.

⁵⁶ Zachary Lesser, *Renaissance Drama and the Politics of Publication: Readings in the English Book Trade* (Cambridge: Cambridge University Press, 2004), 1-4

⁵⁷ Tanya Pollard, *Drugs and Theatre in Early Modern England* (Oxford: Oxford University Press, 2005).

⁵⁸ Andrew Leyshon and Nigel Thrift, eds., *Money/Space: Geographies of Monetary Transactions* (London: Routledge, 1997), 17-18. Here too I should acknowledge their useful terms of "limited purpose" and "special purpose" money which accords with gold coin.

⁵⁹ Cavendish, *The Country Captain* (ca.1641, Malone Society Reprints 162, Oxford, 1999), lines 294-7.

⁶⁰ Compare Alan C. Dessen, "*The Alchemist*: Jonson's 'Estates' Play", *Renaissance Drama 7* (1964): 35-54, which represents Jonson's conservative notions of nobility and clergy standing to their traditional obligations.

⁶¹ Joe Ward will no doubt elucidate Dekker's convictions further.

⁶² Archer, *Pursuit of Stability*; see also, nonetheless, his review article "'Civic Culture' in Later Medieval and Early Modern London", *Journal of Urban History* 34 (2008): 370-9, especially 370 where he discusses the different approaches of historians and literary scholars to their materials.

⁶³ Brooks, "Recent Studies in Ben Jonson", 120, citing Alan Fisher.

⁶⁴ See the judgements of Paul Yachnin commenting on the Middleton/Dekker collaboration on *The Meeting of Gallants at an Ordinary*: Dekker's "moving sympathy which sometimes shades into maudlin sentimentality" and Middleton's "gallows humour", in *Thomas Middleton: The Collected*

Works, ed. Gary Taylor and John Lavagnino (Oxford: Oxford University Press, 2007), 185.

[65] For the suggestion of Middleton's sympathy for the London poor, Chakravorty, *Society and Politics*, 38-41.

[66] *Englishmen for My Money*, lines 28-30 (soliloquy by Pisaro, the City-based Portuguese usurer).

[67] Manley, *Literature and Culture*, 93-8, 308 (the last is a reference to sermon literature which might be considered as a continuation of complaint literature).

[68] Jacques Derrida, *Writing and Difference*, translated with an introduction by Alan Bass (London: Routledge, 2001), 19.

[69] For the intentionality of any text or discourse, Simms, *Paul Ricoeur*, 34-5.

[70] Simms, *Paul Ricoeur*, 65.

[71] Pace, Simms, I take this transformation in the hearer's/reader's consideration to be the "force" in Derrida's "Force and Signification": *Writing and Difference*, 27.

[72] Simms, *Paul Ricoeur*, 73-5.

[73] Wolfgang Iser, *The Range of Interpretation* (New York: Columbia University Press, 2000) remains the best introduction.

5
Eastward Ho. Credit in Virginia

> Would I might lead them to no hotter service
> Till our Virginian gold were in our purses.[1]

When *Eastward Ho* was printed in 1605, a year prior to the royal charter of 1606 establishing the Virginia Company, and two years before the establishment of Jamestown, it predated the establishment of a permanent colony in Virginia. Knowledge of Virginia was tentative, but the characteristics attributed to the colony in *Eastward Ho* invite incredulity. The Virginian expedition arranged by the threadbare knight, Sir Petronel Flash, had expectations of immense quantities of gold, whilst rubies and diamonds would be collected on the seashore. The other attraction to the adventurers of *Eastward Ho* was the absence of political and legal institutions: a *tabula rasa* for the those wishing to escape the regulations of the City.[2]

Accordingly, the adventurers composed a group of wastrels and scoundrels who expected rich pickings for minimal effort: Spendall and Scapethrift described by their monikers, and Sir Petronel, an impoverished knight. They were enraptured by the mythology spun by the hired captain, Seagull, who depicted the prospect of bountiful treasure. The condition of the abandoned colony was, of course, far removed from that paradisaical picture. Before the establishment of Jamestown in May 1607, two years after the printing of the play, the colony was void. The permanent development of the colony is, moreover, still contested, whether with the foundation of Jamestown, or the revocation of the charter and the conversion of the land into a Crown colony.

In the event, the adventurers never reached Virginia, but were washed up by a storm on the Isle of Dogs.[3] Had they achieved their

100   *Social Dramas*

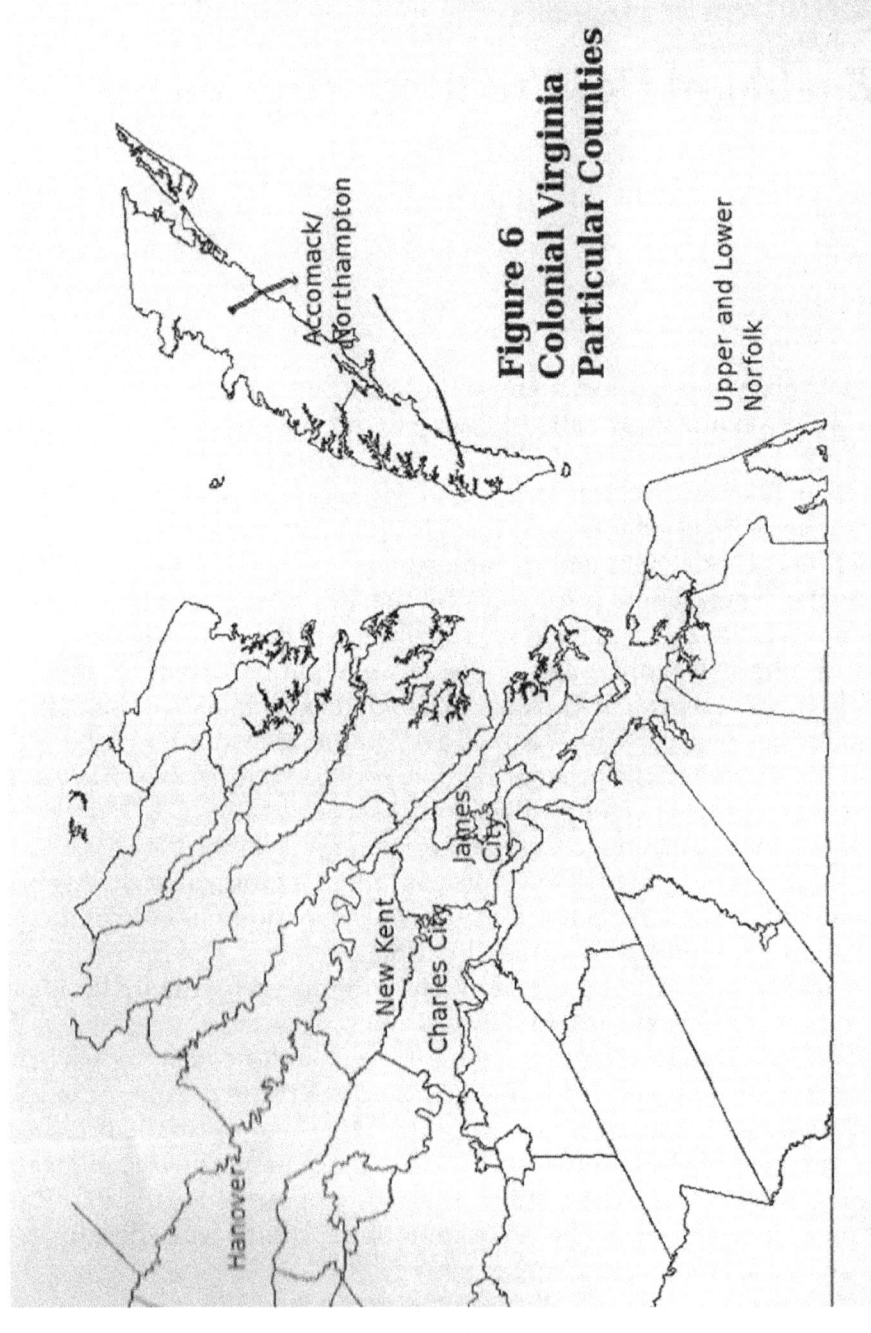

Figure 6
Colonial Virginia
Particular Counties

destination, their lives would have been unimaginably harder, as the colony struggled to survive until the introduction of a sweeter tobacco over a decade later. Only in the middle decades of the seventeenth century was the colony's fate transformed. What follows is a discussion of the credit relationships which Spendall and Scapethrift, as well as Sir Petronel, would have encountered in those middle decades.

Immense questions are still being debated about the early British colonial North American world. Was it an original space of proto-capitalist development or intra-dependent "communities"?[4] Was there a transformational Atlantic world or adaptation to particular circumstances?[5] Much remains to be discovered about these issues from the Chesapeake in the middle decades of the seventeenth century. One commentator has suggested that the Chesapeake pertained to a nexus of "continental staple regions" in comparison with "Atlantic staple regions"; whilst the latter retained strong direct connections with the metropole, the British world, the former developed into more independent, introspective societies.[6] More recently, a more complex understanding of the place of Virginia in this larger picture has been suggested, examining more closely contemporaries' perceptions.[7] The Virginian Chesapeake has an important position in the discussion of these large issues of the nature of the early colonial world and its relationship to the old world.

Perhaps at this point, however, it might be helpful to backtrack and to assess why and how the Virginian colony was "successful" beyond Jamestown. At one, broadly politico-social, level, Roper has succeeded in explaining the consolidation of the colony.[8] The cultivation of tobacco, of course, has been acknowledged as an important ingredient in the mix for success in the first century, if a more ambiguous benefit in the longer run. There remains one aspect, nonetheless, which remains relatively less well explored amongst the variables behind mid-century consolidation, the socio-economic relationship of credit and credit institutions which this contribution attempts to explicate.

Fundamental to the organization of credit was tobacco, of course. During the middle decades of the seventeenth century, tobacco production in the Chesapeake ballooned, from an estimated 400,000 pounds (lbs.) in 1630 to in excess of fifteen million pounds by the late 1660s. Accordingly, the price per pound collapsed, from 1s.-2s. in the 1620s, to 5d., in the 1630s, 2d.-3d. in the early 1650s, 1d.-2d. in the 1660s, and below 1d. after 1680 (despite a decline in output, apart from sweet tobacco, in the last decades of the seventeenth century). The increase in supply, despite a relatively elastic demand, drove down the price. The expansion of production during those middle decades was extraordinary.[9] What has not been considered in this process is the role of a concomitant expansion of credit which enabled this dramatic development of production with a decline in the unit price. The extraordinary circumstance was that tobacco functioned as both commodity and credit.[10] The scarcity of specie (silver coin) meant that tobacco was adopted as a surrogate currency for payment for goods and services and wages. Tobacco occupied a dual role in the society and economy of the Chesapeake: as commodity and currency.[11] The inherent problem of that dual status was that tobacco did not, like metallic coin, fully transcend its commodity status.[12]

The reasons for the adoption of tobacco as the substitute currency have been previously indicated. The effort in the metropole to prevent the export of specie and coin constituted a principal obstacle. Some contemporaries attributed the dearth of coin in the realm to the adverse balance of trade, with the result that preventive measures were investigated. The finger was pointed most directly at the East India Company, but there is little doubt that similar concern surrounded commerce with the N. American colonies. Attempts to establish mints and coinage in these colonies were abrogated; in Virginia, a Crown colony from1625, the prohibition of minting was effective. Whilst the "mercantilists" in the metropole thus complained of scarcity of coin, in the Crown colony coin was almost invisible. The situation, Valenze suggests, was exacerbated after 1684 when the embargo was made explicit.[13] Before then, however, tobacco had already been irrevocably established as the "coinage of the realm" in the Chesapeake, as illustrated by the debt litigation below. The explanation remains, nonetheless, the same, the diffidence of the government in the metropole about the leakage of coin and specie. The issue of the scarcity of coin in the colony had been recognized in 1638, when, as part of a larger concordat, Charles I authorized the provision of copper farthings to lubricate commerce.

The suggestion was rejected by the Burgesses of Virginia who proposed alternatively that the King furnish £5,000 in silver coin annually at ten percent discount.[14] Two years earlier, indeed, the governor, Sir John Harvey, had suggested just such a project of the local issuance of farthing tokens to remedy some of the "many more incommodities" resulting from the want of coin.[15]

Before 1730, the commission system of finance, whereby merchants advanced capital, was insufficiently effective, and before the 1680s non-existent.[16] Before the advent of capital from this direction, credit was the mainstay of Chesapeake society, although the interloping and intervention by some Dutch merchants, despite the Navigation Acts, perhaps facilitated some economic relationships.[17]

The enormous expansion of the production of tobacco to the position of a relative mono-culture thus demanded a substitute currency, but also the exploration of credit relationships and forms of credit.[18] Given the risks involved and the capital investment required combined with labor costs of an intensive agriculture and industry, liquidity of credit was vital.[19] There is then some imperative to examine the forms of credit (mechanisms) and credit relationships that were adopted and forged.

The forms of credit arrangements developed were probably influenced by the particular social organization of the Chesapeake, where the settlement pattern consisted to some extent of dispersed plantations, with a limited number of urban centers.[20] The extent to which such colonization "undermined community by dispersing settlement" has recently been modified, but not controverted.[21] Since there were few port towns, merchants and mariners were compelled to journey upriver to make their contracts and contacts.[22] In 1638, the planters countered Charles I's considerations for a central depot by arguing that "every man's house [was] a store convenient enough for their lading we being all seated by the riverside".[23] At some stage, Virginian society probably conformed to Jack Greene's notion of "essentially yeoman cultures", but the question remains: when and for how long?[24]

The fundamental role of tobacco as a fiduciary instrument is reflected in the valuations in inventories. In the itemization of personal estate in inventories, each constituent was appraised in terms of pounds of tobacco, not as a valuation in cash. This equivalence was introduced in the 1630s and continued through the century.[25]

Goods and services were acquitted in pounds of tobacco. Deferred wages, for example, were defrayed in 100 lbs., 200 lbs., 279 lbs., 330 lbs., 400 lbs., 500 lbs., 645 lbs., 800 lbs., and 1,100 lbs.[26] A list of work performed by Richard Horner for a dozen individuals appraised the work in pounds of tobacco in 1643.[27] Six days of work were recompensed with seventy-two pounds of tobacco.[28] Tobacco was disbursed for the wages of workmen erecting a building.[29] Surgery and the administration of physic similarly involved compensation in pounds of tobacco: 170, 300, 410, 415 and 550 lbs.[30]

When the debts of Gabriel Searle were described in 1648, they totaled 2,096 lbs. of tobacco: for shoes, taxes and duties, a levy for the minister, a hoe, washing, a cow, two knives and a gun.[31] The purchase of a hoe incurred a debt of sixty lbs.[32] A debt relating to a pair of shoes involved fifty-five pounds, another for an iron pot forty, one for a gown 240.[33] Although merely a laborer, the Frenchman Nicolas Perque accumulated debts for goods and services amounting to 4,000 lbs. of tobacco.[34] In a case of non-feasance, the defendant had to recompense the plaintiff in 5,000 lbs. for the costs of plastering a house.[35] When the contract was invited for erecting a new court house for *Charles City County* in 1687, it was awarded to William Bernard and John Baxter for 30,000 lbs. of tobacco.[36]

The county authorities, indeed, regulated the prices of some commodities in terms of pounds of tobacco. In Accomack-Northampton, the authorized price of alcoholic drink was established as fifty pounds per gallon for the best sort and forty for the worst.[37] Rates for the sale of liquor in *Charles City County* were also computed in pounds of tobacco in 1688.[38] One of the earliest injunctions in this new environment was to offer a bounty of one hundred pounds of tobacco to English colonists for killing a wolf.[39] Taxation too was extracted in pounds of tobacco. In the late seventeenth and early eighteenth centuries, the vestries of most parishes imposed their levies in tobacco. When the accounts were drafted, and the disbursements totaled, the entire liability was calculated in pounds of tobacco. This amount was then divided amongst the "tithables" of the parish, resulting in a levy of pounds of tobacco per poll.[40] The levy court of *Charles City County* in 1688, by the same calculation, imposed a subsidy of sixty-two pounds per poll on 957 "tithables".[41] Fifty years earlier, the authority in Lower Norfolk County exacted a levy for particular purposes of ten pounds per poll and two pounds, but subsequently had further recourse to levies of two pounds per poll to maintain one ferry and four pounds per poll for the other.[42] In Accomack-Northampton, the compensation of the sexton and clerk was defrayed through a fee on burials, the sexton to receive fifty pounds of tobacco and the clerk fifteen, in 1636.[43] The House of Burgesses too invoked penalties in tobacco: in 1663, it was enacted that any member "disguised" by drink forfeited one hundred pounds of tobacco, increasing to three hundred and a thousand pounds for subsequent offenses.[44] An Act of the Assembly in 1662 allowed the defraying of quit-rents in tobacco, the weed appraised at 2d. per pound.[45]

In other ways too, indebtedness for quantities of tobacco was incurred through the activity of the courts. Courts imposed fines, costs and punishment in amounts of tobacco. In Harrison v. Shorte in defamation, on the allegation that the plaintiff had stolen and marked all the defendant's hogs, plaintiff demanded damages of 20,000 lbs.; the court in 1688 awarded him 4,000.[46] Failure to assist the constable in his office in 1643 resulted in the derelict being amerced a hundred pounds with fifty pounds for costs and charges.[47] Damages awarded in other cases involved ten, fifty and 800 lbs.[48] Commissioners who defaulted on their obligation to attend court were subject to a forfeiture of 300 lbs.[49] For committing fornication with Mr Edmund Scarburgh's servant in 1648, John Daniell was sentenced to deliver 800 lbs. for detriment to and abuse of Scarburgh's house, exacerbated by another thirty pounds for contempt of court.[50]

Initially, in the 1630s, indebtedness was still expressed in conventional cash terms (sterling), particularly debts to the Crown. In one instance, an agreement between private parties stipulated that £6 sterling would be redeemed in tobacco if the price attained 11d. per pound.[51] In 1639, another debt of £5 sterling was acquitted by 400 lbs. of tobacco.[52] Similarly, £7 sterling in arrears were extinguished by delivery of 160 lbs.[53] In 1642, the court of Lower Norfolk County was permitted to entertain personal cases not exceeding £10 sterling or 600 lbs. of tobacco.[54]

Expressing indebtedness in terms of quantities of tobacco introduced innumerable difficulties perhaps not associated with money, whether real money (either silver or gold) or money of account.[55] Whilst inflation affected the value of money, the rapid collapse of the price of tobacco through the early seventeenth century had more drastic consequences. The value of a pound of tobacco altered radically and swiftly: variously 2d. per pound, 3d., 4d., but sold in New England for 6d.[56] The commodity could, moreover, be supplied in different states of refinement: as leaf; unstripped; stripped; rolled; with (in) the cask (for larger amounts). In Lower Norfolk County debts preponderantly specified stripped and smooth tobacco. Some tobacco there was burned according to an act of the Assembly since it did not attain merchantable standard.[57] Nor was tobacco fungible: a debt might be liquidated from the past or present crop or by a promise on the next crop (a future).[58] Its fungible nature depended too on its being of good, merchantable quality, so that in 1645 depositions in one case attested that the commodity at issue was "good and Marchauntable Tobacco and noe way dampnifyed".[59] Some agreements required a guarantee of the soundness of the tobacco and its replacement if inferior.[60] Debt cases occasionally concerned rotten tobacco.[61] It was alleged in court that Mr Stringer maintained two different stillyards, one for incoming tobacco and one for disbursements, perhaps implying a difference in quality in his payments out.[62]

Reckonings, although a constant mechanism, did not exclude controversy; the balancing process was not always conducted with equanimity. Reckonings consisted of the private balancing of accounts between individuals, comparing their account books for debts accumulated between the two parties. Numerous cases were initiated as a consequence of reckonings. Whilst it is possible that these introductions into court might have consisted simply of a means of recording the balance and the obligations, some of the cases were seemingly acrimonious. In some instances, it is impossible to decipher which objective obtained. William Holmes was ordered to deliver 309 lbs. to John Severne, "all accomptes betweene them beinge ballanced".[63] In the case contested by Cugley and Edmounds, John Fisher testified that the two had conducted a reckoning in Fisher's house in 1636, 600 lbs. due to Edmounds.[64]

One interpretation then might suggest that their resort to the court was intended simply to have or make a court record of their own prior reckoning. When Hunt and Dobey impleaded each other, however, the court adjudged that the accounts between them were out of date and so dismissed both their actions.[65] The imputation of this latter case might then be a real action, although certainty is elusive. Since the court exacted costs and charges, however, the inference might be that these cases involved real differences rather than merely matters of record.[66]

Reckonings thus featured in litigation, sometimes producing any contention, other times resulting from conflict. Reckonings were thus not inevitably amicable processes. In the reckoning between Coghen and Charlton, the court was impelled to appoint an umpire and two arbitrators in 1648.[67] Roberts and Bassett engaged in a reckoning in court with a balance of 1,224 lbs.; the reckoning in court between Conway and Price resulted in a balance of 946 lbs. from Conway who assumed also the costs and charges of the process; the reckoning in court between Connires and Coghen in 1647 involved Coghen's promissory note being entered on the court record; Moore and Downes made a reckoning in court; the court ordered Connaway and Matthewes to conduct a reckoning at the house of Captain Roger or Mr. Clarke. The complexity of the accounts in Yardley esq. v. Moore, mariner, in 1647 vexed the court, which endeavored to resolve "diveres Controversyes of Accontes", attempting to ensure "Concordant equitye and Justice". Their judgment required Yardley to deliver to Moore a bill of Sir Edmund Plowden for 2,160 lbs. and Moore to receive the account for 1,300 lbs. owed by Berry.[68]

Another illustration of the complexity of credit relationships is the reckoning in court between Roger Johns, blacksmith, and Captain Taylor, in which the initial judgment ordered the blacksmith to deliver 923 lbs. in 1645, which was amended upon further investigation of the accounts on oath.[69]

The assignment of bills for tobacco further complicated relationships of credit: "I heare you have turned over my bill to Mr Charleton", exclaimed one debtor in surprise.[70] When William Whittington produced nine pair of gloves for Robert Wright in return for 400 lbs. of tobacco, Wright's obligation consisted of assigning over two bills owed by either Urmstone Foster or John Foster.[71]

Cases of debt which were introduced into the court thus had two principal characteristics: the issue was expressed in quantities of tobacco, regardless of the content of the debt; and the debt had accrued in diverse and sometimes complicated ways. We can now turn to a fuller examination of those debts, their character, and the institutional forum which was responsible for their resolution. It may be useful at this stage to indicate one of the significant features of the statistics below: the prominence of specialties in debt cases.[72] Written instruments continued prominently: in Andrewes v. Drew for 500 lbs. "as by his deed appeared"; in Drew v. Howe for the same amount "under the hand and deead of the syd John Howe", both in 1635, no doubt involving too the assignment of the instrument.[73] This important characteristic will be elucidated further below.

In a large proportion of cases, the judgment in the debt case recited the basis of the debt: confession (acknowledgment by the defendant in court); on oath by account; due by account (proved); *nichil dicit* (not contested by the defendant); by oath and independent testimony (rarely); proved by oath (rarely); by specialty; and by bill.[74] Occasionally, but only so, compound debts were not differentiated: "appering dew by bill and Accompt upon oath".[75] It is then possible to define the minimum level of proceedings upon specialty, since specialty is specifically recorded: for example, 3,000 lbs. owed "by several specialltyes".[76] Some ambiguity might surround debts upon bills, which are often defined separately from specialty (see Table 5). Almost conclusively, however, we can include bills as specialties, as written instruments, if in more rudimentary form than more formal specialties (bonds and obligations). Registration or recording of bills in court assist this conclusion: bills to secure future delivery of 500, 900, 1,700, 1,900, 2,400 lbs., for example.[77]

Recourse to specialty contrasts with traditional forms of debt litigation in the old country (see below for a comparison with debt litigation in an English manorial court). In the statistics below, references to hogsheads are omitted, since this receptacle contained anything from 240 to 360 lbs. Fortunately, debt cases rarely referred to hogsheads, normally recounting numbers of pounds.

Litigation on bills composed a further 13 percent, so that in total perhaps 30 percent of all debt cases depended on a written instrument. Whilst the proportion was considerably lower in contemporary Accomack/Northampton County courts, at 12 percent, the ratio increased to 27 percent in the same county's courts between 1645 and 1651, approximating to the Lower Norfolk County forum. This level of employment of specialties far exceeded their usage in local courts in England.

If we consider the kinds of debt entailed in written instruments, pleas in the Lower Norfolk County courts on specialty involved considerably larger amounts, a mean of more than 1,000lbs., although with a large scatter denoted in the high standard deviation. Despite that wide range, however, it might be concluded that at that time and in that location, specialties were deployed for the largest debts, a rational explanation for the use of this specific written instrument. Bills there, however, were concerned with much more modest amounts of tobacco, a mean of just over 460lbs., an amount not remarkably higher than the 370lbs. or so which constituted the mean amount for informal or oral ("parole") debts.

The situation in the contemporary Accomack/Northampton courts was something of a contrast. Here, there was little difference in the mean amount of tobacco demanded for debts through specialty (447 lbs.) and traditional debt relationships (494 lbs.); indeed, as is revealed, the mean size of orally- conducted debts exceeded that of those incurred by specialty. In the later courts in this county, nonetheless, the respective amounts diverged again, with debts on specialty exceeding oral debts. The mean amount claimed on specialty (860 lbs.) was in the order of 23 percent higher than when not concluded by written instrument (670 lbs.). Where debt litigation was initiated by account, the amount was lower still (just more than 600 lbs.), about 31 percent lower than by specialty. We can perhaps explain the smaller level of debts pursued by account by their being residual debts after some sort of satisfaction of the outstanding amount: in this sense, the parties had already attempted some balancing of their accounts by a reckoning, but one of the parties considered the balancing unsatisfactory and made a claim for more.

Certainly by the 1640s, if not before, debts due on specialties, although a minority of all pleas, had become a normal feature of credit relationships in the Virginian Chesapeake, an unusual situation when compared with debt litigation in England. Other

Table 5 Descriptive Statistics of Debt Cases in Lower Norfolk County Court, 1637-46

Type of debt	Number of cases	Percent of all cases	Total amount tobacco (lbs.)	Mean amount per case (lbs.)	Standard deviation
By specialty	71	17	72277	1018	1633.92
By bill	55	13	25407	462	310.64
Speciality and bill combined	126	30	97684	775	1270.19
Not speciality*	289	70	107379	372	388.16
Totals	415	100	205063		

* includes only twenty-four specifically proved by account

Table 6 Descriptive Statistics of Debt Cases in Accomack/Northampton County Court, 1633-40

Type of debt	Number of cases	Percent of all cases	Total amount of tobacco (lbs.)	Mean amount per case (lbs.)	Standard deviation
By specialty	48	12	21436	447	377.02
Not specialty	339	88	167302	494	741.44
Totals	387	100	188738		

Table 7 Descriptive Statistics of Debt Cases in Northampton County Court, 1645-51

Type of debt	Number of cases	Percent of all cases	Total amount of tobacco (lbs.)	Mean amount per case (lbs.)	Standard deviation
By specialty	233	27	200834	862	1016.35
By account	98	12	59299	605	648.07
Other not specialty	522	61	349813	670	935.03
Total	853	100	609946		

differences existed too: in the nature of the forum in which debts were resolved; and in the actions involved in the litigation. To employ the concept of James Horn, debt litigation in the Virginian Chesapeake does indeed reflect adaptation to a new world.

If we compare first the juridical structure of the Virginian Chesapeake and the old country, the former had adopted a single, unitary court of competence, the county court, with appeal to a superior court in James City.[78] In contrast, a multiplicity of courts operated by tradition in the old country: manorial courts, often limited, if not franchisal with special privileges, to claims below 40s.; borough courts in those towns which had been incorporated as boroughs; and the common law and equity courts, including, importantly, King's Bench.⁷⁹ Although an immense increase in litigation occurred in the central courts in Westminster, the local courts (manorial and borough) equally entertained a vast amount of litigation, particularly on debt.⁸⁰ The structure of "civic" jurisdiction was thus much simplified when translated to the new dominion, as in the other N. American colonies.

In the central common law courts, particularly King's Bench, debt issues proceeded predominantly on written instruments, estimated at about 90 percent of the debt litigation in actions of debt in the contemporary common law courts in Westminster. "Furthermore, so-called actions of debt on specialty were a very reliable means of seeking legal remedy."⁸¹ Whilst bonds insinuated into local credit relationships during the seventeenth century, they remained a minor element in credit relationships and were associated with larger amounts of money.⁸²

In the local courts of England, claims had traditionally been pursued by action of debt (*placitum de debito*–plaint or plea of debt), which obtained for amounts owed by both written and oral agreement. The action of debt was adjudicated by jury or by wager of law, in the latter case by the use of compurgators (vouchees). From the late sixteenth century, however, the action of trespass on the case was increasingly employed, since it abrogated compurgation and its potential abuses, encompassed parole agreements, and awarded damages for the breach of contract conceived inherent in the debt.⁸³ "The importance of *assumpsit* [trespass on the case] was that it relaxed the strict common law requirements for written evidence of agreements between parties and it also offered the prospect of getting a defendant to pay damages for the loss he caused the plaintiff by failing to fulfill his promise".⁸⁴ The local courts in England thus entertained two forms of action concerned with debt in contradistinction, it seems, to the unitary action in Virginian county courts.

The proportion of the two forms of action in the lowest courts in England can be illustrated by litigation in the manorial court of Loughborough, a small town in the north of the county of Leicestershire. This court is selected because it was fairly representative of the sort of jurisdiction which predominantly obtained in England where borough courts did not intervene. Borough courts existed in incorporated urban places, the larger towns which had received royal charters to conduct their own affairs and government. For purposes of the personal actions (debt, trespass, and covenant/ "contract"), the local courts which entertained these actions were usually manorial courts, the courts of the lords of manors for their tenants. Although Loughborough was developing as an urban center, with a sizable population, it remained an unincorporated borough with extensive rural environment and its court remained the seigniorial court.

The manorial jurisdiction was restricted to pleas below 40s., whilst the Virginian county courts were competent for larger amounts. The court rolls for Loughborough's manorial court survive for 1558-1564, 1599-1602, and 1607-1612. The courts thus antedate the Virginian county court records, but illustrate the nature of the predecessor courts in the old country.[85] Of the 526 pleas, 426 (about 79 percent) consisted of pleas of debt and 100 trespass on the case (11 percent). In the Virginian county courts there was ostensibly no such differentiation in the forms of action: the plaintiff simply claimed a debt, whether on specialty, by promise, or by account.

The incidence of trespass on the case in the manorial court certainly antedated Slade's Case, an important piece of case law for the action in 1603, by at least a couple of years.[86] The earliest cases were construed as theft of chattels for which damages were demanded.[87] The amounts requested did not exceed those demanded in pleas of debt: 23s. 6d., 8s. 8d., 6s. 7d., for example, in the earliest extant prosecutions.[88] As with debt, it seems probable that the upper limit of competence for the court in trespass on the case was 40s., for Thomas Monck claimed 39s. 11d. against John Wycloppe, whilst Hugh Webster demanded 39s. 11½d from Richard Colson, and Robert Wollandes 39s. from Thomas Burbage.[89] The first extant plaints were initiated against the miller, John Gyles, all in the same court, by three different plaintiffs, suggesting failure to perform (non-feasance), malfeasance, or peculation of the grain of tenants who were obliged to send their grain to the lord's mill for grinding. The imputation of failure to perform is implicit also in the trespass on the case introduced by Robert Hutchenson of Shepshed against John Hall, tanner, for an outstanding remainder from 53s. 4d. to be acquitted by 1 August some five years previously.[90]

Since the court record is usually laconic, the impact of trespass on the case often remains obscure. About a year before Slade's Case, however, in Joan Keighley v. Thomas Hull, the record is more explicit, as the case was referred to a jury of twelve whose verdict is recited in some detail. The consideration of the jurors merits quotation.

> *Qui ad veritatem De infracontenta dicenda electi triati & Jurati dicunt super Sacramentum suum quod predictus Thomas Hull assumpsit modo & forma &c Et assident dampna Occasione transgressionis predicta ultra missericordiam & Custagia sua per ipsum Circa sectam suam predictam in hac parte apposita Ad vj.s. Et pro missericordia & Custagiis illis ad ij.s. Sed Curia hic se advisare vult de Judicio suo hic usque ad proximam Curiam hic &c.*[91]

["Which jurors elected to find the truth about the recited claim say on their oath that the said Thomas Hull was obliged in the way and form &c And they assess damages caused by the said trespass over and above the fine and costs incurred on his plea as 6s. And for the fine and costs at 2s. But the court wishes to take counsel about its judgment until the next court.]

We see then that the simplification of the process in the new world extended too to the language of record of the courts. In all the jurisdictions in England–lower as well as higher–the language of record of the courts in litigation over debt continued to be Latin, a higher, written, register of language use, as, indeed, illustrated immediately above: that is to say, whilst the parties in Loughborough conducted their oral plaint and defense in the vernacular, English, the court record was composed in Latin. We can illustrate this persistence from the very lowest level of the courts, again that of the manorial court of Loughborough, limited to pleas below 40s. The process in debt was fairly straightforward, much as in other manorial courts. The plaintiff claimed debt (*quod Reddat ei*–"that he return to him"), proceeded with a count (*narratio*), and the defendant requested a copy of the count: *et Narrauit ... et predictus Robertus petit copiam Narracionis* ("and he counts ... and the aforesaid Robert [defendant] asks for a copy of the count").[92] It seems likely that the count and counter-plea were committed to writing, although there are no extant copies.

> *Et modo hic venerunt tam predictus Ricardus Cranwell et quam predicta Margeria Welles per Concilium suum in lege eruditum et argumentaverunt et dederunt argumenta in scriptis in Curia.*[93]
>
> ["And thus came both the aforesaid Richard Cranwell and the aforesaid Margery Welles through their counsel and pleaded and gave their arguments in written forms to the court"]
>
> *De placito predicto de Audiendo inde Judicio suo inde quia Curia ulterius se Aduisare vult usque ad proximam Curiam De Judicio suo inde Reddendo eo quod Curia hic inde nondum &c.*[94]
>
> ["About the hearing of the aforesaid plea and giving its judgment, the court wishes to seek advice between now and the next court"]
>
> *Et quia Curia hic se advisare vult de & super omnia & premissa priusquam inde Judicium suum inde Reddat.'*[95]
>
> ["And because the court wishes to take advice on all matters and premises before it gives its judgment"]
>
> *predictus Magnus dicit quod non debet prefato Willelmo predictos x.s. nec aliquem inde denarium in forma qua Idem Willelmus versus eum Narrauit.*[96]
>
> ["the aforesaid Magnus said that he didn't owe the said William the said 10s. nor any other money in the way that William pleaded against him"]

In complete contrast, the record of the Virginian county courts was compiled in the vernacular.

One of the characteristics of the Virginian courts, by contrast, was the registration of intermittent delay (in total about sixteen occurrences), but it had a definite, and distinctly different, character. The forbearance related to the deferment of repayment for a number of years, usually one or two, exceptionally three or four.[97] No compromise was involved in these deferrals, however, for the debtor was committed to interest at the current legal rate of 8 percent per annum.[98] The intention in these cases must approximate to the plaintiffs' forbearance to demand repayment now, that is, the plaintiff's agreement to the delay in the repayment, but not at any cost, rather at the going rate of interest. Forbearance retained a commercial edge; it involved none of trust, harmony or concession.

Nor was the plaintiff expecting to claim damages as a consequence of the non-payment, as in trespass on the case; the costs of late redemption were already introduced into the arrangement.

There is little doubt that, despite the dangers of mono-culture which were, indeed, subsequently encountered, the success of the early Chesapeake resulted from the development of tobacco as a staple crop and its commerce. That exploitation was facilitated by the adoption of tobacco as currency as well as commodity, in the context of the dearth of money. Credit relationships were enabled by the use of tobacco as exchange. The fortunes of this venture depended also, however, on the regulation of credit relationships through legal institutions. In the old country, the existing legal framework, although fragmented and complicated, provided a traditional forum which assured the operation of trust and credit in its wider socio-economic senses. The Chesapeake lacked that existing institutional framework. Chesapeake society, moreover, was topographically less face-to-face than in the old country; its individuals, furthermore, had no embedded social relationships in which credit could be integrated. An institutional framework was necessary to assure credit which could not exist simply through conditions of trust. The rapid introduction of a simplified court structure which expedited judgment in debt cases was essential to the fundamental working of the Chesapeake credit economy. The judicial framework for credit in the old country was traditional and well-established, but dilatory, so that it was important that credit involved trust and social credit.[99] In the Chesapeake, trust was a rarer commodity in the context of the formation of a new and disparate society, so that expeditious remedy at law was a prerequisite. Whilst in the old country, contractual notions were gradually encroaching on trust and social credit, the Chesapeake was probably a contractual society from its formation, exhibited in entitlement to land, indentured servant-hood, and commercial ideas.[100] These institutional factors allied with the currency of tobacco were formative influences in the establishment of the Chesapeake and its economy in the middle decades of the seventeenth century.[101]

Notes

[1] *Eastward Ho*, Act III, scene ii, lines 324-5.

[2] *Eastward Ho*, Act III, scene iii, lines 12-47.

[3] Interestingly, *The Isle of Dogs* (1597), a collaborative play begun by Nashe and finished by Jonson, brought Jonson into his first conflict with the Lord Chamberlain: Riggs, *Ben Jonson*, 44-5.

[4] Cathy Matson, "A House of Many Mansions: Some Thoughts on the Field of Economic History," in *The Economy of Early America: Historical Perspectives and New Directions*, ed. Matson (University Park, PA: Pennsylvania State University Press, 2006), 11, 33, addresses the literature.

[5] David Armitage and Michael Braddick, eds., *The British Atlantic World, 1500-1800* (Basingstoke: Palgrave, 2002), especially Armitage, "Three Concepts of Atlantic History", 11-27; Elizabeth Mancke and Carole Shammas, eds., *The Creation of the British Atlantic World* (Baltimore, MD: Johns Hopkins University Press, 2005); Peter C. Mancall, ed., *The Atlantic World and Virginia, 1550-1624* (Chapel Hill, NC: University of North Carolina Press, 2007). For a counter suggestion for the higher geographical entity, J. Douglas Deal: "Intense localism and parochialism of many, if not most, American colonists", in his review of R. Applebaum and J. W. Sweet, eds., *Envisioning Empire: Jamestown and the Making of the North Atlantic World* (Philadelphia, PA: University of Pennsylvania Press, 2005), in *The Journal of Southern History* [JSH], 73 (2007), 674. For recent responses addressing material culture in the Chesapeake, W. Graham, C. L. Hudgins, C. R. Lounsbury, F. D. Neiman, and J. F. Whittenburg, "Adaption and Innovation: Archaeological and Architectural Perspectives on the Seventeenth-century Chesapeake", *William and Mary Quarterly* [WMQ], 3rd series 64 (2007): 451-522, and C. Carson, J. Bowen, W. Graham, M. McCartney and L. Walsh, "New World, Real World: Improvising English Culture in Seventeenth-century Virginia", *JSH* 74 (2008): 31-88.

[6] Stephen J. Hornsby, *British Atlantic, American Frontier: Spaces of Power in Early Modern British America* (Hanover, NH, and London: University Press of New England, 2005), esp. 88-111. For the potential for criticism of the "staples" thesis, Matson, "A House of Many Mansions", 14.

[7] Lou H. Roper, *The English Empire in America, 1602-1658: Beyond Jamestown* (London: Pickering and Chatto Publishers, 2009).

[8] Roper, *English Empire in America*.

[9] James Horn, *Adapting to a New World: English Society in the Seventeenth-century Chesapeake* (Chapel Hill, NC: University of North Carolina Press, 1994), 142; Russell R. Menard, "The Tobacco Industry of the Chesapeake, c. 1617-1730: An Interpretation', *Research in Economic History* 5 (1980): 109-77, particularly 111 (Figure 1) for the movement of prices and exports, 113 for the output numbers in 1630 and the late 1660s, 129, 142 for prices

at interstitial points. Per capita consumption in the main export area, England, is considered by Carole Shammas, *The Pre-Industrial Consumer in England and America* (Oxford: Oxford University Press, 1990), 77-81.

[10] Or, as J-J. Goux suggests, "commodity with exchange-value": *Symbolic Economies: After Marx and Freud*, trans. J. C. Gage (Ithaca, NY: Cornell University Press, 1990), 61; for exchange-value, *Symbolic Economies*, 19.

[11] Galbraith regarded specie coinage–with its intrinsic value–as but another commodity, but the role of tobacco as both commodity and currency is still rather different. Galbraith also remarked upon the phenomenon of tobacco as currency in some southern states. John K. Galbraith, *A History of Economics: The Past as the Present* (London: Penguin, 1991 edn.), 14 and 14n. Deborah Valenze, *The Social Life of Money in the English Past* (Cambridge: Cambridge University Press, 2006), 44-47, remarks on the problems of coinage and its substitutes in the N. American colonies.

[12] Goux, *Symbolic Economies*, 22.

[13] Valenze, *Social Life of Money*, 44; see, for more detail, but really confined to the 1680s to 1720s, C. P. Nettels, *The Money Supply of the American Colonies before 1720* (repr. New York: Kelley, 1964), ch. VI (160-78) for general comments on currency and coinage; 206-7 for Maryland and Virginia; 209 for the purpose of legal status of "commodity currency" including tobacco.

[14] Lou H. Roper, "Charles I, Virginia, and the Idea of Atlantic History', *Itinerario* 30 (2006), 35, 37.

[15] The National Archives, London, CO1/9, fol. 41r.: this reference was generously supplied to me by Lou Roper who also kindly furnished me with a copy of his paper in note 11.

[16] R. C. Nash, "The Organization of Trade and Finance in the British Atlantic Economy, 1600-1830", in *The Atlantic Economy during the Seventeenth and Eighteenth Centuries: Organization, Operation, Practice, and Personnel*, ed. P. A. Coclanis (Columbia, SC: University of South Carolina Press, 2005), 106-8, 122-3.

[17] A. L. Hatfield, "Dutch and New Netherland Merchants in the Seventeenth-century Chesapeake", in *Atlantic Economy*, ed. Coclanis, 205-28.

[18] For contemporary (1649) critique of the direction towards monoculture, Peter Thompson, "William Bullock's 'Strange Adventure': A Plan to Transform Seventeenth-century Virginia", *WMQ*, 3rd series 61 (2004), 107-28. In fact, in the early decades of the seventeenth century, Indian corn figured appreciably in debt cases.

[19] Menard, "The Tobacco Industry", 142-6.

[20] D. Meyers and M. Perreault, eds., *Colonial Chesapeake: New Perspectives* (Lanham, MD, 2006), introduction; T. W. Tate and D. L. Ammerman,

eds., *The Chesapeake in the Seventeenth Century* (Chapel Hill, NC: University of North Carolina Press, 1979); L. G. Carr, P. D. Morgan and J. B. Russo, eds., *Colonial Chesapeake Society* (Chapel Hill, NC: University of North Carolina Press, 1988); Billings, ed., *The Old Dominion in the Seventeenth Century: A Documentary History of Virginia, 1606-1689* (Chapel Hill, NC: University of North Carolina Press, 1975). For population estimates, Menard, "The Tobacco Industry", 119 (Figure 5).

[21] Anthony McFarlane, *The British in the Americas 1480-1815* (London: Longman 1992), 70 (for the quotation) and referring to James R. Perry, *The Formation of Society on Virginia's Eastern Shore 1615-1655* (Chapel Hill, NC: University of North Carolina Press, 1990), ch. 7.

[22] April L. Hatfield, *Atlantic Virginia: Intercolonial Relations in the Seventeenth Century* (Philadelphia, PA: University of Pennsylvania Press, 2004). For Virginian society in the late seventeenth century, Peter Thompson, "The Thief, the Householder, and the Commons: Languages of Class in Seventeenth-century Virginia", *WMQ*, 3rd series 63 (2006): 253-80, concerning social relationships in Isle of Wight County, and who perceives the economy of makeshifts obscured by the emphasis on the economy of the plantation.

[23] Cited by Roper, "Charles I, Virginia and the Idea of Atlantic History', 37.

[24] Jack P. Greene, "Early Modern South Eastern North America and the Broader Atlantic and American Worlds', *JSH* 73 (2007), 529.

[25] A. G. Walter, ed., *Lower Norfolk County, Virginia Court Records: Book "A", 1637-1646 & Book "B", 1646-1651/2* (Baltimore, MD: Genealogical Publishing Co., 1994) (hereafter *LNC*), 42, 44-5, 50-1; Susan M. Ames, ed., *County Court Records of Accomack-Northampton, Virginia, 1632-1640* (Washington, D.C.: American Historical Association, 1964) (hereafter *AccI*), 62-8 (inventory of William Smith, 1636); H. M. Mackey and M. A. H. Groves, eds., *Northampton County Virginia Record Book, Orders, Deeds, Wills &c Volume 4 1645-1651* (Camden, ME: Picton Press, Inc, 2000) (hereafter *Northampton III*), 171-4, 176, 251, 266-8, 275-77, 286-88, 299, 314, 329-30, 349- 52, 422-8.

[26] *Northampton III*, 275, 341, 430, 450, 452.
[27] *LNC*, 125.
[28] *LNC*, 125.
[29] *LNC*, 125.
[30] *Northampton III*, 434, 437, 440, 441.
[31] *Northampton III*, 329.
[32] *Northampton III*, 42.
[33] *AccI*, 13, 26.
[34] *Northampton III*, 239, 247.

³⁵ B. B. Weisiger III, ed., *Charles City County, Virginia, Court Orders, 1687-1695* (Athens, GA: Iberian Publishing Co., 1992) (hereafter *Charles City County*), 108.

³⁶ *Charles City County*, 4. See Carl R. Lounsbury, *The Courthouses of Early Virginia: An Architectural History* (Charlottesville, VA, 2005).

³⁷ *AccI*, 73.

³⁸ *Charles City County*, 33.

³⁹ Virginia D. Anderson, "Animals into the Wilderness: The Development of Livestock Husbandry in the Seventeenth-century Chesapeake", *WMQ*, 3rd series 59 (2002), 377.

⁴⁰ C. G. Chamberlayne, ed., *The Vestry Book and Register of St Peter's Parish, New Kent and James City Counties, Virginia, 1684-1786* (Richmond, VA., 1937), 3-4, 6-7, 11-12; Chamberlayne, ed., *The Vestry Book of St Paul's Parish, Hanover County, Virginia, 1706-1786* (Richmond, VA., 1940), 8-9, 13-15, 19-21, 28-30.

⁴¹ *Charles City County*, 33. In general, John K. Nelson, *A Blessed Company: Parishes, Parsons and Parishioners in Anglican Virginia, 1690-1776* (Chapel Hill, NC: University of North Carolina Press, 2001).

⁴² *LNC*, 10.

⁴³ *AccI*, 54.

⁴⁴ Sharon Salinger, *Taverns and Drinking in Early America* (Baltimore, MA: Johns Hopkins University Press, 2002), 92.

⁴⁵ Nettels, *Money Supply of the American Colonies*, 216.

⁴⁶ *Charles City County*, 31. For attempts to prevent hog-stealing, Anderson, "Animals into the Wilderness", 396.

⁴⁷ *LNC*, 138.

⁴⁸ *Northampton III*, 50, 206.

⁴⁹ *Northampton III*, 336-7.

⁵⁰ *Northampton III*, 297.

⁵¹ Susan M. Ames, ed., *County Court Records of Accomack-Northampton, Virginia, 1640-1645* (Charlottesville, VA: University of Virginia Press, 1973) (hereafter *AccII*), 57-8.

⁵² *AccII*, 146.

⁵³ *LNC*, 90.

⁵⁴ *LNC*, 95.

⁵⁵ Nettels, *Money Supply of the American Colonies*, 210-28, explains the numerous problems of "commodity currency" and (213-20) tobacco in particular.

⁵⁶ *Northampton III*, 195 (2d.); *LNC*, 31, 155; *AccI*, 46. For contact between Virginia and the other colonies of the eastern seaboard, Hatfield, *Atlantic Virginia*.

⁵⁷ *LNC*, 27. For this form of regulation of the industry to protect quality,

Menard, "The Tobacco Industry", 130.

[58] For example only, from the next crop, *Northampton III*, 252 (730 lbs.); additionally, for example again, 60, 110. "A market economy requires an adequate system of credit at its base; and a sophisticated credit system requires that debts should be largely fungible": Patrick S. Atiyah, *The Rise and Fall of Freedom of Contract* (Oxford: Oxford University Press, 1979, repr. 1988), 135 on the fungibility (i.e. transferability or assignment) of credit.

[59] *AccII*, 397.

[60] *AccI*, 122.

[61] *AccI*, 85.

[62] *Northampton III*, 457.

[63] *AccI*, 116.

[64] *AccI*, 65.

[65] *Charles City County*, 78.

[66] *Northampton III*, 63 (for example).

[67] *Northampton III*, 50, 63, 147, 229, 235, 258-9.

[68] *Northampton III*, 141-2.

[69] *Northampton III*, 21.

[70] *Northampton III*, 284.

[71] *Northampton III*, 48.

[72] For example, *AccI*, 66, 75.

[73] *AccI*, 27.

[74] *Northampton III*, 13 ("it appering dew by Account upon oath"), 103 (by account proved upon oath–260 lbs.), 106-9 (example of confession; on oath and testimony), 377 (proved by oath).

[75] *Northampton III*, 14, for example. For other illustrations, pp. 405 (1,345 lbs. due by bill and account), 431, 449.

[76] *Northampton III*, 100; sometimes the specialty is further defined: 388 for 3,410 lbs. owed on an obligation.

[77] *Northampton III*, 20, 41, 95, 122, 134, 363; Hugh Yeo, merchant, had recorded in court about eighteen bills for smaller and larger amounts of tobacco: 80, 82, 150, 267, 300, 330, 400, 430, 435, 450, 640, 900, 1,000, 1,500, 1,600 lbs.: 144-7 (these commercial bills such as Yeo's have been omitted from the statistics below). For their nature, Atiyah, *Rise and Fall of Freedom of Contract*, 154-6. LNC, 1637-46, debts incurred explicitly by specialty comprised 17 percent of all debt pleas.

[78] For analysis of the divergence of county courts in the colonies from the ancient juridical structure in England, and the local solutions for jurisdictions and process in the colonies, Peter C. Hoffer, *Law and People in Colonial America* (Baltimore, MA: Johns Hopkins University, 1992), ix, 24-6, 28-38.

[79] Christopher Brooks, *Pettyfoggers and Vipers of the Commonwealth: The*

'Lower Branch' of the Legal Profession in Early Modern England (Cambridge: Cambridge University Press, 1986), remains the comprehensive treatment of the central courts in Westminster.

[80] Muldrew, *Economy of Obligation*, esp. 203.

[81] Brooks, *Pettyfoggers and Vipers*, 67.

[82] Muldrew, *Economy of Obligation*, 112-13: the evidence is extracted from probate inventories rather than litigation and it is suggested that the inventories pertained to the wealthiest in local society.

[83] For the precise nature of these damages, Atiyah, *Rise and Fall of Freedom of Contract*, 198-205.

[84] Muldrew, *Economy of Obligation*, 206-7; Brooks, *Pettyfoggers and Vipers*, 88 for the quotation.

[85] Huntington Library, San Marino, CA, Hastings Manuscripts (hereafter HL HAM) Box 25, folders 3, 9, 11.

[86] HL HAM Box 25, folder 3, court book section, p. 59 (16 December 43 Eliz.). For the implications of Slade's Case, David Harris Sacks, "The Promise and the Contract in Early Modern England: Slade's Case in Perspective", in *Rhetoric and Law in Early Modern Europe*, ed. V. A. Kahn and L. Huston (New Haven, CT: Yale University Press, 2001), xx-xx.

[87] HL HAM Box 25, folder 3, court book section, p. 69.

[88] HL HAM Box 25/4, court book section, pp. 69-70; also p. 99: 14s. 8d. and 25s. 10d.; HL HAM Box 25/9, court book section, p. 150: 20s.

[89] HL HAM Box 25, folder 9, court book section, pp. 77, 129, 193.

[90] HL HAM Box 25, folder 3, court book section, p. 90 (court of 26 Jan. 48 Eliz.)(*pro Residuo Liij.s. iiij.d. solvendo primo die Augusti* [43 Eliz.]... *Et petit processum*.

[91] HL HAM Box 25, folder 3, court book section, p. 126 (August 44 Eliz.).

[92] For example, HL HAM Box 25, folder 3, court book section, p. 89.

[93] HL HAM Box 25, folder 3, court book section, p. 95.

[94] HL HAM Box 25, folder 3, court book section, p. 110.

[95] HL HAM Box 25, folder 3, court book section, p. 113 (Cowley v. Welles).

[96] HL HAM Box 25, folder 3, court book section, p. 129.

[97] *Northampton III*, 7, 11, 27, 30, 109.

[98] For the reduction of the rate from 10 to 8 percent in 1623: Atiyah, *The Rise and Fall of Freedom of Contract*, 66.

[99] Muldrew, *Economy of Obligation*.

[100] For the context of each of these particular notions, Horn, *Adapting to a New World*. For the suggestion of the gradual supplanting of credit by contract, Muldrew, *Economy of Obligation*, ch. 10 (315-33), but compare Atiyah, *Rise and Fall of Freedom of Contract*, 36-60, and throughout, who

suggests that contractual ideas were slightly different and more deferred.

[101] For the importance of institutional frameworks and transaction costs, Douglas North, *Institutions, Institutional Change and Economic Performance* (Cambridge: Cambridge University Press, 1990).

6
Northern Speech

He wille whit _gou all' this[1]

Hight Hobbinol gan thus to him areed.[2]

INTRODUCTION

In 1344, two incumbents expressed their desire to exchange benefices, one in the diocese of Carlisle, the other in Lincoln diocese. Presented earlier to the parish church of Moorby in the latter diocese, Roger de Kyrkoswald–a toponymic byname reflecting his origins–offered two reasons for returning to his homeland in the diocese of Carlisle: improvement of his health through breathing the air amongst his kinsmen; and performing better his service in God's church by exercising the cure of souls back there rather than in Lincolnshire because of his native dialect.[3] The implication was the difficulty of understanding his dialect even in Lincolnshire where northern dialect elements extended, although not from the N.W. We might assume that between the fourteenth and the sixteenth century, the expansion of East Midlands dialect and Chancery Standard had eroded differences and caused some leveling, but in fact multiple differences of lexis (vocabulary and word usage) remained.[4]

The playwrights of the late-sixteenth and early-seventeenth century attempted to replicate dialect languages and to indicate their difference.[5] To a large extent, they reproduced stereotypes, with stock characters, and, for rural counterparts, quite often some brogue of Mummerset. Constance, the "Northern lasse", might fall into this category, but there are senses in which northern English retained a distinctness in early-modern language use, not only in phonemes (sounds) but also lexis (vocabulary).[6]

During the later middle ages, some standardization developed in the English language, whereas there had previously been more dialect difference by region and locality. This development of common forms of speech, however, has mainly been documented for the south Midlands and "Home counties" through the adoption of East Midlands Middle English. A conundrum remains: what was happening in other regions? Indeed, how did speech sound in other localities in the early-modern era? What differences persisted–if any–in those other localities through the late middle ages and into the early-modern period?

At least one redaction (one copy of an original manuscript) of "Christ's Burial and Resurrection" retained the form "whit". The likely provenance of the original text from the Charterhouse in Hull confirms the association of "whit" with northerly areas, with Yorkshire in particular. This usage signifies the retention of a word which had a particular association with Yorkshire (and other parts of the "North"). The extent of the dialect difference of the "North" from southern regions has often been debated.[7] Recently, Katie Wales has demonstrated how northern language was not always categorized as peculiar or archaic before the further normalization of language in the eighteenth century. Although Chancery Standard and London pronunciation developed in the later middle ages, the attitude to other dialects was only to notice their difference, not to ridicule them. Indeed, aspects of northern speech infiltrated London language.[8]

With reference to the verb "to whit", we can infer that dialect consisted not only in pronunciation but also in lexical content (vocabulary). Much previous investigation of late-medieval dialect has been predicated on phonemes and graphemes–the bits of sound (phonemes) as represented in written form (graphemes).[9] Although Wales examined some of the lexical evidence, much of her approach was concerned with appraising references to northern characters in early-modern drama and to northern speech in other contemporary literary works, since her purpose was predominantly to demonstrate the benign intention of this contemporary comment. There is then some room to consider further lexical items as they appeared in "ordinary" language use: common speech as recorded in written form (and therein, of course, lie dangers).

One of the difficulties is whether one takes–in anthropological language–an etic (insider's) or an emic (outsider's) perspective. The view from inside might concentrate on the differences within–the dialect differences of particular localities within the north. In contrast, the perception from outside might focus on the commonality of dialect across a zone by comparison with other dialect "regions".[10]

One way around this problem is to consider smaller spaces and localities. The intention here is to consider some lexical items in their local context in Yorkshire in the late fifteenth through to the early sixteenth centuries. The examination concentrates on testaments–loosely wills–which provide by far the largest body of contemporary material which was produced locally. The writers of wills are likely, by and large, to have been local and to have used local terms.

In 1584, Ralph Baocke of Harrogate, a yeoman, bequeathed 40s. to be disbursed at his burial for his neighbours and the "poure of the parishinge". Other testators in this locality also benefited "the poore of the parishinge", including John Stubbe in 1593 (13s. 4d.).[11] Many years earlier–in 1545–William Wilson of Howgill had described his abode as "in the parishinge of Kendall".[12] The writer of the will of Helen Mowr, of Eckington (Derbyshire), furthermore, employed the same form in 1541: "Item to the por pepull of our paryschyng Wher neydys xxd."[13] What is, moreover, interesting about this last example is that it occurred in the very north of Derbyshire, below the presumed southern extremity of northern England, perhaps denoting the southernmost occurrence of the term. To return to our first lexical item, although many of these will-makers employed the verb "to give" in making their bequests and legacies, a small proportion (certainly in the early sixteenth century) had a preference for "I wytt" rather than "I gyffe".[14] In referring in his will to arrangements for his burial, Lancelot Claxton desired that he be "brought forthe accordyng to my degre".[15] This phrase ("brought forth" for burial) also has connotations with Yorkshire. All these terms (wit; parishing; bring forth) seem, then, to belong to a linguistic tradition in Yorkshire (and some in further parts of the

"North") and the intention here is to explore how far they allow us to refer to a Yorkshire speech community and to delineate its southern dialect boundary based on these three lexical items.[16] There are a number of linguistic items which seem to characterize northern language use in the late-medieval and early-modern Yorkshire. These three lexical items, however, permit some further understanding of the characteristics of local speech and language use. "I wytt" derives from the present verb infinitive "witen" which, whilst it had many uses, in this present context meant "to bestow, confer or bequeath".[17] In these testators' wills, "parish" increasingly replaced "parishing", but the latter form persisted into the late sixteenth century. It can be considered to be formed with the denominal noun suffix *-ing*, a category usually indicating an abstract quality, and often associated with place or abode.[18] We might conclude from the sporadic incidence of these particular terms that they represented a conservative element of a local speech community's language use in the sixteenth century. The terms are certainly distinctive. Their sporadic usage and their gradual eclipse by "to give" and "parish" suggest that they belonged to an older tradition which, although under pressure from outside, was stubbornly retained by some local inhabitants. The continuous use of 'bring forth' for burial reinforces this idea of a particular local use of language.

"Wit"

Wills of the Leeds area of Yorkshire allow some insight into this language use. Jane Sykerwham of Addle in 1503 commenced her will: "Fyrst I commend and wittes my synfull saule to the mercy of god almughty..." and subsequently in the bequests used the form "I witt" seventeen times and "I bewitt" once.[19] A number of succeeding testators also employed "witt" for their bequests: one in 1504; another in 1505; one in ?1513; two in 1520; eight in 1521; one in 1523; another in 1524; one in 1526; three in 1527; three in 1528; three in 1529; one in 1530; one in 1531; and two in 1538.[20] Almost equal numbers used "witt" and "bewitt". An interesting variation occurred when some testators referred to their residuary legacy as all their goods which were "unwitt" (i.e. "unbequeathed", not already disposed earlier in their will as specific legacies), as did John Webster, of Preston, husbandman, in 1527.[21]

We can also perceive that, certainly in the reaches of Yorkshire, "(be)witt" has no associations with any particular social group in the fifteenth century. The verb peppered the will (1437) of Richard Shirburn, esquire, Dame Matilda Ever (1467), and Dame Alice Nevile.[22] In the will of Dame Alice Nevile, widow of Sir Thomas, knight, in 1479, "wit" was consistently used for dispositions.[23] In 1502, the will of the vicar of Otley, William Taylyoure, similarly deployed "wit" throughout.[24] A comparison with slightly later transactions might suggest that when it began to be employed less frequently towards the middle of the sixteenth century, "(be)wit" was being used residually by lower social groups, although even in the 1540s the making of a will perhaps implied a "middling" status. It was only during its decline during the sixteenth century that, as a residual usage, it became associated with less wealthy testators.

Thereafter, however, the use of "witen" declined, although reappearing sporadically. A will of 1539 referred to the "residue of all my goodes unbequest and not witt..."[25] The will of Elizabeth Talior, widow, consistently employed "wit" in the same year, as did six Sherburn wills in 1540-1.[26] The verb–either as wit or bewit–emerged also in wills of 1541 (Pudsey), 1542 (Woodkirk), 1543 (Sherburn – x3; Arthington), 1544 (Sherburn), 1545 (Woodkirk), 1546 (Barkston, Sherburn), 1547 (Methley), 1548 (Milford), and 1550 (Wakefield Hill; Tong).[27] In this residual use, two features are prominent: localization, particularly around Sherburn; and lower (non-elite) social status. For example, the final will in the series in 1550 belonged to Robert Morvell, a husbandman of Tong.[28] As late as 1558, John Roger's will–relating to Methley–consistently used "bewit", concluding with "The residew of all my goodes not bewite..."[29] The inference might be made that these testators were relying on older scribes to write their wills which thus reproduced an older, but persistent, form of language.

The concentration of the employment of "(be)wit" was in Yorkshire (particularly the West Riding), with an extension into north Lincolnshire.[30] What is demonstrated here is the close association of north Lincolnshire with Yorkshire in Middle English dialect. Both "(be)wit" and "parishing" are obfuscated by the predominance of the Latin for wills for much of the later middle ages. The sporadic intrusion of the vernacular, however, allows some visibility of both terms. We can detect, for example, from the vernacular will of the York chandler John of Croxton in 1393 that "I wyte" was consistently deployed in some final requests.[31]

"Parishing"

In 1521, William Barker of Tadcaster, pronounced in his will: "Also I witto the hye Alter viijd. to the behove of the parishynge".[32] About a year earlier, John Goodhale had described himself in his will as "of the parishynge of Brystall [Birstall–metathesis]..."[33] Those two forms constitute the principal means of reference in wills to "parishing": bequests to the parish(ing) and habitation within the parish(ing). Another occasional association was with requests for burial: "my bodie to be beriede in the Kirke yerde of the parishyng of Ledesham".[34] In 1532, furthermore, Agnes Hemsworth, widow, made a legacy "to every householder within the parishing of Swyllington havyng noo corne grouyng one stroke of wheate", she having described herself as "within the parishing of Swyllington".[35] About this time, Richard Grave of Rothwell declared in his will: "And also I bequeth to the said Rauf xxvjs. viijd. that Olyuer Bynnys of the parishyng of Elande owe unto me for ij fatt oxen".[36] Eleven years later–in 1544–William Chamber of Collingham left 4d. to every husbandman "within the parishinge of Collingham".[37] Another testator made an allowance of a quarter of wheat "to the pore within the parishinge of Bramham".[38] Forty years earlier, William Taylyoure, vicar of Otley, bequeathed 20s. towards the purchase of a coucher, but "if the parischynge by nott this said Cowcher", then his executors to deploy the money to other purposes.[39] Another West Riding testator bequeathed 1s. "to the poore people of the ... parishing in Almes".[40] Robert Abbott of Awsthorpe also remembered in the same way in his will: "And forthermer I will that the parishing of Blagburn have vjs. viijd. to the reparacion of their kirk..." as well as allowing burial "in what parishing that it pleaseth God to take me to hys mercy".[41]

The most frequent incidence, however, related to place of habitation: "of the parishing of Harwod"; "of Holbeke in the parishyng of Ledes..." (1531); "of the parishyng of Thorpparche" (1533); "of Wyke within the parochyn of Harwode" (1533); a formula which was repeated by testators in 1534, 1535, 1536, 1537 and 1538, the places represented in Figure 7.[42]

In this part of the West Riding, then, parishing had a significant use–alongside parish. Testaments from other parts of the north illustrate its deployment–occasionally–elsewhere. Willmakers described themselves in their preambles as of the parishing of: Chester-le-Street (1573); Croft (1551); Esh (1590); Fingall (1547); Grinton (1542); Houghton in the Spring (1597); Kirkby in Kendal (1543, 1563); Lanchester (1598); Lowther (1553); Middleton Tyas (1543); Patrick Brompton (1558); Thornton (1543); York, St Peter the Little (1525); and Well (1558).[43] Other testators made reference in other contexts: "my detts within the parichengs of Thornton and Engleton" (1543); "with all the pressts belonyng to the parryssyng" (1547); 6d. to the "clerks of the parishing" (1558); 2d. to every poor person "withyn this paryssen" (1558); £20 to be distributed amongst the poor "of the parishynges of Rychemonde and Bedall" (1562); 20s. to the "pore folkes in Elvett parishinge" (1578); 13s. 4d. "unto the poore people of my parishinge" (1587); bequests to the poor in the parishings of Jarrow, Houghton, Easington, Pittington, Kirkleatham, Cockwold and St Andrew Auckland (1597–in a will which referred to parishing four times); and 20s. to the poor householders in the parishing of Lanchester and 6s. 8d. to the poor of the parishing of Esh (1598).[44] Perhaps the most demonstrative context of this "northern-ness", however, is contained in the last bequests of Robert Colynson, mercer of York, in 1436: to twelve "pure folke in ilke parissyn underwretyn...the whilke parisshins are thes..."[45]

Further association of the form "parishing" with a northern zone is exhibited in a copy of a letter in the York House Books from John Conyers, knight, to the mayor of York, defending the nationality of John Harington against the defamation that he was a Scot: "bot aswele a gentilman borne in the parishing of Estrington".[46]

There was, however, a distinction in the use of parishing and parish. The former was used mainly as an abstraction. The noun parishing was employed when referring to the parish as a space and community. In other contexts, however, parish was preferred. To illustrate this difference, we might consider the will of James Birtbie of Birkenshaw who located himself "within the paroshing of Bristall" [Birstall–this frequent reversal of i and r known linguistically as metathesis] in 1534, but requested burial in the "paroche churche" of Birstall.[47] That same differentiation occurred in the will of Richard Pollard "of the parishing of Guysley", soliciting burial in the parish church.[48]

"Bringing forth"

Within northern wills, funeral arrangements were consistently described as "bringing forth" (verb) the body or "forthbringing" (noun) of the body. In 1540, for example, Nicholas Lounde of Calverley allocated £3 6s. 8d. for his "forthe bringinge".[49] The term recurred in wills in the West Riding: "I honestlie broughe forth"; "my forth bringinge"; "to bringe me forth honestlie"; "to bringe me forth honestlie according to my degre"; "at the day of my buriall to be brought forthe like an honest man of myne owne parte". The last prescription brings into relief the association of the bringing forth with the (male, married) testator's own part, his third of his personal estate, for his appropriate funeral and burial, the other thirds or parts devolving one part to his wife/widow and one third to his children–the so-called *legitim*.[50] Confirmation is contained in a testator's setting aside "one parte to my forthbringinge".[51]

We might suspect that the "forthbringing" marked the transition from "private" grief around the body in the household to a "public" accompaniment of the body to the church. "If the vigil was the more private part of the funeral ceremony, the convoy brought the body into the light of day and the public space of street and church".[52] In other words, the body was presented before local society. A death of a member was a concern for the whole of local society, a rupture, indeed, in its continuous existence. The tolling of the bell before and after interment was sometimes known as the "forthfare".[53]

We can compare this lexis with testamentary evidence from the north Midlands. In Leicestershire, from over 1,100 wills between 1522 and 1546, the consistent vocabulary involved some variation of honestly brought to the ground. In fewer than thirty instances, the testator desired to be (honestly) brought home. Brought forth did not exist in the local speech community.[54]

A more pertinent illustration is the language use of testators in the large diocese of Lichfield, which extended through northern

(Arden) Warwickshire, northern Shropshire, and through the whole of Staffordshire and Derbyshire. (Although the archdeaconry of Chester belonged to the diocese before 1540, it exercised much autonomy and for the most part had an independent probate jurisdiction).[55] In Lichfield diocese, more than 700 testators referred to their funeral and burial as their being brought home: "sche [his widow and executor] to bryng me Whome honestylly"; "I broght onestly to my long home"; "I broght home as a Cristent man hoght to be"; "to se that I be honestlie browgh Whome"; "to be brought to my longer home"; four marks allocated "to the bryngyng off me home"; "on parte to brynge me home"; and so on.[56] Over 250 parishes are represented by wills with this formula, of being brought home. In the northernmost part of the diocese, however, especially in the far north of Derbyshire, we encounter again in wills the preference for being brought forth. The intermediate location of north Derbyshire is, also, reflected in some mixed and compound expressions: "I wylle that I be brogthe forth homme"; "to bryng me forthe & Home"; and "afthar I be brothe forth home".[57]

Brought forth (as above) signified the bringing of the body back into local society. It was the opportunity of local inhabitants to commemorate the passing of one of their own. It had a further resonance, however, perhaps better indicated in the "forthfare": the reception of the body alongside the bodies of deceased neighbors in the churchyard. That implication is more directly expressed, perhaps, in bringing home: the body is transferred to its longer home, but also a home amongst departed neighbors. Although the lexis differs, the intention was the same. The admixture of the terms in a hybrid manner in north Derbyshire confirms the similarity of meaning.

Conclusion

The forms which have been considered above are not without ambiguity. In the context of parishing, we might remark that other words in the northern speech community/ies were ostensibly pronounced in a similar manner: "chylderyng" (children); "cosing"/ "coussyngs"; "kytchinge"; for example.[58] No doubt dialect pronunciation interfered in the formation of "parishing", but the most formative influence was a preference for a denominal noun suffix

-ing for expressing abstract entities. Equally, although "bewit" might have developed to some extent from the variable sounding of *-w-* and *-qu-*, that explanation will not readily extend to *wit* ("quit" would seem anomalous and inappropriate in the context of bequests and legacies). In both cases, therefore, we seem to be confronted by distinctive dialect lexis which persisted in local and regional vocabulary through into the early sixteenth century and lingered to the end of that century. In the case of *(be)wit*, what had earlier been a verb used equally by all of society, perhaps became associated during the course of the sixteenth century more with lower (and perhaps rural) social groups. During the sixteenth century, the continuing use of these lexical items might have represented a conservative aspect of language use in some parts of the local speech community.

The three items of language use—"parishing", "(be)wit", and "brought forth"—were all distinctive of the West Riding of Yorkshire. Like many items of language, however, they were not simply contained within one locality, but also spilled out in different directions. The limits of particular dialect terms are called isoglosses; each term had a different isogloss, although all were current within the West Riding. One usage extended into Lincolnshire, associating again the north of that county with some aspects of more northerly dialect: "(be)wit" specifically with usage in parts of the West Riding of Yorkshire. Although the "North" was internally divided into dialect localities—those intimate *espaces vécus*—an overall coherence to the "North" was produced by some language use which extended across the "North": "parishing".[59] What the divergent distributions of the three items seem to indicate is the difficulty of establishing clearly defined dialect boundaries in this sense: that dialect boundaries are constituted of congruent bundles of isoglosses of particular terms, that is, we can only speak of dialect boundaries when the limits of a number of dialect items coalesce. With our three items that was not the case. On the other hand—and perhaps more importantly—we can look at where they were concentrated and occurred together rather than just at their limits. Together they contributed to the local speech of the West Riding of Yorkshire in a distinctive manner.

Table 8 Numbers of Testators in "Leeds and District" Described as of the "Parishing"

Decade	Number of testators	Parishes
1520s	1	Birstall
1530s	15	Birstall, Harewood, Kippax, Leeds, Sherburn-in-Elmet, Swillington, Thorpe Arch,
1540s	43	Ardsley, Batley, Birstall, Calverley, Collingham, Featherstone, Guiseley, Kippax, Ledsham, Leeds, Normanton, Otley, Sherburn-in-Elmet, Thorner, Wakefield, Woodkirk
1550s	61	Aberforth, Bardsey, Batley, Birstall, Bramham, Garforth, Guiseley, Harewood, Kippax, Ledsham, Leeds, Methley, Normanton, Otley, Pontefract, Rothwell, Sherburn, Swillington, Thorner, Wakefield, Weston. Woodkirk
1560-1	8	Adel, Birstall, Guiseley, Monk Friston, Spofforth, Wakefield

Table 9 Distribution of "Brought Home" and "Brought Forth", 1528-46, in Lichfield Diocese

Parish/township	Brought home	Brought forth
Ashover	7	1
Barlborough	0	1
Barlow	0	1
Bolsover	11	2
Brampton	2	2
Dronfield	9	20
Eckington	1	10
Duckmanton	0	2
Glossop	4	1
Glenton	0	1
Handley	0	1
North Wingfield	2	2
Pinxton	0	1
Pleasley	1	2
Sheen	1	2
Staveley	0	12
Whittington	2	2
Whitwell	1	1

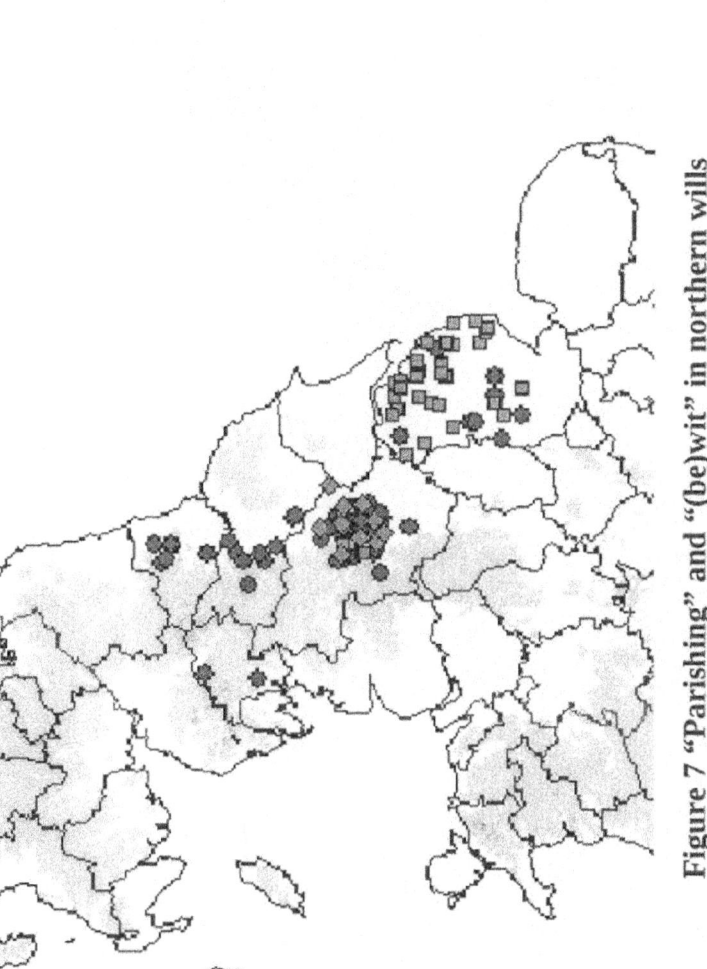

Figure 7 "Parishing" and "(be)wit" in northern wills

In this figure, the dots indicate occurrences of "parishing"; squares represent instances of "(be)wit"; and triangles reflect the combination of both items. "Parishing" here relates only to testators' description of their place of habitation in the *incipit* of wills.

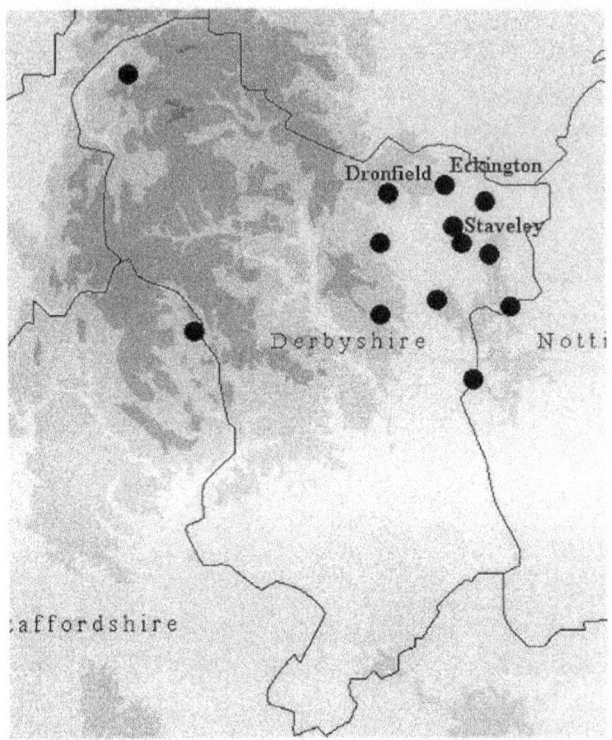

Figure 8 'Brought Forth' in Wills, 1528-46, Lichfield Diocese

Notes

[1] D. C. Baker, J. L. Murphy and L. B. Hall, eds., *The Late Medieval Religious Plays of Bodleian MSS Digby 133 and E Museo 160*, Early English Text Society, 283 (1982), 167; F. J. Furnivall, ed., *The Digby Plays*, EETS Extra Series 70, (1896), 199/850. The ͡g is the Middle English character yogh.

[2] Edmund Spenser, *Colin Clouts Come Home Again*, line 15. [1591]

[3] R. L. Storey, ed., *Register of John Kirkby, Bishop of Carlisle, 1332-1352, and the Register of John Ross, Bishop of Carlisle, 1325-1332, 1*, Canterbury and York Society, 79 (1992), 158-9.

[4] For this development, Laura Wright, *Sources of London English: Medieval Thames Vocabulary* (Oxford: Oxford University Press, 1996).

[5] For example, the Northern Merchant in *Bartholomew Fair*, Act IV, scene iv.

[6] Richard Brome, *The Northern Lasse*, ed. Harvey Fried (New York and London: Garland Publishing, Inc., 1980) (originally published in ?1629).

[7] Summarized by Helen M. Jewell, *The North-South Divide: The Origins of Northern Consciousness in England* (Manchester: Manchester University Press, 1994), 198-201; D. Burnley, "Lexis and Semantics", in *The Cambridge History of the English Language*, II, 1066-1476, ed. N. Blake (Cambridge: Cambridge University Press, 1992), 411.

[8] Katie Wales, *Northern English: A Cultural and Social History* (Cambridge: Cambridge University Press, 2006), 66-93.

[9] See note 4 above and also Gillis Kristensson, *A Survey of Middle English Dialects 1290-1350: the Six Northern Counties and Lincolnshire*, Lund Studies in English, 35 (1967). Further definition is also given in Dave Postles, "Defining the 'North' : Some Linguistic Evidence", *Northern History* 38 (2001), 27-9.

[10] These differences of perspective might explain–at least to some extent–the divergence between the earlier S. Moore, S. B. Beech, and H. Whitehall, *Middle English Dialect: Characteristics and Dialect Boundaries* (Ann Arbor, MI: University of Michigan, 1935) and the later A. McIntosh, M. L. Samuels, and M. Benskin, *A Linguistic Atlas of Late Mediaeval English* 4 vols (Aberdeen: Aberdeen University Press, 1986). For the nature of this difference of approach, Michael Benskin, "Description of Dialect and Areal Distribution", in *Speaking in Our Tongues: Medieval Dialectology and Related Disciplines*, ed. M. Lang and K. Williamson (Cambridge: Cambridge University Press, 1994), 169-92. At issue, is whether there was a dialect "continuum" or distinctive dialect "regions". The two might not be incompatible. For the latest word, as it were, J. Milroy, "Middle English Dialectology", in *Cambridge History*, II, 182-91.

[11] *Wills and Administrations from the Knaresborough Court Rolls*, volume I, Surtees Society, civ (1902), 145, 194; see also pp. 27, 58, 117 for the noun "parishinge".

[12] J. W. Clark, ed., *North Country Wills 1383 to 1558*, Surtees Society, cxvi (1908), 198 (cxliv).

[13] Lichfield Record Office (LRO) B/C/11 Helen Mowr 1541.

[14] For example, *Knaresborough Wills*, 8, 12, 15, 16, 27, 36; R. Cook, "Wills of the Parishes of Rothwell, Saxton ...", *Miscellanea*, Thoresby Society, 33 (1935), 35-7 (1502, 1510).

[15] Clark, *North Country Wills*, 124-5.

[16] For a succinct elucidation of early-modern regional variation, M. Gorläch, "Regional and Social Variation", in *Cambridge History of the English Language*, volume III, 1476-1776, ed. Roger Lass (Cambridge: Cambridge University Press, 1999), 486-514.

[17] *Middle English Dictionary* volume 13 W-Z, ed. R. E. Lewis et al. (Ann

Arbor, MI: University of Michigan Press, 1999), 705 witen v. (2) cites testamentary contexts, mainly from Lincolnshire and Yorkshire, without commenting on the significance of this localization.

[18] At one of the "Parish" symposia at the University of Warwick, Steve Hindle and Patrick Collinson alluded to the use of "righting" for "right" in receiving communion in the north-west of England.

[19] W. Brigg, "Testamenta Leodiensia", *Miscellanea*, Thoresby Society 4 (1895) (hereafter "TL" 4), 7-9.

[20] Brigg, "TL" 4, 9, 15-16, 141; G. D. Lumb, "Testamenta Leodiensia", *Miscellanea*, Thoresby Society 9 (1899), 163-7, 170-1, 177, 183, 188, 256-7, 260-4, 267, 271, 272 (hereafter "TL" 9); Lumb, "Testamenta Leodiensia 1531 to 1534", *Miscellanea*, Thoresby Society 11 (1904) (hereafter "TL" 11), 46-7, 64; Lumb, "Testamenta Leodiensia", *Miscellanea*, Thoresby Society 15 (1909) (hereafter "TL" 15), 16, 23.

[21] "TL" 9, 261. Also "TL" 9, 262, 267 ("not wit(t)"); "TL" 11, 47, 64.

[22] James Raine, ed., *Testamenta Eboracensia Part II*, Surtees Society 30 (1855), 75, 284-5; Raine, ed., *Testamenta Eboracensia Part III*, Surtees Society 45 (1864), 244-5.

[23] R. Cook, "Wills of Leeds and District", *Miscellanea*, Thoresby Society 24 (1919), 61-2.

[24] Cook, "Wills of Leeds and District", 333-4.

[25] Lumb, *Testamenta Leodiensia ... 1539 to 1553*, Thoresby Society 19 (1913), 2.

[26] Lumb, *Testamenta Leodiensia ... 1539 to 1553*, 11, 22, 23, 24, 25, 26, 107-8.

[27] Lumb, *Testamenta Leodiensia ... 1539 to 1553*, 38, 73, 83, 91, 92, 95, 114, 134-5, 142, 186-7, 192-3, 201, 213-14, 265-6.

[28] Lumb, *Testamenta Leodiensia ... 1539 to 1553*, 265-6.

[29] Lumb, *Testamenta Leodiensia ... 1553 to 1561*, Thoresby Society 27 (1930), 236.

[30] The Lincolnshire occurrences during the early sixteenth century are located in Figure 7, the sources for which are: C. W. Foster, ed., *Lincoln Wills Registered in the District Probate Registry at Lincoln*. Vol.1, 1271 to 1526, Lincoln Record Society, 5 (1914); Foster, ed., *Lincoln Wills Registered in the District Probate Registry at Lincoln*. Vol.2, 1505 to May, 1530, LRS, 10 (1918); Foster, ed., *Lincoln Wills Registered in the District Probate Registry at Lincoln*. Vol.3, 1530 to 1532, LRS, 24 (1930); and David Hickman, ed., *Lincoln Wills 1532-1534*, LRS, 89 (2001).

[31] Raine, James, ed., *Testamenta Eboracensia Part I*, Surtees Society 4 (1836), 184 (cxlviii).

[32] "TL" 9, 166.

[33] "TL" 4, 95 (1520).

[34] "TL" 9, 176 (Robert Milson, 1521).
[35] "TL" 11, 49 (1532).
[36] "TL" 11, 53.
[37] Lumb, *Testamenta Leodiensia ... 1539 to 1553*, 119.
[38] Lumb, *Testamenta Leodiensia ... 1539 to 1553*, 330.
[39] Cook, "Wills of Leeds and District", 337-40.
[40] Lumb, *Testamenta Leodiensia ... 1553 to 1561*, 10.
[41] Cook, 'Wills of the Parishes of Rothwell, Saxton ...', 52. For the "parishing" of Halifax in 1533: J. W. Clay and E. W. Crossley, eds., *Halifax Wills* (Halifax, 1904), 87 (177).
[42] "TL" 11, 40, 49, 51, 54, 295, 301, 311, 315, 318, 320; "TL" 15, 12, 23.
[43] Raine, ed., *Wills and Inventories from the Registry of the Archdeaconry of Richmond...*, Surtees Society 26 (1853), 10 (viii), 25 (xxvi), 27 (xxviii), 31 (xxxi), 33 (xxxii), 49 (xlv), 50 (xlviii), 66 (lxii), 71 (lxviii), 73 (lxx), 123 (cvi), 124 (cvii), 167 (cxxxvii), 258 (clxxxix); W. Greenwell, ed., *Wills and Inventories from the Registry at Durham Part II*, Surtees Society 38 (1860), 284 (cxxvi), 337-8 (cl); J. Hodgson, ed., *Wills and Inventories from the Registry at Durham Part III*, Surtees Society 112 (1906), 67, 140, 148.
[44] Raine, *Wills and Inventories from the Registry of the Archdeaconry of Richmond....*, 51 (xlviii), 63 (lviii), 104 (xciii), 124 (cvi), 157 (cxxxv); Greenwell, *Wills and Inventories from the Registry at Durham Part II*, 105 (xlix), 337-8 (cl); Hodgson, *Wills and Inventories from the Registry at Durham Part III*, 79, 142.
[45] Raine, ed., *Testamenta Eboracensia Part II*, Surtees Society 30 (1855), 217.
[46] Raine, ed., *A Volume of English Miscellanea Illustrating the History and Language of the Northern Counties*, Surtees Society 85 (1890), 48.
[47] "TL" 11, 295.
[48] "TL" 11, 318–there are many other examples.
[49] "TL" 19, 17.
[50] Alice Wolfram (Yale University) will examine the persistence of the legitim in London and the diocese of York in her PhD dissertation.
[51] "TL" 19, 5, 17, 20, 27, 28, 32, 34, 36, 38, 42, 45, 48, 53, 56, 57, 60, 61, 62-3, 66, 67, 68, 69, 70, 74, 76, 77, 78, 79, 81, 86, 88, 90, 92, 94, 95, 101, 111–for example!
[52] Vanessa Harding, "Whose Body? A Study of Attitudes Towards the Dead Body in Early Modern Paris", in *The Place of the Dead: Death and Remembrance in Late Medieval and Early Modern Europe*, ed. Bruce Gordon and Peter Marshall (Cambridge: Cambridge University Press, 2000), 180.
[53] Clare Gittings, *Death, Burial and the Individual in Early Modern England* (Beckenham: Croom Helm, 1984), 134.
[54] Record Office for Leicestershire, Leicester and Rutland: all probate

140   *Social Dramas*

material examined between these dates–see http://www.le.ac.uk/ee/pot/wills/leicswillsfram.html

[55] The following is based on Lichfield Record Office B/C/11wills and inventories before 1547 (see http://www.le.ac.uk/ee/pot/lichfield/lichwillsfram.html).

[56] LRO B/C/11 William Bratt, Colton, 1539; Robert Balle, Aston, 1535; William Lace, Ilkeston, 1538; Robert Herryson, Smisby, 1542; William Wylmer, Sowe, 1540; Thomas Kempson, Walsall, 1536; and Roger Ferrers, Walton, 1535. The association of "long(er) home" and testament is dramatically confirmed by Heywood: [Sir Charles] "Thou shalt to thy long home. Or I will want my will!": *Woman Killed with Kindness*, scene iii, line 38.

[57] LRO B/C/11 Richard Schae, Brampton, 1537; Richard Hethe, Brampton, 1543; and John Stevenson, Brampton.

[58] Examples are: Raine, *Wills and Inventories from the Registry of the Archdeaconry of Richmond*, 225, 235, 239, 251; Greenwell, *Wills and Inventories from the Registry at Durham Part II*, 105 (xlix); Hodgson, *Wills and Inventories from the Registry at Durham Part III*, 9 ("chylderyng" in the will of "Helyng" [i.e. Helen] Muschaunce, 1551); 37 ("childring", 1567); 16 ("fyrmynges" [i.e. Farms], 1558); 61 ("cossing", 1571); 69 ("tokinge" [i.e. token], 1574)..

[59] For *espace vécu*, Pierre Claval, *An Introduction to Regional Geography*, translated by Ian Thompson (Oxford: Blackwell, 1998), 22, 138-60: this phenomenology of living in the world embraces speech and language use.

7
The Drama of the Cockfight

[SIR BOUNTEOUS] Tomorrow your lordship shall see my cocks, ...[1]

[SIR BOUNTEOUS] Ha, ha, I have fitted her; an old knight and a cock o'th' game still; I have not spurs for nothing, I see.[2]

Most recent discussions of the cockfight have been formulated as an expression of or reaction to the seminal article by Clifford Geertz on the Balinese cockfight in which he deployed his hermeneutic anthropological method to interpret the cultural significance of the contest. Geertz addressed the action of the cockfight and read off the event as a text. The ritualization of the contest, for him, revealed a homogeneous cultural situation.

More recently, although acknowledging the significance of Geertz's significant analysis, Thomas Hamill has taken some inspiration from James Clifford's "ethnographic authority" of literary devices, dissecting the allegorical mode of literature on the cockfight, as a rhetorical construction and reflection of social relations, and as male subject-formation. In this process, Hamill examined two literary texts, the one a prescriptive conduct manual and the other a husbandry manual.[3] In 1607 was printed a biblically-based justification for cockfighting, *The Commendation of Cockes...*, composed by George Wilson, vicar of Wretton in Norfolk, which adduced through exegesis the importance of cockfighting for the cultivation of masculine virtue, "male subject-formation", through the nurturing of the cock and the animal's valour. That duty of care and respect for the animal was evoked also by Gervase Markham's *The Second Booke of the English Husbandman* (1614). Hamill's elucidation is predicated, however, on the prescriptive and advice literature, "as signifying texts", so a return to the action and activity of the cockfight merits further attention to balance these discursive and rhetorical literary texts. In so doing, however, we are concerned less with the cockfight as text in the manner of Geertz, but with the various meanings of the action of the cockfight in its historical context.

Gentry, the urban and urbane

After the establishment of the royal cockpit in Whitehall by Henry VIII, the cockfight assumed even greater status in gentry life.[4] At this level, cockfighting remained an event with social cachet, cultural, social and political capital. Matches were arranged between individual gentry as social contests at an elite level, with elaborate rules of engagement encompassed in private articles of agreement.[5]

By the later sixteenth century, it had become desirable for all boroughs to have a cockpit, not merely for the entertainment of its own townspeople, but to attract the local gentry into the urban centre for consumption, social liaison and association between the urban magistracy and the local notables. The importance of this facility was made evident by the mayor and burgesses of Liverpool who in 1568 resolved that "it [is] nedfull That theare be an handsome cockefeight pit made" "for the further & greater Repayre of gentilmen & others to this towne"[6] About the same time, it was resolved to establish a cockpit in York to attract those of gentle status to frequent the city more often and consume there:

> that dyvers worshipfull gentylmen was muche desyerous to have a cokk pytt mayd in this Citie that they myght resorte unto for there pastyme and to spend money here that they were wont to spend in other places. And these presens consideryng that the same wold be a commoditie to this Citie and occacion to cause much money to be spent bothe emongs vyttelers and other craftsmen...[7]

So the common council authorized a cockpit to be constructed on a piece of ground in the former garden of the dissolved house of Austin Friars near the Common Hall.

Even such a relatively small borough as Congleton invested in such a facility to attract the local gentry of its part of Cheshire.[8] Between 1583 and 1633, the urban authority constantly prepared the cockpit: straw for the cockpit; a thatcher of the cockring; getting clods for the cockfight; piles for the cockpit from time to time; constant repair with clods and re-thatching; a gallon of wine bestowed on Mistress Egerton at the great cockfight in 1599; half a pound of sugar also bestowed on Mistress Egerton and Mistress Willbram at the great cockfight; wine bestowed on the gentlemen at the great cockfight; wine and sugar bestowed on Sir John Savage knight and the gentlewomen the first day of the great cockfight; the same bestowed in great cockfight week on Mr. John Brereton and his kinsmen in his "Companye"; wine for Sir John Savage knight and his followers and Mr. Wilbram at a cockfight; wine for Sir John Savage and Sir Brian Leeghe, knights, and gentlewomen at the schoolhouse on the last day of the great cockfight; carpentry repair to the cockpit in 1601; and claret wine for the gentlemen at the great cockfight (1614); amongst many examples of such borough expenditure.

Gentlemen attending with Sir William Wrey the cockfights at Lostwithiel in Cornwall were similarly entertained with wine from the mayor's account in 1635-6.[9] The mayor and burgesses of the small borough of Bodmin in Cornwall in 1603 entered into an agreement to lease to William Collier, sadler, of the same place, a small plot of land called "The Fryers", 54 feet wide, with the cockpit which had been erected there by Collier.[10]

Undoubtedly, as Hamill elucidates, the cockfight thus had an allegorical connection with gentry culture and the representation of masculinity. A courtesy manual printed in 1684 in London included cockfighting amongst the desirable recreational activities of the gentleman: *The School of Recreation; Or, The Gentlemans Tutor, To Those Most Ingenious Exercises...*, describing hunting, racing, hawking, riding, cockfighting, fowling, fishing, shooting, bowling, tennis, ringing and billiards.[11] The author devoted eleven pages to the rearing and preparation of fighting cocks. The elaborate procedures involved time and expense. Unlike Wilson's admonitions, the author has no patriarchal advice, but concentrates on the relationship between the gentleman and the cock. The cock is nurtured, but purposefully. After the practise sparring, for example, the perspiring cock should receive a balm of butter, finely-chopped rosemary, and white sugar candy, with an additional allowance of walnut, "which will scower, strengthen and prolong Breath". After the administration of that admixture, the cock should be enveloped in a deep straw basket. At five in the evening, the cock should be lifted out and the owner "lick his Head and Eyes with your Tongue"; after replacing the cock in the straw basket, the owner should fill the basket with manchet and hot urine. Thenceforth, the cock's feed should consist of cakes made from wheat, oat-meal, ale, whites of eggs, and butter.[12]

Whilst the close connection between owner and cock is thus emphatic in the advice, there is no presumption of a patriarchal relationship nor any such allegorical implication. The association between cock and hens is barely mentioned, except for the circumspection that the cock's virility might be debilitated by the availability of too many hens, which must be limited to three. Masculinity is thus predicated, but moreso the preparation needed for the purpose. The point is to preserve the honor of the gentleman owner through attention to detail and skill in preparing the cock. Despite the intensive attention lavished on the cock, there is no conception here of the owner as mother or nurturer, but simply of rearing for a purpose.

It is in this last sense that the cockfight conforms to the residual and lingering concept of masculinity and gentry violence. Indeed, at least one tragedy acted out in the theater suggested how privately-arranged competition in recreational activity between the gentry might dissolve into direct violence. In *Woman Killed with Kindness*, Sir Francis Acton and Sir Charles Mountford agree to a hawking contest.[13] In the heat of the competition, the two contestants fell into mutual abuse, resulting in a confrontation between the followers of the two camps, in which Sir Charles and his retinue kill Sir Francis's men, which felony through rage begins the downfall of Sir Charles.[14] Whilst a culture of restraint and civility was developing, there remained nonetheless opportunities for the legitimate exercise of violence through the spectacle and competition of the cockfight, a discourse which might have pervaded society, not just the gentry, as a sort of "hegemonic masculinity".[15] The cockfight perpetuated masculine identity as a continuous process, not the achievement of manhood through a ritual rite of passage, but its constant maintenance.[16]

RITUAL GOING AWRY

As mentioned above, the cockfight was regulated by customary or conventional rules or by articles of agreement between the parties. Where the cockfight existed as a local, annual event, the procedures were conventional; when the event was a contest between private parties rather than a regular public event, the rules were negotiated between the parties and engrossed in precise articles of agreement.[17] Formally regulated in this manner, the cockfight became a ritualized performance. As is acknowledged, such ritual events did not always conform to their prescriptive circumstances: occasionally, unforeseen outcomes occurred. Ritual could not always be contained. Contests for power derailed the ritual, the ritual occasion was appropriated, or the event became the *locus* of the settling of scores, a convenient occasion for the channelling of rancour.[18]

This form of derogation of the cockfight as a ritual event happened at Winwick in Lancashire in the early sixteenth century. During the later middle ages, this village in Lancashire had developed as the place for a weekly cockfight on Saturdays.[19] A violent event there resulted in a suit in the court of the Duchy of Lancaster in 1515, a plaint by Thomas Boteler, esquire, against Thomas Gerard, knight, and his accomplices. The complaint reveals how the annual, ritualized event became the *locus* for a dispute between contestants with local status. The cockfight event at Winwick had become established as an annual celebration on the Saturday of Easter (Holy) week, intermingling the sacred and the profane in popular festivities. The regulations for the occasion had already been established by custom or convention "after the maner of the Cuntrey there used" and "aftre accustumable maner of the Cuntrey", country signifying here the locality.[20] The cockfight commenced at 10 a.m. and lasted most of the day, an occasion for all the tenants as well as the gentlemen, the tenants wearing their best clothes ("theire Clene geere").[21] Boteler himself had a retinue of a dozen people and children who carried the cocks. Several other gentlemen arrived with similar retinues, totalling about another fifty people.

The complaint of Boteler, as the "Orator" or complainant, must be situated within the context of the rhetoric of all complainants in the *Duchy Court*. The narrative no doubt contains not only legal *formulae* appropriate to the form of action, but also other rhetorical devices to make a compelling case.[22] In the count or narration of his accusation, Boteler denounced Gerard with five other named gentlemen, two named yeomen and others, known and unknown, amounting to more than eighty armed persons ("his said riottuous cumpany") of setting an ambush for the plaintiff about a quarter of a mile from the cockpit on the road from the plaintiff's house to the event. The ambushers advanced on the cockfight to attack Boteler and his small number of companions, the intervention of Sir John Southworth, who requested observance of the king's peace, being of no avail, until afforced by two priests despatched to quell the riot.[23]

CULTURAL COHERENCE?

Despite the potential for ambiguities about the cockfight, there was, nonetheless, some degree of cultural coherence. In the events at Winwick, the gentry were accompanied by their retinue and servants and by children carrying the cocks. No doubt numerous villagers attended the spectacle too. Although some competitions were arranged by and reserved for the local elite, other lesser contests involved other social groups, the "middling" and "lower sorts" who engaged in cockfighting. So, in 1576, Mark Haslonde was examined in Devizes (Wiltshire) about a game cock which he had found in his cellar feeding on his peas. When the cock was not claimed, he took it to Urchfont to his father-in-law, but then it returned to its owner, John Watt. Apparently, there had been a dispute about the cock between Watt and another inhabitant, Stephen Flower.[24]

CULTURAL INCOHERENCE?

The substance of the suggestions by Geertz and Hamill is that there obtained a homologous culture of the cockfight. From the late sixteenth century, the cockfight was not without opponents. The opposition was formulated not on the grounds of cruelty or violence, but on an attempt to eradicate those aspects of popular culture distasteful to the "Puritan" elite. The antagonism to the cockfight, like all recreational activities, was informed by an insistence on moral reform and rectitude satisfactory to God's word. In 1654, Oliver Cromwell prohibited cockfights.[25]

It is interesting that in the case of George Wilson, we have simply an Anglican clergy's perception of allegorical force of the cockfight. In fact, the symbolism of the cockfight was appropriated into politico-religious discourse in a tract of 1647:

> *A battaile fought between a Presbyterian cock of the right breed, and a craven of the Independent breed. With the cravens desire, that the quarrell may be ended, either upon Tower-Hill, or at the narrow place turning up to Padington. Also the sad complaint the craven made to some of his friends at his death, that he could not be buryed, and intomb'd as Presbytery John was, he therefore only desires one of the beadles of the Bride-Well to be his excequetor. With the Presbyterian cocks epistle to the heads-man.*[26]

By 1646, the Presbyterians had established *de facto* a shadow ecclesiastical structure to replace the defunct Anglican ecclesiology. In attempting to impose this model, resistance was encountered from the Independent sects. The Presbyterians submitted a proposal to Parliament in August 1646, a scheme accepted by the that authority in December.[27] The woodcut on the title page of the tract illustrates Presbyterian John "revived" and the Independent Craven "a dying". The analogy is with the cockpit and struggle, with viciousness and intolerance. The pamphlet is involved in the disputation between the Presbyterians and the Independents in 1646, instigated by the publication in 1646 of *Gangraena* by Thomas Edwards, referring to the sectarian allegiances and intolerance. The Presbyterian Edwards contended that physical punishment could correct heretical depravity.[28] In 1647, the Presbyterians contrived to gain control of the militia in London "in the increasingly tense political atmosphere".[29] By this action, the Presbyterians forged an alliance with the City authorities, Parliament and the militia.

148 *Social Dramas*

Thereafter, the Presbyterians and the Independents continued a contest for influence over Parliament. London thus became a cockpit. The dispute over sectarianism contained violence, punishment and unmitigated defeat, the suppression experienced in the cockpit when the defeated cock crowed its last.

Last thoughts
We should not be surprised that contemporaries appropriated the metaphor of the cockfight for their particular purposes. Allegory remained a constant resource for political comment. When violence was at issue, invoking cockfights and bear-baiting was a natural recourse. "Whether violence involves the use of animals... [involves] issues which cover the changing means by which violence is perpetrated, as well as the bodily and emotional control this involves."[30] Masculinity and politics retained a measure of covert violence. The cultural, as has been predicated, cannot be divorced from the political.[31]

Notes
[1] *Mad World*, Act II, scene ii, line 16.
[2] *Mad World*, Act III, scene ii, lines 79-80.
[3] Thomas A. Hamill, "Cockfighting as Cultural Allegory in Early Modern England", *Journal of Medieval and Early Modern Studies* 39 (2009): 375-406, which recites Geertz and the attendant literature. Clifford Geertz, "Deep Play: Notes on the Balinese Cockfight", in his *The Interpretation of Cultures* (New York: Basic Books, 1973), 412–15 and Fred Inglis, *Clifford Geertz: Culture, Custom and Ethics* (Cambridge: Polity Press, 2000), 84–9; Vincent Pecora, "The Limits of Local Knowledge", in *The New Historicism*, ed. H. Aram Veeser (London: Routledge, 1989), 243–76; William Roseberry, "Balinese Cockfights and the Seduction of Anthropology", *Social Research* 49 (1982): 1013–28, but compare Geertz, *Available Light: Anthropological Reflections on Philosophical Topics* (Princeton: Princeton University Press, 2000), xi-xiii; A. Biersack, "Local Knowledge, Local History: Geertz and Beyond", in *The New Cultural History*, ed. Lynn Hunt (Berkeley: University of California Press,1989), 72–96; Talad Asad, "Anthropological Conceptions of Religion: Reflections on Geertz", *Man* new series 18 (1983): 237–59; and William Sewell, "Geertz, Cultural Systems, and History: From Synchrony to Transformation", in *The Fate of Culture: Geertz and Beyond*, ed. Sherry Ortner (Berkeley: University of California Press, 1999).

⁴ *The School of Recreation; Or, The Gentlemans Tutor, To Those Most Ingenious Exercises* (London, 1684), 64, confers the description "Royal-Sport" on the cockfight; Felicity Heal and Clive Holmes, *The Gentry in England and Wales 1500-1700* (Basingstoke: Macmillan Press Ltd., 1994), 308-9, 311.

⁵ Articles of agreement are extant from the eighteenth century in particular: Staffordshire and Stoke on Trent Archives Service William Salt Library 49/146/44, articles of agreement between Lord Gower and the Earl of Exeter for their cockfight at Ashbourne in Derbyshire in 1728; Lancashire Record Office DDX 346/1, similar between John Auton, of Clotherholm, Yorkshire, and Henry Avision, of Hampsthwaite, Yorkshire, both gentlemen, for a cockfight at Leeds in 1731; West Yorkshire Archives Service Bradford SpSt/12/1/9 draft articles of agreement between John Lambert, of Leeds, gent., on behalf of Lord Viscount Down, and John Stanhope, of Horsforth, esq., for a cockfight in Bradford, 1756 (the Spencer-Stanhope papers contain numerous references to their interest in cocks and cockfighting); occasionally, the rules of engagement were established in court, as between Thomas Cust, of Danby Hall, gent., with Ralph Thompson and Martin Dunn, for a cockfight in Bishop's Auckland (Durham) (The National Archives, London, E134/22Geo2/Mich5).

⁶ David George, ed., *Records of Early English Drama [REED]: Lancashire* (Toronto: University of Toronto Press, 1991), 38.

⁷ Angelo Raine, ed., *York Civic Records VI*, Yorkshire Archaeological Society Record Series 112 (1948 for 1946), 135.

⁸ E. Baldwin, L. Clopper and D. Mills, eds., *REED: Cheshire including Chester*, vol. 2 (Toronto: University of Toronto Press, 2007), 617-60.

⁹ Sally L. Joyce and Evelyn S. Newton, eds., *REED: Cornwall* (Toronto: University of Toronto Press, 1999), 499.

¹⁰ Joyce and Newlyn, *REED: Cornwall*, 475.

¹¹ Printed for H. Rodes in London, 1684.

¹² *The School of Recreation*, 59 (the section on the cockfight is 54-64).

¹³ *Woman Killed with Kindness*, scene i, lines 80-115.

¹⁴ *Woman Killed with Kindness*, scene iii.

¹⁵ For masculinity and violence in general in early-modern England, Alexandra Shepard, *Meanings of Manhood in Early Modern England* (Oxford: Oxford University Press, 2003), 140-51, especially for the codification of violence; for "hegemonic masculinity", R. W. Connell, *Masculinities* (Cambridge: Polity Press, 1995), 37, 76-81 (on "the social organization of masculinity"); in a still largely agrarian society, it is probable that the discourse of masculinity would involve the substitution of animals for humans, so the attainment of manhood in Crete was until recently associated with the theft of sheep: Michael Herzfeld, *The Poetics of Manhood: Contest*

and Identity in a Cretan Mountain Village (Princeton, NJ: Princeton University Press, 1985), esp. 45-50 (the village is Glendi).

[16] For the difference between the attainment of manhood and its perpetuation, David D, Gilmore, *Manhood in the Making: Cultural Concepts of Masculinity* (New Haven, CT: Yale University Press, 1990), esp. 220-31; to be even more specific, there are two different aspects of manhood: becoming a man, through a once-for-all rite of passage which in itself qualifies one forever as a man; and maintaining manhood through constant attention, repeated proving that one is a man in the approved manner.

[17] For a reference to the conventions as "Cock-Pitt Law", *The School of Recreation...*, 64.

[18] Edward Muir, *Ritual in Early Modern Europe* (Cambridge: Cambridge University Press, 1997), 4, 85, 92, 112-13, for how early-modern ritualized events might have entirely unexpected, violent consequences.

[19] *Pleadings and Depositions in the Duchy Court of Lancaster Volume I Time of Henry VII and Henry VIII [Duchy Court]*, Lancashire and Cheshire Record Society 32 (1896), 108.

[20] *Duchy Court*, 106-8.

[21] *Duchy Court*, 109.

[22] Hayden White, "The Value of Narrativity in the Representation of Reality", in *On Narrative*, ed. W. J. T. Mitchell (Chicago: University of Chicago Press, 1981), 1-23.

[23] *Duchy Court*, 108-9.

[24] B. Howard Cunnington, ed., *Some Annals of the Borough of Devizes* (Devizes: George Simpson and Co., 1925), xx.

[25] Christopher Durston, "Puritan Rule and the Failure of Cultural Revolution, 1645-1660", in *The Culture of English Puritanism, 1560-1700*, ed. Durston and Jacqueline Eales (Basingstoke: Macmillan Press, 1996), 217, 229.

[26] British Library, London, Thomas Tracts 63/E.400[15] (London, 1647).

[27] John Spurr, *English Puritanism 1603-1689* (Basingstoke: Macmillan Press, 1998), 108-9.

[28] Ann Hughes, *Gangraena and the Struggle for the English Revolution* (Oxford: Oxford University Press, 2004); for the vicissitudes of toleration and intolerance, Alexandra Walsham, *Charitable Hatred: Tolerance and Intolerance in England 1500-1700* (Manchester: Manchester University Press, 2006).

[29] Michael Braddick, *God's Fury, England's Fire: A New History of the English Civil Wars* (London: Penguin, 2008), 491.

[30] Jonathan Fletcher, *Violence and Civilization: An Introduction to the Work of Norbert Elias* (Cambridge: Polity Press, 1997), 50.

[31] Patrick Collinson, "De Republica Anglorum: Or History with the Politics Put Back", repr. in his *Elizabethans* (London: Hambledon and London, 2003), 1-29 (originally published 1990); Keith Wrightson, "The Politics of the Parish in Early Modern England", in *The Experience of Authority in Early Modern England*, ed. Paul Griffiths, Adam Fox, and Steve Hindle (Basingstoke: Macmillan Press Ltd., 1996), 10-46.

Conclusion

> Yet thus far he thinks meet to let you know
>   Before you see't, the subject is so low
>   That to expect high language or much cost
>   Were a sure way now to make all be lost.¹

The Prologue to *The Sparagus Garden* (1632) by Richard Brome, one of the "sons of Ben [Jonson]", illustrates how closely drama of the seventeenth century attempted consciously to replicate at least some aspects of "ordinary" existence. In the same dramatist's *The Covent Garden Weeded* (also 1632), Rooksbill, the builder, expresses his hopes for his prospective tenants ("worthy persons") in his new buildings, to which Cockbrain responds: "Phew, that will follow. What new plantation was ever peopled with the better sort at first?"² The language of "sorts" of people appeared in dramatic vocabulary. Although complicated by poetic self-consciousness, early-modern drama affords a window onto the quotidian. Dekker, Jonson and Middleton had, in particular, close experience of that reality. By the turn of the century, the influence of the scholar-poets such as Greene and Nashe, had forfeited popular acclaim to the "artisanal culture of playwrights", whose background belonged in the City.³ Some of their plays were appropriations of popular literature which exulted the City crafts, such as Dekker's almost instantaneous conversion of the prose-fiction of Deloney's *The Gentle Craft* (1597/8) into *Shoemaker's Holiday* (1599).⁴ In this "age of cultural appropriation", the craftsmen of the theater engaged with their social environment.⁵

Despite the profession of Richard Brome in the quotation above ("the subject is so low"), the encounter with characters of genuinely "low" status, even in the comedies, is intermittent. Our preceding discussion thus engages with "low subjectivity" to a lesser degree than "middling" social position and the social and political encounter between citizens and gentry.[6] The most continuous addressing of "low" status occurs in *Bartholomew Fair*, carnivalesque in its approach and intensity.[7] Jonson offers some further depiction through Cob, the water-carrier, and his wife, Tib (Isabel), in *Every Man in His Humour*, somewhat idiosyncratic in his profession of his genealogy indicated by his moniker (cob as herring) and his aversion to tobacco. The single mother (Wench) who disencumbers herself of her child in *Michaelmas Term* affords further insight into the poorest sector of society, not least because of her sharp wit in gulling the Promoters (searchers for meat), lumbering them with the child.[8] The junior journeyman, Firk, in *Shoemaker's Holiday*, belongs to this social category too, as does Audrey, the somewhat assertive servant of Dampit, in *Trick to Catch the Old One*.[9] As Jonson's acolyte, Richard Brome conceived of characters of lower status. Overall, however, we may need to exploit the plays more extensively for that "low subjectivity" as imagined by the playwrights whose own status was, indeed, not too far removed.

Perhaps it is appropriate to leave the final word to Thomas Middleton, whose song, voiced by The Bawd in *Fair Quarrel*, intimates the value of the City comedies for elucidating aspects of early-modern social and cultural experience.

> Whate'er we get by gulls,
>   Of country or of city,
>   Old flat-caps or young heirs,
>   Or lawyers' clerks so witty,
>   By sailors newly landed,
>   To put in for fresh waters,
>   By wandering gander-mooners,
>   Or muffled late night-walkers.[10]

Notes

[1] Richard Brome, *The Weeding of Covent Garden* and *The Sparagus Garden*, ed., Donald S. McClure (NY: Garland Publishing, Inc., 1980): prologue to *The Sparagus Garden*.

² *Weeding of Covent Garden*, Act I, scene i, lines 21-5.

³ Paul Yachnin, *Stage-wrights: Shakespeare, Jonson, Middleton, and the Making of Theatrical Value* (Philadelphia: University of Pennsylvania Press, 1997), xii.

⁴ Elizabeth Rivlin, "Forms of service in Thomas Deloney's *The Gentle Craft*", *English Literary Renaissance* 40 (2010): 191-214, esp. 209-12.

⁵ Ian Munro, "Knightly Complements: *The Malcontent* and the Matter of Wit", *English Literary Renaissance* 40 (2010), 237.

⁶ Patricia Fumerton, *Unsettled: The Culture of Mobility and the Working Poor in Early Modern England* (Chicago: University of Chicago Press, 2006), 4.

⁷ Peter Stallybrass and Allon White, "The Fair, The Pig, Authorship", in their *The Politics and Poetics of Transgression* (London: Methuen & Co. Ltd., 1986), 27-79 (Chapter 1).

⁸ *Chaste Maid in Cheapside*, Act II, scene ii, lines 145-212.

⁹ *Trick Catch...Old One*, Act III, scene iv, for example.

¹⁰ Taylor and Lavagnino, eds., *Thomas Middleton: The Collected Works*, 1241 (*A Fayre Quarrell*, Act IV, scene iv, lines 130-7). For night-walkers, Paul Griffiths, "Meanings of Nightwalking in Early Modern England", *Continuity and Change* 3 (1988): 273-90.

Works cited

Primary Sources: MSS.

Lichfield Record Office
    B/C/11 wills, ca.1528-1546
Huntington Library, San Marino, California
    Hastings Manuscripts Box 25, folders 3, 4, 9, 11
Record Office for Leicestershire, Leicester and Rutland
    Wills, ca.1522-1546

Primary Sources: Printed

Note: most plays are listed in the **Abbreviations** at the front of the volume.

Ames, Susan M., ed. *County Court Records of Accomack-Northampton, Virginia, 1632-1640*. Washington, D.C.: American Historical Association, 1964.
Ames, Susan M., ed. *County Court Records of Accomack-Northampton, Virginia, 1640-1645*. Charlottesville: University of Virginia Press, 1973.
[Anon.],*The School of Recreation; Or, The Gentlemans Tutor, To Those Most Ingenious Exercises*. London, 1684.
Baker, D. C., J. L. Murphy and L. B. Hall, eds. *The Late Medieval Religious Plays of Bodleian MSS Digby 133 and E Museo 160*. Early English Text Society 283, 1982.
Baldwin, E., L. Clopper and D. Mills, eds. *Records of Early English Drama: Cheshire including Chester, vol. 2*. Toronto: University of Toronto Press, 2007.
Brigg, W. "Testamenta Leodiensia", *Miscellanea*. Thoresby Society 4, 1895.
Brinkworth, E. R., ed. *The Archdeacon's Court*: Liber Actorum *1584 Volume 1*. Oxfordshire Record Society 23, 1942.
Brome, Richard. *The Weeding of Covent Garden* and *The Sparagus Garden*, edited by Donald S. McClure. New York: Garland Publishing, Inc.,

1980.

Chamberlayne, C. G., ed. *The Vestry Book and Register of St Peter's Parish, New Kent and James City Counties, Virginia, 1684-1786*. Richmond, VA., 1937.

Chamberlayne, C. G., ed. *The Vestry Book of St Paul's Parish, Hanover County, Virginia, 1706-1786*. Richmond, VA., 1940.

Clark, J. W., ed. *North Country Wills 1383 to 1558*. Surtees Society 116, 1908.

Clay, J. W., and E. W. Crossley, eds. *Halifax Wills*. Halifax, 1904.

Cook, R. "Wills of Leeds and District", *Miscellanea*. Thoresby Society 24, 1919.

Cook, R. "Wills of the Parishes of Rothwell, Saxton...", *Miscellanea*. Thoresby Society 33, 1935.

Cunnington, B. Howard, ed. *Some Annals of the Borough of Devizes*. Devizes: George Simpson and Co., 1925.

Foster, C. W., ed. *Lincoln Wills Registered in the District Probate Registry at Lincoln. Volume 1, 1271 to 1526*. Lincoln Record Society 5, 1914.

Foster, C. W., ed. *Lincoln Wills Registered in the District Probate Registry at Lincoln. Volume 2, 1505 to May, 1530*. Lincoln Record Society 10, 1918.

Foster, C. W., ed. *Lincoln Wills Registered in the District Probate Registry at Lincoln. Volume 3, 1530 to 1532*. Lincoln Record Society 24, 1930.

Furnivall, F. J., ed. *The Digby Plays*. Early English Text Society Extra Series 70, 1896.

Gardiner, S. R., ed. *Reports of Cases in the Courts of Star Chamber and High Commission*. Camden Society new series 39, 1886.

George, David, ed. *Records of Early English Drama: Lancashire*. Toronto: University of Toronto Press, 1991.

Greenwell, William, ed. *Wills and Inventories from the Registry at Durham Part II*. Surtees Society 38, 1860.

Hickman, David, ed. *Lincoln Wills 1532-1534*. Lincoln Record Society 89, 2001.

Hodgson, J., ed. *Wills and Inventories from the Registry at Durham Part III*. Surtees Society 112, 1906.

Joyce, Sally L., and Evelyn S. Newton, eds. *Records of Early English Drama: Cornwall*. Toronto: University of Toronto Press, 1999.

Lewis, R. E., et al. *Middle English Dictionary* volume 13 W-Z. Ann Arbor: University of Michigan Press, 1999.

Lumb, G. D. "Testamenta Leodiensia", *Miscellanea*. Thoresby Society 9, 1899.

Lumb, G. D. "Testamenta Leodiensia 1531 to 1534", *Miscellanea*. Thoresby Society 11, 1904.

Lumb, G. D. "Testamenta Leodiensia", *Miscellanea*. Thoresby Society 15, 1909.

Lumb, G. D. *Testamenta Leodiensia...1539 to 1553.* Thoresby Society 19, 1913.
Mackey, H. M., and M. A. H. Groves, eds. *Northampton County Virginia Record Book, Orders, Deeds, Wills &c Volume 4 1645-1651.* Camden, ME: Picton Press, Inc, 2000.
Raine, Angelo, ed. *York Civic Records VI.* Yorkshire Archaeological Society Record Series 112, 1948 for 1946.
Raine, James, ed. *Testamenta Eboracensia Part I.* Surtees Society 4, 1836.
Raine, James, ed. *Wills and Inventories from the Registry of the Archdeaconry of Richmond...* Surtees Society 26, 1853.
Raine James, ed. *Testamenta Eboracensia Part II.* Surtees Society 30, 1855.
Raine, James, ed. *A Volume of English Miscellanea Illustrating the History and Language of the Northern Counties.* Surtees Society 85, 1890.
Stone, E. D., and B. Cozens-Hardy, eds. *Norwich Consistory Court Depositions, 1499-1512 and 1518-1530.* Norfolk Record Society 10, 1938.
Storey, R. L., ed. *Register of John Kirkby, Bishop of Carlisle, 1332-1352, and the Register of John Ross, Bishop of Carlisle, 1325-1332, 1.* Canterbury and York Society 79, 1992.
Walter, A. G., ed. *Lower Norfolk County, Virginia Court Records: Book "A", 1637-1646 & Book "B", 1646-1651/2.* Baltimore: Genealogical Publishing Co., 1994.
Weisiger, B. B. III, ed. *Charles City County, Virginia, Court Orders, 1687-1695.* Athens, GA: Iberian Publishing Co., 1992.
Wills and Administrations from the Knaresborough Court Rolls, volume I. Surtees Society 104, 1902.

Secondary Works

Agnew, Jean-Christophe. *Worlds Apart: The Market and the Theater in Anglo-American Thought, 1550-1750.* Cambridge: Cambridge University Press, 1986.
Amussen, Susan. *An Ordered Society: Gender and Class in Early Modern England.* Oxford: Basil Blackwell, 1988.
Amussen, Susan. "Punishment, Discipline and Power: The Social Meanings of Violence in Early Modern England". *Journal of British Studies* 34 (1995), 1-34.
Anderson, Virginia D. "Animals into the Wilderness: The Development of Livestock Husbandry in the Seventeenth-century Chesapeake". *William and Mary Quarterly*, 3rd series 59 (2002): 377-48.
Archer, Ian. *The Pursuit of Stability: Social Relations in Elizabethan London.* Cambridge: Cambridge University Press, 1991.
Archer, Ian. "'Civic Culture' in Later Medieval and Early Modern London". *Journal of Urban History* 34 (2008): 370-9.

Armitage, David, and Michael Braddick, eds. *The British Atlantic World, 1500-1800*. Basingstoke: Palgrave, 2002.
Asad, Talad. "Anthropological Conceptions of Religion: Reflections on Geertz". *Man* new series 18 (1983): 237–59.
Aston, Trevor H., and C. H. E. Philbin, eds. *The Brenner Debate: Agrarian Class Structure and Economic Development in Pre-industrial Europe*. Cambridge: Cambridge University Press, 1985.
Atiyah, Patrick S. *The Rise and Fall of Freedom of Contract*. Oxford: Oxford University Press, 1979, repr. 1988.
Austin, John L. *Philosophical Papers*. 3rd edn., Oxford: Oxford University Press, 1979.
Bardsley, Sandy. *Venomous Tongues: Speech and Gender in Late Medieval England*. Philadelphia: University of Pennsylvania Press, 2006.
Barry, Jonathan, and Christopher Brooks, eds. *The Middling Sort of People. Culture, Society and Politics in England, 1550–1800*. Basingstoke: Macmillan Press, 1994.
Barry, Jonathan. "Civility and Civic Culture in Early Modern England: The Meanings of Urban Freedom". In *Civil Histories: Essays Presented to Sir Keith Thomas*, edited by Peter Burke, Brian Harrison and Paul Slack, 181-96. Oxford: Oxford University Press, 2000.
Barton, Anne. "*The New Inn* and The Problem of Jonson's Late Style". *English Literary Renaissance* 9 (1979): 395-418.
Bate, Jonathan. *Soul of the Age: The Life, Mind and World of William Shakespeare*. London: Penguin, 2008.
Bayman, Anna. "Rogues, Conycatching and the Scribbling Crew". *History Workshop Journal* 63 (2007): 1-17.
Beier, A. L. (Lee). "Engine of Manufacture: the Trades of London". In *The Making of Metropolitan London 1500–1700*, edited by Beier and R. Finlay, 141-67. Harlow: Longman, 1986.
Beier, A. L. (Lee). "Anti-language or Jargon? Canting in the English Underworld in the Sixteenth and Seventeenth Centuries". In *Languages and Jargons: Contributions to a Social History of Language*, edited by Peter Burke and Roy Porter, 64-101. Cambridge: Polity Press, 1995.
Bennett, Susan. *Theatre Audiences: A Theory of Production and Reception*. 2nd edn., New York: Routledge, 2001.
Benskin, Michael. "Description of Dialect and Areal Distribution". In *Speaking in Our Tongues: Medieval Dialectology and Related Disciplines*, edited by Margaret Lang and K. Williamson. Cambridge: Cambridge University Press, 1994.
Biersack, Aletta. "Local Knowledge, Local History: Geertz and Beyond". In *The New Cultural History*, edited by Lynn Hunt, 72-96. Berkeley: University of California Press, 1989.

Billings, Warren, ed. *The Old Dominion in the Seventeenth Century: A Documentary History of Virginia, 1606-1689.* Chapel Hill: University of North Carolina Press, 1975.
Bourdieu, Pierre. *Distinction: A Social Critique of the Judgement of Taste*, translated by Richard Nice. London: Routledge, 1986.
Braddick, Michael. *The Nerves of State: Taxation and the Financing of the English State, 1558-1714.* Manchester: Manchester University Press, 1996.
Braddick, Michael. *God's Fury, England's Fire: A New History of the English Civil Wars.* London: Penguin, 2008.
Brooks, Christopher. *Pettyfoggers and Vipers of the Commonwealth: The 'Lower Branch' of the Legal Profession in Early Modern England.* Cambridge: Cambridge University Press, 1986.
Brooks, Douglas A. "Recent Studies in Ben Jonson (1991-mid-2001)". *English Literary Renaissance* 33 (2003): 110-52
Bruster, Douglas. *Shakespeare and the Question of Culture: Early Modern Literature and the Cultural Turn.* Basingstoke: Palgrave Macmillan, 2003.
Burnley, David. "Lexis and Semantics". In *The Cambridge History of the English Language. II, 1066-1476*, edited by Norman Blake, 409-99. Cambridge: Cambridge University Press, 1992.
Cameron, Deborah. *Feminism and Linguistic Theory.* Basingstoke: Palgrave, 1985.
Euan Cameron. "'Civilized Religion' from Renaissance to Reformation and Counter-Reformation". In *Civil Histories: Essays Presented to Sir Keith Thomas*, edited by Peter Burke, Brian Harrison and Paul Slack, 49-66. Oxford: Oxford University Press, 2000.
Capp, Bernard. *When Gossips Meet: Women, Family, and Neighbourhood in Early Modern England.* Oxford: Oxford University Press, 2003.
Carr, Lois G., Philip D. Morgan and Jean B. Russo, eds. *Colonial Chesapeake Society.* Chapel Hill, NC: University of North Carolina Press, 1988.
Carson, C., J. Bowen, W. Graham, M. McCartney and L. Walsh. "New World, Real World: Improvising English Culture in Seventeenth-century Virginia". *Journal of Southern History* 74 (2008): 31-88.
Chakravorty, Swapan. *Society and Politics in the Plays of Thomas Middleton.* Oxford: Oxford University Press, 1996.
Clarke, Sandra. *Renaissance Drama.* Cambridge: Polity Press, 2007.
Claval, Pierre. *An Introduction to Regional Geography*, translated by Ian Thompson. Oxford: Blackwell, 1998.
Coleman, Julie. *A History of Cant and Slang Dictionaries Volume I 1567-1784.* Oxford: Oxford University Press, 2004.
Collinson, Patrick. "*De Republica Anglorum*: Or History with the Politics Put Back". In his *Elizabethans*, 1-29. London: Hambledon and London, 2003.

Connell, R. W. *Masculinities*. Cambridge: Polity Press, 1995.
Crawford, Patricia. *Blood, Bodies and Families in Early Modern England*. Harlow: Longman, 2004.
Crystal, David. *"Think on My Words": Exploring Shakespeare's Language*. Cambridge: Cambridge University Press, 2008.
Derrida, Jacques, *Writing and Difference*, translated with an introduction by Alan Bass. London: Routledge, 2001.
Dessen, Alan C. "*The Alchemist*: Jonson's "Estates" Play". *Renaissance Drama* 7 (1964): 35-54.
Dillon, Janette. *The Cambridge Introduction to Early Modern Theatre*. Cambridge: Cambridge University Press, 2006.
Dowd, Michelle M. and Julie A. Eckerlie. "Recent Studies in Early Modern English Life Writing". *English Literary Renaissance* 40 (2010): 132-62.
Durston, Christopher. "Puritan Rule and the Failure of Cultural Revolution, 1645-1660". In *The Culture of English Puritanism, 1560-1700*, edited by Durston and Jacqueline Eales, 210-33. Basingstoke: Macmillan Press, 1996.
Eley, Geoff. *A Crooked Line: From Cultural History to the History of Society*. Michigan: University of Michigan Press, 2005.
Eley, Geoff, and Keith Nield. *The Future of Class in History: What's Left of the Social?* Michigan: University of Michigan Press, 2007.
Fischer, David H. *The Great Wave: Price Revolutions and the Rhythm of History*. New York: Oxford University Press, 1996.
Fisher, F. J. (Jack). "The Development of London as a Centre of Conspicuous Consumption in the Sixteenth and Seventeenth Centuries". Repr. in *London and the English Economy 1500–1700*, edited by Penny J. Corfield and Negley B. Harte, 105-18. London: Hambledon, 1990.
Fletcher, Anthony. *Gender, Sex and Subordination in England 1500-1800*. New Haven and London: Yale University Press, 1995.
Fletcher, Jonathan. *Violence and Civilization: An Introduction to the Work of Norbert Elias*. Cambridge: Polity Press, 1997.
Fowler, Alistair. "Transformations of Genre". Repr. in *Modern Genre Theory*, edited by David Duff, 232-49. Harlow: Longman, 2000.
Fowler, Alistair. "Georgic and Pastoral: Laws of Genre in the Seventeenth Century". In *Culture and Cultivation in Early Modern England: Writing and the Land*, edited by Michael Leslie and Timothy Raylor, 81-8. London: University of Leicester Press, 1992.
Fox, Adam. *Oral and Literate Culture in England 1500-1700*. Oxford: Oxford University Press, 2000.
French, Henry. "Social Status, Localism and the "Middle Sort of People" in England, 1620-1750". *Past and Present* 166 (2000): 66-99.
French, Henry. *The Middle Sort of People in Provincial England 1600-1750*.

Oxford: Oxford University Press, 2007.
Fumerton, Patricia. *Unsettled: The Culture of Mobility and the Working Poor in Early Modern England*. Chicago: University of Chicago Press, 2006.
Galbraith, John Kenneth. *A History of Economics: The Past as the Present*. London: Penguin, 1991 edn.
Gaskill, Malcolm. *Crime and Mentalities in Early Modern England*. Cambridge: Cambridge University Press, 2000.
Geertz, Clifford. "Deep Play: Notes on the Balinese Cockfight". In his *The Interpretation of Cultures*, 412-53. New York: Basic Books, 1973.
Geertz, Clifford. *Available Light: Anthropological Reflections on Philosophical Topics*. Princeton: Princeton University Press, 2000.
Gent, Lucy, ed. *Albion's Classicism: Visual Art in Britain, 1550-1660*. New Haven: Yale University Press, 1995.
Gilmore, David. *Manhood in the Making: Cultural Concepts of Masculinity*. New Haven: Yale University Press, 1990.
Gittings, Clare. *Death, Burial and the Individual in Early Modern England*. Beckenham: Croom Helm, 1984.
Goodman, Jennifer R. *British Drama Before 1660*. Boston, MA: Twaine Publishers, 1990.
Gorläch, M. "Regional and Social Variation". In *The Cambridge History of the English Language, Volume III, 1476-1776*, ed. Roger Lass, 486-514. Cambridge: Cambridge University Press, 1999.
Gossett, Suzanne. "Marston, Collaboration and *Eastward Ho!*" *Renaissance Drama* new series 33 (2004): 181-200.
Gottlieb, Bernard. *The Family in the Western World: From the Black Death to the Industrial Age*. Oxford: Oxford University Press, 1993.
Goux, J-J. *Symbolic Economies: After Marx and Freud*, translated by J. C. Gage. Ithaca, NY: Cornell University Press, 1990.
Gowing, Laura. *Domestic Dangers: Women, Words, and Sex in Early Modern London*. Oxford: Oxford University Press, 1996.
Graham, W., C. L. Hudgins, C. R. Lounsbury, F. D. Neiman, and J. F. Whittenburg. "Adaption and Innovation: Archaeological and Architectural Perspectives on the Seventeenth-century Chesapeake". *William and Mary Quarterly*, 3rd series 64 (2007): 451-522.
Greenblatt, Stephen. *Renaissance Self-fashioning: From More to Shakespeare*. Chicago: University of Chicago Press, 1980.
Griffiths, Paul. "Meanings of Nightwalking in Early Modern England". *Continuity and Change* 3 (1988): 273-90.
Griffiths, Paul. *Lost Londons: Change, Crime and Control in the Capital City, 1550-1660*. Cambridge: Cambridge University Press, 2008.
Gurr, Andrew. *The Shakespearean Stage, 1574-1642*. Cambridge: Cambridge University Press, 1982.

Hamill, Thomas A. "Cockfighting as Cultural Allegory in Early Modern England". *Journal of Medieval and Early Modern Studies* 39 (2009): 375-406.
Harding, Vanessa. "Whose Body? A Study of Attitudes Towards the Dead Body in Early Modern Paris". In *The Place of the Dead: Death and Remembrance in Late Medieval and Early Modern Europe*, ed. B. Gordon and Peter Marshall, 170-87. Cambridge: Cambridge University Press, 2000.
Hatfield, April L. *Atlantic Virginia: Intercolonial Relations in the Seventeenth Century.* Philadelphia: University of Pennsylvania Press, 2004.
Hattaway, Michael. *An Introduction to Early Modern English Literature.* Oxford: Blackwell Publishing, 2005.
Heinemann, Margot. *Puritanism and Theatre: Thomas Middleton and Opposition Drama under the Early Stuarts.* Cambridge: Cambridge University Press, 1980.
Herzfeld, Michael. *The Poetics of Manhood: Contest and Identity in a Cretan Mountain Village.* Princeton: Princeton University Press, 1985.
Hoffer, Peter C. *Law and People in Colonial America.* Baltimore: Johns Hopkins University, 1992.
Holmes, Janet. *Women, Men and Politeness.* Harlow: Longman Group Ltd., 1995.
Horn, James. *Adapting to a New World: English Society in the Seventeenth-century Chesapeake.* Chapel Hill, NC: University of North Carolina Press, 1994.
Hornsby, Stephen J. *British Atlantic, American Frontier: Spaces of Power in Early Modern British America.* Hanover, NH, and London: University Press of New England, 2005.
Hughes, Ann. *Gangraena and the Struggle for the English Revolution.* Oxford: Oxford University Press, 2004.
Hughes, Geoffrey. *A History of English Words.* Oxford: Blackwell, 2000.
Hulton, Mary. *Coventry and its People in the 1520s.* Dugdale Society 38, 1999.
Inglis, Fred. *Clifford Geertz: Culture, Custom and Ethics.* Cambridge: Polity Press, 2000.
Ingram, Martin. "Sexual Manners: The Other Face of Civility in Early Modern England". In *Civil Histories: Essays Presented to Sir Keith Thomas*, edited by Peter Burke, Brian Harrison and Paul Slack, 87-109. Oxford: Oxford University Press, 2000.
Iser, Wolfgang. *The Range of Interpretation.* New York: Columbia University Press, 2000.
Jewell, Helen M. *The North-South Divide: The Origins of Northern Consciousness in England.* Manchester: Manchester University Press, 1994.
Jones, Ann R., and Peter Stallybrass. *Renaissance Clothing and the Materials*

of Memory. Cambridge: Cambridge University Press, 2000.
Jűtte, Robert. *Poverty and Deviance in Early Modern Europe.* Cambridge: Cambridge University Press, 1994.
Kamensky, Jane. *Governing the Tongue: The Politics of Speech in Early New England.* Oxford: Oxford University Press, 1997.
Kaplan, Joel L. "Virtue's Holiday: Thomas Dekker and Simon Eyre". *Renaissance Drama* new series 2 (1969): 103-22.
Kinney, Arthur F. ed. *Renaissance Drama: An Anthology of Plays and Entertainments.* Oxford: Blackwell Publishing, 1999.
Kinney, Arthur F. ed. *A Companion to Renaissance Drama.* Oxford: Blackwell Publishing, 2002.
Kristensson, Gillis. *A Survey of Middle English Dialects 1290-1350: The Six Northern Counties and Lincolnshire.* Lund Studies in English 35, 1967.
Lakoff, George, and Martin Johnson. *Metaphors We Live By.* Chicago: University of Chicago Press, 1980.
Lesser, Zachary. *Renaissance Drama and the Politics of Publication: Readings in the English Book Trade.* Cambridge: Cambridge University Press, 2004.
Leyshon, Andrew, and Nigel Thrift, eds. *Money/Space: Geographies of Monetary Transactions.* London: Routledge, 1997.
Lounsbury, Carl R. *The Courthouses of Early Virginia: An Architectural History.* Charlottesville, VA, 2005.
McCrea, Adriana. *Constant Minds: Political Virtue and the Lipsian Paradigm in England, 1584-1650.* Toronto and London: University of Toronto Press, 1997.
McFarlane, Anthony. *The British in the Americas 1480-1815.* London: Longman 1992.
McIntosh, Angus, M. L. Samuels, and M. Benskin. *A Linguistic Atlas of Late Mediaeval English.* 4 volumes, Aberdeen: Aberdeen University Press, 1986.
McLuskie, Kathleen. *Dekker and Heywood.* Basingstoke: Macmillan Press Ltd., 1994.
McLuskie, Kathleen. *Renaissance Dramatists.* Hemel Hempstead: Harvester Wheatsheaf, 1989.
Macpherson, C. B. *The Political Theory of Possessive Individualism.* Oxford: Oxford University Press, 1962.
Mancall, Peter C., ed. *The Atlantic World and Virginia, 1550-1624.* Chapel Hill, NC: University of North Carolina Press, 2007.
Mancke, Elizabeth and Carole Shammas, eds. *The Creation of the British Atlantic World.* Baltimore: Johns Hopkins University Press, 2005.
Mandler, Peter. "The Problem with Cultural History". *Cultural and Social History* 1 (2004): 94-117.

Manley, Lawrence. *Literature and Culture in Early Modern London*. Cambridge: Cambridge University Press, 1994.

Matson, Cathy. "A House of Many Mansions: Some Thoughts on the Field of Economic History". In *The Economy of Early America: Historical Perspectives and New Directions*, edited by Matson. University Park, PA: Pennsylvania State University Press, 2006.

Martin, Matthew R. *Between Theater and Philosophy: Skepticism in the Major City Comedies of Ben Jonson and Thomas Middleton*. Newark, Delaware: University of Delaware Press, 2001.

Martinet, Marie-Madeleine. "Le vocabulaire de l'or dans les appelations satiriques au temps de la Renaissance anglaise". In *L'Or au Temps de la Renaissance: Du Mythe a l'Économie*, edited by M. T. Jones-Davies, 99-104. Paris, 1978.

Maus, Katharine Eisaman. "Satiric and Ideal Economies in the Jonsonian Imagination". *English Literary Renaissance* 19 (1989): 42-64.

Menard, Russell R. "The Tobacco Industry of the Chesapeake, c. 1617-1730: An Interpretation". *Research in Economic History* 5 (1980): 109-77.

Meyers, D., and M. Perreault, eds. *Colonial Chesapeake: New Perspectives*. Lanham, MD, 2006.

Muir, Edward. *Ritual in Early Modern Europe*. Cambridge: Cambridge University Press, 1997.

Mukherji, Subha. "Women, Law and Dramatic Realism in Early Modern England". *English Literary Renaissance* 35 (2005): 248–72.

Moore, S., S. B. Beech, and H. Whitehall. *Middle English Dialect: Characteristics and Dialect Boundaries*. Ann Arbor: University of Michigan, 1935.

Muldrew, Craig. "'Hard Food for Midas': Cash and Its Social Value in Early Modern England". *Past and Present* 170 (2001): 78-120.

Muldrew, Craig. *The Economy of Obligation: The Culture of Credit and Social Relations in Early Modern England*. Basingstoke: Palgrave, 1998.

Mullaney, Steven. *The Place of the Stage: License, Play and Power in Renaissance England*. Chicago: University of Chicago Press, 1988.

Nash, R. C. "The Organization of Trade and Finance in the British Atlantic Economy, 1600-1830". In *The Atlantic Economy During the Seventeenth and Eighteenth Centuries: Organization, Operation, Practice, and Personnel*, edited by P. A. Coclanis. Columbia, SC: University of South Carolina Press, 2005.

Nelson, John K. *A Blessed Company: Parishes, Parsons and Parishioners in Anglican Virginia, 1690-1776*. Chapel Hill, NC: University of North Carolina Press, 2001.

Nettels, C. P. *The Money Supply of the American Colonies before 1720*. Repr. New York: Kelley, 1964.

Norbrook, David. *Poetry and Politics in the English Renaissance*. Oxford: Oxford University Press, 2002.

North, Douglas. *Institutions, Institutional Change and Economic Performance.* Cambridge: Cambridge University Press, 1990.
Palmer, Daryl W. *Hospitable Performances: Dramatic Genre and Cultural Practices in Early Modern England.* West Lafayette, IN: Purdue University Press, 1992.
Parker, John. *Structuration.* Buckingham: Open University Press, 2000.
Partridge, Eric. *Dictionary of Historical Slang.* Harmondsworth: Penguin, 1972.
Patterson, W. Brown. *King James VI and I and the Reunion of Christendom.* Cambridge: Cambridge University Press, 1997.
Pearlman, E. "Ben Jonson: An Anatomy". *English Renaissance Literature* 9 (1979): 364-93.
Pecora, Vincent. "The Limits of Local Knowledge". In *The New Historicism*, edited by H. Aram Veeser, 243-76. London: Routledge, 1989.
Perry, James R. *The Formation of Society on Virginia's Eastern Shore 1615-1655.* Chapel Hill, NC: University of North Carolina Press, 1990.
Phillips, Kim M. "Masculinities and the Medieval English Sumptuary Laws". *Gender and History* 19 (2007): 22–42.
Pickering, Michael. *Stereotyping: The Politics of Representation.* Basingstoke: Palgrave Macmillan, 2001.
Pollard, Tanya. *Drugs and Theatre in Early Modern England.* Oxford: Oxford University Press, 2005.
Rappaport, Steven. *Worlds Within Worlds: Structures of Life in Sixteenth-century London.* Cambridge: Cambridge University Press, 1989.
Riggs, David. *Ben Jonson: A Life.* Cambridge, MA: Harvard University Press, 1989.
Rivlin, Elizabeth. "Forms of Service in Thomas Deloney's *The Gentle Craft".* *English Literary Renaissance* 40 (2010): 191-214.
Roche, Daniel. *A History of Everyday Things: The Birth of Consumption in France, 1600–1800.* Cambridge: Cambridge University Press, 2000.
Roper, Lou H. "Charles I, Virginia, and the Idea of Atlantic History'. *Itinerario* 30 (2006):
Roper, Lou H. *The English Empire in America, 1602-1658: Beyond Jamestown.* London: Pickering and Chatto Publishers, 2009.
Roseberry, William. "Balinese Cockfights and the Seduction of Anthropology". *Social Research* 49 (1982): 1013–28.
Sacks, David Harris. "The Promise and the Contract in Early Modern England: Slade's Case in Perspective". In *Rhetoric and Law in Early Modern Europe*, edited by Victoria. A. Kahn and Lorna Hutson. New Haven: Yale University Press, 2001.
Salinger, Sharon. *Taverns and Drinking in Early America.* Baltimore: Johns Hopkins University Press, 2002.

Schneider, J. "Fantastical Colors in Foggy London. The New Fashion Potential of the Late Sixteenth Century". In *Material London, ca. 1600*, edited by Lena C. Orlin, 109-27 Philadelphia: University of Pennsylvania Press, 2000.
Scott, Michael. "Ill-mannered Marston". In *The Drama of John Marston: Critical Re-Visions*, edited by T. F. Wharton, 212-30. Cambridge: Cambridge University Press, 2000.
Scott-Warren, Jason. *Early Modern English Literature.* Cambridge: Polity Press, 2005.
Searle, John. *Mind, Language and Society: Philosophy in the Real World.* London: Penguin, 1999.
Sewell, William. "Geertz, Cultural Systems, and History: from Synchrony to Transformation". In *The Fate of Culture: Geertz and Beyond*, edited by Sherry Ortner, 35-55. Berkeley: University of California Press, 1999.
Shammas, Carole. *The Pre-Industrial Consumer in England and America.* Oxford: Oxford University Press, 1990.
Shepard, Alexandra. *Meanings of Manhood in Early Modern England.* Oxford: Oxford University Press, 2003.
Simms, Karl. *Paul Ricoeur.* London: Routledge, 2003.
Spufford, Margaret. *Small Books and Pleasant Histories: Popular Fiction and Its Readership in Seventeenth Century England.* Cambridge: Cambridge University Press, 1985.
Spufford, Peter. *Money and its Uses in Medieval Europe.* Cambridge: Cambridge University Press,, 1988.
Spurr, John. *English Puritanism 1603-1689.* Basingstoke: Macmillan Press, 1998.
Supple, Barry. *Commercial Crisis and Change in England, 1600-1642: A Study in the Instability of a Mercantile Economy.* Cambridge: Cambridge University Press, 1957
Stallybrass, Peter, and Allon White. *The Politics and Poetics of Transgression.* London: Methuen & Co. Ltd., 1986.
Synnott, Anthony. *The Body Social: Symbolism, Self and Society.* London: Routledge, 1993.
Tate, T. W., and D. L. Ammerman, eds. *The Chesapeake in the Seventeenth Century.* Chapel Hill, NC: University of North Carolina Press, 1979.
Taylor, Charles. *A Secular Age.* Cambridge, MA, and London: Harvard University Press, 2007.
Thomas, Jenny. *Meaning in Interaction: An Introduction to Pragmatics.* Harlow: Longman Group Ltd., 1995.
Thompson, Peter. "William Bullock's 'Strange Adventure': A Plan to Transform Seventeenth-century Virginia". *William and Mary Quarterly*, 3rd series 61 (2004): 107-28.

Thompson, Peter. "The Thief, the Householder, and the Commons: Languages of Class in Seventeenth-century Virginia". *William and Mary Quartlery*, 3rd series 63 (2006): 253-80.

Tittler, Robert, ed. *Accounts of the Roberts Family of Boarzell, Sussex, c. 1568-1582*. Sussex Record Society 71, 1979.

Tittler, Robert. "Freemen's Gloves and Civic Authority: the Evidence from Post-Reformation Portraiture". *Costume* 40 (2006): 13–20.

Tittler, Robert. "Civic Portraiture and Political Culture in English Provincial Towns, ca. 1560–1640". *Journal of British Studies* 37 (1998): 306–29.

Turner, Henry S., ed. *The Culture of Capital: Property, Cities, and Knowledge in Early Modern England*. London: Routledge, 2002.

Valenze, Deborah. *The Social Life of Money in the English Past*. Cambridge: Cambridge University Press, 2006.

Walby, Sylvia. *Theorizing Patriarchy*. Oxford: Blackwell, 1990.

Wales, Katie. *Northern English: A Cultural and Social History*. Cambridge: Cambridge University Press, 2006.

Walsham, Alexandra. *Charitable Hatred: Tolerance and Intolerance in England 1500-1700*. Manchester: Manchester University Press, 2006.

Ward, Joseph P. *Metropolitan Communities: Trades, Guilds, Identity and Change in Early Modern London*. Stanford, CA: Stanford University Press, 1997.

Watt, Tessa. *Cheap Print and Popular Piety, 1550-1640*. Cambridge: Cambridge University Press, 1991.

Wayne, Don E. *"Drama and Society in the Age of Jonson*: An Alternative View". *Renaissance Drama* new series 13 (1982): 103-29.

White, Hayden. "The Value of Narrativity in the Representation of Reality". In *On Narrative*, edited by W. J. T. Mitchell, 1-23. Chicago: University of Chicago Press, 1981.

Williams, Gordon. "Mediation and Contestation: English Classicism from Sidney to Jonson". In *Renaissance Poetry*, edited by Christine Malcolmson, 178-202. Harlow: Longman, 1998.

Williams, Patrick R. "Ben Jonson's Satiric Choreography". *Renaissance Drama* new series 9 (197): 121-45.

Withington, Phil. *The Politics of Commonwealth: Citizens and Freemen in Early Modern England*. Cambridge: Cambridge University Press, 2005.

Withington, Phil. "Company and Sociability in Early Modern England". *Social History* 32 (2007): 291-307.

Woodbridge, Linda, ed. *Money in the Age of Shakespeare: Essays in New Economic Criticism*. Basingstoke: Palgrave Macmillan, 2004.

Worden, Blair. "Ben Jonson Among the Historians". In *Culture and Politics in Early Stuart England*, edited by Kevin Sharpe and Peter Lake, 67-89. Basingstoke:Macmillan Press, 1994.

Wright, Laura. *Sources of London English: Medieval Thames Vocabulary.* Oxford: Oxford University Press, 1996.

Wright, Laura, ed. *The Development of Standard English 1300-1800.* Cambridge: Cambridge University Press, 2000.

Wrightson, Keith. "'Sorts of People' in Tudor and Stuart England". In *The Middling Sort of People: Culture, Society and Politics in England, 1550-1800*, edited by Jonathan Barry and Christopher Brooks, 28-51. Basingstoke: Palgrave, 1994.

Wrightson, Keith. "The Politics of the Parish in Early Modern England". In *The Experience of Authority in Early Modern England*, edited by Paul Griffiths, Adam Fox, and Steve Hindle, 10-46. Basingstoke: Macmillan Press Ltd., 1996.

Yachnin, Paul. *Stage-wrights: Shakespeare, Jonson, Middleton, and the Making of Theatrical Value.* Philadelphia: University of Pennsylvania Press, 1997.

Zagorin, Perez. *Ways of Lying: Dissimulation, Persecution and Conformity in Early Modern Europe.* Cambridge: MA: Harvard University Press, 1990.

Zelizer, Viviana. *The Social Meaning of Money: Pin Money, Paychecks, Poor Relief and Other Currencies.* New York: Basic Books, 1994.

Index

Notes. The titles of plays are in italics; the abbreviations used here are explained at pp. vii-xi, where also the dates of first performance or printing of the plays are given. Where *dramatis personae* are listed in the index, the title of the play in which they appear is given in parenthesis.

Alchemist 12, 22, 25, 28, 30, 35
argot, see canting
Aristotelian unities 1
Arnold (Nottinghamshire) 50

Bartholomew Fair 2, 5, 12, 15, 28, 30, 86 154
Beaumont, Francis (1584-1616/17) 4, 13, 34, 35, 51, 69, 70
bills (financial) 108-111
bonds, see specialties
bring forth, see funeral
Brome, Richard (ca.1590-1653) 153-4
burial, see funeral

Candido (*Honest Whore*) 5, 63-8
canting 25-6
caps, flat 5, 43-56, 154

Changeling 11, 12, 29
Chaste Maid 12, 24, 28, 70
City, see London
civility 15, 43-56, 68-9, 143
cockfight 141-8
coin, see money
company 16-19, 83, 143, 146
Congleton (Cheshire) 143
conjugal relations, see marriage
Cornwall (county) 143
courts (Virginia) 99-115
courts (Loughborough) 111-14
Coventry (Warwickshire) 53
cozen(age) 20, 21-2, 83
credit (financial) 99-115
culture, see gentry
culture, popular 148
cunning 15, 22
Cynthia's Revels 12, 35

debt, see credit
Dekker, Thomas (ca.1572-1632) 2, 3, 5, 12-13, 17, 22, 25, 29, 30, 31-2, 44, 45, 51, 52, 55-6, 63-8, 72-4, 80, 81-2, 83, 90-1, 153
Derbyshire 131, 134, 136, 149
Devil is an Ass 12, 22, 24, 28, 30
dialect 6, 123-36
dissemble 15, 22-4
dissimulation, see dissemble

Duchess of Malfi 11, 13, 29, 31, 53
dull 24, 48, 50
Durham (county) 129, 149

Eastward Ho 6, 10, 12, 24, 27, 28, 48, 53-4, 70, 82-3, 99-101
Eckington (Derbyshire) 125
Epicoene 3, 12, 28, 30, 35
Every Man in his Humour 12, 27, 28, 35, 154
Every Man out of his Humour 12, 35
Eyre, Simon (*Shoemaker's Holiday*) 10, 17, 55, 63-8, 74, 81-2, 83, 86
Eyre, Margery (Madge) (*Shoemaker's Holiday*) 63-8, 73

Fair Quarrel 154
fashion (to fashion, fashioning) 15-16, 43-56
Fletcher, John (1579-1625) 4, 35, 51
forthbringing, see funeral
funeral 130-1, 134, 136

Game at Chess 11, 12, 22-3, 28
genre 11, 75, 80
gentry (culture) 141-8
George, grocer (*Knight of the Burning Pestle*) 69
gold, see money
groat (4d.) 87-9, 97

Harrogate (Yorkshire) 125
Heywood, Thomas (ca.1570-1641) 4, 11, 13, 21, 29, 143
honesty 14-15
Honest Whore 5, 12, 29, 51, 52, 63-8
honor 11, 143
household, see marriage
hypergamy 67-8
hypogamy 67-8

idiom, see speech

Jonson, Ben (1572-1637) 1, 2, 3, 5, 6, 7, 10, 12, 13, 15, 16, 18, 22, 24, 25, 27, 28, 30, 34, 35, 44, 45, 46, 47, 48, 53-4, 55-6, 70, 79, 80, 82-3, 84, 86, 91, 99-101, 153-4
Jovial Crew 3, 30

Knight of the Burning Pestle 34, 51, 69-70, 73

language, see vocabulary
Leeds (Yorkshire) 126, 128, 133, 149
lexis, see vocabulary
Lincoln (Lincolnshire) 88
Lincolnshire 123, 127
Lipsius, Justus (1547-1606) 5, 68, 77
Liverpool (Lancashire) 142
London passim
Loughborough (Leicestershire) 111-14
Lutterworth (Leicestershire) 96

Madge (Margery) Eyre, see Eyre
Mad World 12, 17, 28, 33, 47, 54, 71
Malcontent 13, 26, 29, 34
makeshift, see shift
manhood 150
marriage 61-74
Marston, John (1576-1634) 4, 6, 10, 11, 13, 26, 27, 28-9, 34, 48, 53-4, 70, 82-3, 99-101
masculinity 141-9
meta-theatricality 3
metaphor 11, 26, 49, (money as) 79-92
Michaelmas Term 12, 18, 19, 20, 21, 28, 46, 47, 48, 83, 154
Middleton, Thomas (ca.1570-1623) 2, 3, 11, 12, 15, 17, 18, 19, 20, 21, 22-3, 24, 25, 26, 27, 28-9, 30, 31-2, 33, 44, 54, 55-6, 70-1, 79, 80, 83, 84, 86, 91, 153-4

Moll Cutpurse, see *Roaring Girl*
money, see also groat and see also tobacco 79-92

Nell, wife of George (*Knight of the Burning Pestle*) 69
Neo-Stoicism, see Stoicism
New Inn 5, 12, 13, 16, 24, 26, 28, 30, 34, 46
North (of England) 123-36
No Wit... 12, 28

parish(ing) 125-6, 128-30, 132, 133, 135
patriarchy 63-8, 71, 76, 88, 143-4
Poetaster 2, 5, 12, 15, 28, 35
popular culture, see culture

Queniborough (Leicestershire) 96

Revenger's Tragedy 11, 12, 28
rhyme (verse) 27-34
ritual 145-6
Roaring Girl 2, 12, 17, 25, 29, 30, 31-2
Rowley, William (ca.1585-1637) 2, 4, 11, 12, 13, 26, 28-9

Sejanus 12, 28, 35
Shoemaker's Holiday 10, 17, 44, 55, 63-8, 81-2, 153-4
shift (to make shift) 19
silver, see money
Slade's Case (1603) 112
sorts (of people) 11-14, 26, 79-80, 90, 153
specialty (financial instrument) 108-111
speech, see also dialect

speech, idiomatic 10
speech, Northern 123-36
speech, speech acts 63-8, 85-7
Stafford (Staffordshire) 49
Staple of News 2, 12, 15, 18, 25, 28, 45-6
stereotyping 62-3, 76, 77
Stockerston (Leicestershire) 96
Stoicism 5, 68-9, 77

tobacco 49, (fiduciary and commercial role) 99-115
Trick...Old One 12, 28, 33, 154

vocabulary (dialect lexis) 123-36
vocabulary (poetic, playwrights') 7-36
Viola, wife of Candido (*Honest Whore*) 63-8, 73
violence (masculine) 141-9
Virginia (N. American colony) 82-3, 99-115
Volpone 12, 28, 35

Webster, John 11, 13, 29, 31, 53
Westward Hoe 52
White Devil 11, 13, 29
wills (testaments) 123-36
Winwick (Lancashire) 145-6
wit(en) (to give) 125-8
Witch of Edmonton 2, 13, 29
Woman Killed with Kindness 11, 13, 21, 29, 143
Women Beware Women 11, 12, 20, 28, 33

York (city) 142
Yorkshire 123-36, 149

www.ingramcontent.com/pod-product-compliance
Lightning Source LLC
Chambersburg PA
CBHW020800160426
43192CB00006B/396